G000136553

BRITAIN'S *Best*
HOTELS 2012
PERFECT PLACES TO STAY

Typeset by AA Lifestyle Guides

Printed and bound by DZS Grafik, d.o.o, Slovenia

Editorial contributor: Philip Bryant

A CIP catalogue record for this book is available from the British Library

ISBN: 978-0-7495-7213-6

Published by AA Publishing, which is a trading name of AA Media Limited, whose registered office is:
Fanum House, Basing View, Basingstoke,
Hampshire RG21 4EA
Registered number 06112600

theAA.com/shop

A04801

Contents

Welcome

The selection of establishments in Britain's Best Hotels have all been professionally inspected by the AA to ensure the highest standards of hospitality, accommodation and food.

The hotels

This guide covers over 200 town and country houses, small hotels and restaurants with rooms. Every establishment has received a star rating and percentage merit score following a visit by an AA inspector. This indicates that you can expect a friendly welcome, comfortable surroundings, excellent food and good service. Further details about the AA scheme, inspections and awards and rating system can be found on pages 10–11 of this guide.

Before you travel

Some places may offer special breaks and facilities not available at the time of going to press. If in doubt, it's always worth calling the hotel before you book. See also the useful information provided on pages 12–13, and visit theAA.com for up-to-date establishment and travel information.

How to use the guide

The main section of the guide is divided into four parts, covering England, Channel Islands, Scotland and Wales. The counties within each of these sections are ordered alphabetically as are the town or village locations (shown in capital letters as part of the address) within each county. Finally, the establishments are listed alphabetically under each location name. Town names featured in the guide can also be located in the map section at the back of the guide.

❶ Grading and awards

All entries in the guide have been inspected by the AA and, at the time of going to press, are rated under the AA Hotel Scheme.

Stars: Each establishment has 3, 4 or 5 stars ★ and a high merit score (%). The very best hotels in each of these categories have been given red stars ★ . For full details see page 10.

Rosettes ⍟: The AA's award for food excellence. For full details see page 11.

❷ Designator

For full details see page 11.

❸ Address details

❹ Contact details

For further details see page 8.

❺ Map reference

Map page number followed by a 2-figure National Grid reference. For full details see page 8.

❻ Directions

Brief details of how to find the hotel.

❼ Rooms

Accommodation information. For full details see page 8.

Prices

These are indications only. Please check before booking. Charges shown are per night including VAT, unless otherwise stated.

❽ Facilities

Includes satellite TV, Wi-fi & leisure facilities. For full details see page 8.

❾ Parking

The number of parking spaces available at the property. For further details see page 8.

❿ Notes

Details relating to children, dogs, and Wi-fi. For further details see page 8.

⓫ Description

Includes background information, brief history, room information, special features and description of the food if an award has been given.

⓬ Recommended in the area

Local places of interest, activities and potential day trips.

Langley Castle

❶ ★★★★ 82% ◉◉ HOTEL ❷
❸ **Address:** Langley, HEXHAM, NE47 5LU
❹ **Tel:** 01434 688888
Fax: 01434 684019
E-mail: manager@langleycastle.com
Website: www.langleycastle.com
❺ **Map ref:** 11, NY96
❻ **Directions:** From A69 S on A686 for 2m.
Hotel is on right
❼ **Rooms:** 27 (18 annexe) (8 fmly) (9 GF)
❽ **Facilities:** STV Wi-fi
❾ **Parking:** 70
❿ **Notes:** ⊗

⓫ A genuine 14th-century castle, restored and transformed into a magnificent and comfortable hotel, set in its own 12-acre woodland estate. The guest bedchambers have private facilities, and some boast window seats set into 7ft-thick walls, four-poster beds, and even a sauna and spa bath. CastleView and CastleView Lodge, converted Grade I listed buildings within the grounds, offer additional guest rooms. All the bedrooms have draped canopies over the beds, satellite TV and stunning views up to the main castle. The splendid drawing room, with blazing log fire, traceries and stained glass, together with the oak-panelled cocktail bar, complement the intimate atmosphere of the Josephine Restaurant. The food served here is of the highest order, making the most of fresh, local produce, with fish and game a speciality on the table d'hôte menu. For early diners the Early Knight menu offers sophisticated choices between lunchtime and 6pm. The exclusive nature of the castle makes Langley the perfect destination to be pampered in unique surroundings, and it's ideally located for discovering the delights of Hadrian's Wall, Bamburgh Castle, Holy Island and the Scottish Borders. The Castle is only 30 minutes from Newcastle city centre and 40 minutes from Newcastle Airport.

Recommended in the area ⓬
Hadrian's Wall; Bamburgh Castle; Hexham Abbey

Key to symbols

★	Black stars (see page 10)
★	Red stars (see page 10)
%	Merit score
◉	AA Rosette (see page 11)
3, TQ28	Map reference
S	Single room
D	Double room
GF	Ground floor room
Family	Family room

⊗	No dogs allowed (assist dogs should be allowed)
🚼	Children not allowed
Wi-fi	Wireless network
STV	Satellite television
FTV	Freeview television
⊕	Indoor heated swimming pool
⊰	Outdoor swimming pool
⊰	Outdoor heated swimming pool
CONF	Conference facilities available

How to use the guide continued

Contact details

The establishment address includes a locator or place name in capitals (e.g. NORWICH). Within each county, entries are ordered alphabetically first by this place name and then by the name of the establishment.

Telephone and fax numbers, and e-mail and website addresses are given where available. The telephone and fax numbers are believed correct at the time of going to press but changes may occur. The latest establishment details are on the Hotel pages at **theAA.com**.

Map reference

Each establishment in this guide is given a map reference for a location which can be found in the atlas section at the back of the guide. It is composed of the map page number and the two-figure map reference based on the National Grid.

For example: **Map 5, SU48**
5 refers to the page number of the map section at the back of the guide
SU is the National Grid lettered square (representing 100,000sq metres) in which the location will be found
4 is the figure reading across the top and bottom of the map page
8 is the figure reading down each side of the map page
Maps locating each establishment and a route planner are available at **theAA.com**.

Room information

The entries show the number of en suite letting bedrooms available. Bedrooms that have a private bathroom adjacent may be included as en suite. Further details of facilities provided in the rooms are listed in the main entry description.

Prices: Prices are per room per night including VAT (unless otherwise specified) and are provided by the hoteliers in good faith. These prices are indications and not firm quotations. Always check before booking.

VAT (Value Added Tax) is payable in the UK and in the Isle of Man, on basic prices and additional services. VAT does not apply in the Channel Islands.

Payment: Most hotels now accept credit or debit cards. Credit cards may be subject to a surcharge – check when booking if this is how you intend to pay. Not all hotels accept travellers' cheques.

Facilities

This section lists a selection of facilities offered by the hotel including sports facilities such as indoor and outdoor swimming pools, golf, tennis and gym; options for relaxation such as spa, jacuzzi and solarium, and services such as satellite TV and Wi-fi. Use the key to the symbols on page 7 to help identify what's available at a particular hotel.

Additional facilities, or notes about other services may be listed here. Some hotels have restricted service during quieter months, and at this time some of the listed facilities will not be available. If unsure, contact the hotel before your visit.

Parking

This shows the number of parking spaces available. Other types of parking (on road or Park and Ride) may also be possible; check the descriptions for further information.

Notes

This section provides specific details relating to:

Smoking policy: Smoking in public places is banned in England, Scotland and Wales.

The proprietor can designate one or more bedrooms with ventilation systems where the occupants can smoke, but communal areas must be smoke-free.

Dogs: Although many hotels allow dogs, they may be excluded from some areas of the hotel and some breeds, particularly those requiring an exceptional license, may not be acceptable at all. Under the Equality Act 2010 access should be allowed for guide dogs and assistance dogs. Please check the hotel's policy when making your booking.

Children: 🚼, means children cannot be accommodated, or a minimum age may be specified, e.g. 🚼 **under 4**, means no children under four years old. The main description may also provide details about facilities available for children.

Establishments with special facilities for children may include a babysitting service or baby-intercom system, playroom or playground, laundry facilities, drying and ironing facilities, cots, high chairs and special meals.

Best quality

All entries in Britain's Best Hotels have excelled in several categories set by the AA inspection team. Red stars are awarded to the very best establishments in each star category and signify that the hotel offers the finest accommodation available.

High standards

Hotels recognised by the AA should:

- have high standards of cleanliness
- keep proper records of booking
- give prompt and professional service to guests, assist with luggage on request, accept and deliver messages
- provide a designated area for breakfast and dinner, with drinks available in a bar or lounge
- provide an early morning call on request
- have good quality furniture and fittings
- provide adequate heating and lighting
- undertake proper maintenance

The hotels in Britain's Best Hotels all have a three, four or five black or red star rating. The following is a brief guide to some of the general expectations for each star classification:

★★★ Three star

- Management and staff smartly and professionally presented and usually wearing a recognisable uniform
- A dedicated receptionist on duty at peak times
- At least one restaurant or dining room open to residents and non-residents for breakfast and dinner whenever the hotel is open
- Last orders for dinner no earlier than 8pm
- Remote-control television, direct-dial phone
- En suite bath or shower and WC

★★★★ Four star

- A formal, professional staffing structure with smartly presented, uniformed staff anticipating and responding to your needs or requests
- Usually spacious, well-appointed public areas
- Reception staffed 24 hours by well-trained staff
- Express checkout facilities where appropriate
- Porterage available on request
- Night porter available
- At least one restaurant open to residents and non-residents for breakfast and dinner seven days per week, and lunch to be available in a designated eating area
- Last orders for dinner no earlier than 9pm
- En suite bath with fixed overhead shower and WC

★★★★★ Five star

- Luxurious accommodation and public areas with a range of extra facilities. First time guests shown to their bedroom
- Multilingual service
- Guest accounts well explained and clearly presented
- Porterage offered
- Guests greeted at hotel entrance, full concierge service provided
- At least one restaurant open to residents and non-residents for all meals seven days per week
- Last orders for dinner no earlier than 10pm
- High-quality menu and wine list
- Evening service to turn down the beds
- Remote-control television, direct-dial telephone at bedside and desk, a range of luxury toiletries, bath sheets and robes
- En suite bathroom incorporating fixed overhead shower and WC

★ Inspectors' Choice

Each year the AA selects the best hotels in each rating. These hotels stand out as the very best in the British Isles, regardless of style. The Inspectors' Choice hotels in this guide are identified by red stars.

Designator (types of hotel)

The majority of establishments in this guide come under the category of Hotel; other categories are listed below:

Town house hotel:
A small, individual city or town centre property, which provides a high degree of personal service and privacy.

Country house hotel:
These are quietly located in a rural area.

Small hotel:
Has less than 20 bedrooms and is managed by the owner.

Restaurant with rooms:
This category of accommodation is now assessed under the AA's Guest Accommodation scheme. Some of them have been awarded yellow stars, which indicates that they are among the top ten percent of their star rating. Most Restaurants with Rooms have been awarded AA Rosettes for their food.

AA Rosette Awards

Out of the many thousands of restaurants in the UK, the AA identifies some 2,000 as the best. The following is an outline of what to expect from restaurants with AA Rosette Awards. For a more detailed explanation of Rosette criteria please see **theAA.com**

◉ Excellent local restaurants serving food prepared with care, understanding and skill, using good quality ingredients.

◉◉ The best local restaurants, which aim for and achieve higher standards, better consistency and where a greater precision is apparent in the cooking. There will be obvious attention to the selection of quality ingredients.

◉◉◉ Outstanding restaurants that demand recognition well beyond their local area.

◉◉◉◉ Amongst the very best restaurants in the British Isles, where the cooking demands national recognition.

◉◉◉◉◉ The finest restaurants in the British Isles, where the cooking stands comparison with the best in the world.

Useful information

If you're unsure about any of the facilities offered, always check with the establishment before you visit or book accommodation.

Hints on booking your stay

It's always worth booking as early as possible, particularly for the peak holiday period from the beginning of June to the end of September. Bear in mind that Easter and other public holidays may be busy too, and in some parts of Scotland, the ski season is a peak holiday period.

Some hotels will ask for a deposit or full payment in advance, especially for one-night bookings. And some hotels charge half-board (bed, breakfast and dinner) whether you require the meals or not, while others may only accept full-board bookings. Not all hotels will accept advance bookings for bed and breakfast, overnight or short stays. Some will not take reservations from midweek.

Once a booking is confirmed, let the hotel know at once if you are unable to keep your reservation. If the hotel cannot re-let your room you may be liable to pay about two-thirds of the room price (a deposit will count towards this payment). In Britain a legally binding contract is made when you accept an offer of accommodation, either in writing or by telephone, and illness is not accepted as a release from this contract. You are advised to take out insurance against possible cancellation, for example AA Single Trip Insurance. Visit theAA.com or call 0845 092 0606 for details.

Booking online

Booking a place to stay can be a very time-consuming process, but you can search quickly and easily online for a place that best suits your needs. Simply visit our website (**www.theAA.com/travel**) to search for a hotel, then click on Book online on the hotel's own page to check availability.

Prices

The AA encourages the use of the Hotel Industry Voluntary Code of Booking Practice, which aims to ensure that guests know how much they will have to pay and what services and facilities are included, before entering a financially binding agreement. If the price has not previously been confirmed in writing, guests should be given a card stipulating the total obligatory charge when they register at reception.

Facilities for disabled guests

The Equality Act 2010 means that service providers may have to make permanent adjustments to their premises. For further information, see the government website www.disability.gov.uk

Please note: AA inspectors are not accredited to make inspections under the National Accessibility Scheme. We indicate in the entries if an establishment has ground floor rooms; and if a hotel tells us that they have disabled facilities this is included in the description.

The establishments in this guide should all be aware of their responsibilities under the Act. We recommend that you always phone in advance to ensure that the establishment you have chosen has appropriate facilities.

Licensing laws

Licensing laws differ in England, Wales, Scotland, the Republic of Ireland, the Isle of Man, the Isles of Scilly and the Channel Islands. Public houses are generally open from mid morning to early afternoon, and from about 6 or 7pm until 11pm, although closing times may be earlier or later and some pubs are open all afternoon. Unless otherwise stated, establishments listed are licensed. Hotel residents can obtain alcoholic drinks at all times, if the licensee is prepared to serve them. Non-residents eating at the hotel restaurant can have drinks with meals. Children under 14 may be excluded from bars where no food is served. Those under 18 may not purchase or consume alcoholic drinks. Club license means that drinks are served to club members only. Forty-eight hours must lapse between joining and ordering.

Fire safety

The Fire Precautions Act does not apply to the Channel Islands, Republic of Ireland, or the Isle of Man, which have their own rules. As far as we are aware, all hotels listed have applied for and not been refused a fire certificate.

Smoking regulations

Smoking in public places is banned in England, Scotland, Wales and the Channel Islands. If a bedroom is allocated for smokers, the hotel is obliged to clearly indicate that this is the case.

Bank and Public Holidays 2012

New Year's Day	1st January
New Year's Holiday	3rd January (Scotland)
Good Friday	6th April
Easter Monday	9th April
Early May Bank Holiday	7th May
Spring Bank Holiday	4th June
Diamond Jubilee Holiday	5th June
August Holiday	6th August (Scotland)
Summer Bank Holiday	27th August
St Andrew's Day (Scotland)	30th November
Christmas Day	25th December
Boxing Day	26th December

theAA.com

Go to theAA.com to find more AA listed guest houses, hotels, pubs and restaurants – There are around 12,000 establishments on the site.

- The AA's easy-to-use route planner is on the home page.

- Simply enter your postcode and the establishment postcode given in this guide and click 'Find Route'. You will have a detailed route plan to take you from door-to-door.

- Use the Travel section to search, either by name or location, for Hotels, B&Bs, Restaurants and Pubs rated or selected by the AA.

Why not spend less and relax more on UK breaks?

cottages4you
property ref: GRL

Make AA Travel your first destination and you're on the way to a more relaxing short break or holiday.

AA Members and customers can get great deals on accommodation, from B&Bs to farmhouses, inns and hotels.

You can also save up to 10% at cottages4you, enjoy a 5% discount with Hoseasons, and up to 60% off the very best West End shows.

Thinking of going further afield?

Check out our attractive discounts on car hire, airport parking, ferry bookings, travel insurance and much more.

Then simply relax.

These are just some of our well-known partners:

cottages4you   Hoseasons   Hertz   holiday extras   P&O Ferries

Visit theAA.com/travel

AA For the road ahead

ENGLAND

Runswick Bay, North York Moors National Park

Bedfordshire

The small town of Ampthill, near Bedford, seen from Laurel Wood

Icon Hotel

★★★ 81% HOTEL

Address: 15 Stuart St, LUTON, LU1 2SA
Tel: 01582 722123
Fax: 01582 722424
E-mail: reservations@iconhotelluton.com
Website: www.iconhotelluton.com
Map ref: 3, TL02
Directions: Approx 1m from M1 junct 10A. Take next left into Hasting St
Rooms: 60 (7 fmly) (5 GF) **S** £78-£156; **D** £87-£227 (incl. bkfst) **Facilities:** FTV Gym Therapy treatments by prior arrangement ♫ Wi-fi
Parking: 18 **Notes:** ⊗

It's a short linguistic step from icon to iconic, which Italian, Franco Anacreonte, and his Greek wife, Lefi, surely had in mind for their coolly designed boutique hotel. Even the door handles have style, and look around the walls at the alternative art from world-renowned illustrators. The hotel is well placed in the heart of Luton's business and leisure district, within 10 minutes or less of junction 10 of the M1, the railway station, and the airport. If you're worried about noise, don't be, as particular attention was paid to soundproofing when it was converted from two former offices in 2009. Suites and rooms have all the facilities you would expect from a hotel of this calibre, and then some, as well as the latest energy-saving features. Luton's hat-making past

is recalled in Capello's, the bistro-style restaurant, which means 'hat' in both Italian and Greek. The Mediterranean shows its hand on the menu with modern dishes, some British-influenced, including *baccala* (poached cod); and *manzo alla Stroganoff* (classic beef stew with rice). The restaurant incorporates the Snug Lounge and Piano Bar, a very comfortable place to relax after a meal. Gym facilities are available for residents to use.

Recommended in the area

Woburn Abbey; Whipsnade Wild Animal Park and Tree Cathedral; Berkhamsted Castle

The Inn at Woburn

★★★ 81% ◉◉ HOTEL

Address: George St, WOBURN, Milton Keynes, MK17 9PX
Tel: 01525 290441
Fax: 01525 290432
E-mail: inn@woburn.co.uk
Website: www.woburn.co.uk/inn
Map ref: 3, SP93 **Directions:** M1 junct 13, towards Woburn. In Woburn left at T-junct, hotel in village
Rooms: 55 (7 annexe) (4 fmly) (21 GF) **S** £118;
D £138 **Facilities:** FTV ♨ 54 Concessionary rate to access Woburn Safari Park & Woburn Abbey Wi-fi
Parking: 80

Occupying centre stage in what has been described as 'a Georgian town of village proportions', this former coaching inn is part of the estate belonging to the Duke of Bedford, whose home, Woburn Abbey, has been the family seat for nearly 400 years. The village is noted for its fine architecture, antique and gift shops, tea rooms, restaurants and the surrounding parkland. The Inn at Woburn has wide-ranging appeal – rooms, from singles to executive king, have satellite TV, radio, direct-dial telephone and kettle. Across the courtyard are seven cottages, five with their own individual sitting room. Olivier's is the hotel's two AA Rosette-awarded restaurant, where contemporary English and Continental cuisine is offered, typified by carpaccio of Woburn venison with roasted beetroot and basil dressing; and daily specials, all of which make good use of local produce. Brunch and snack menus, available according to the hour, offer sandwiches, salads, wraps and a 'dish of the day'. The informal Tavistock Bar is a convivial place to relax with an ale or a fine wine. A concierge service will arrange everything from a restaurant booking to a birthday cake. Overnight guests can enjoy concessionary entry to Woburn Abbey and Woburn Safari Park.

Recommended in the area

Woburn Safari Park; Woburn Abbey; Woburn Golf Club

Berkshire

Windsor Castle, Windsor

Donnington Valley Hotel & Spa

★ ★ ★ ★ 84% ◎◎ HOTEL

Address: Old Oxford Rd, Donnington, NEWBURY,
RG14 3AG

Tel: 01635 551199 **Fax:** 01635 551123

E-mail: general@donningtonvalley.co.uk

Website: www.donningtonvalley.co.uk

Map ref: 3, SU36 **Directions:** M4 junct 13; A34 to
Newbury. Take exit signed Donnington/Services; at
rdbt take 2nd exit. Left at next rdbt. Hotel 2m on right

Rooms: 111

Facilities: Spa STV ⊛ ⌁ 18 Putt green Gym
Aromatherapy Sauna Steam room Dance studio Wi-fi

Parking: 150 **Notes:** ⊗

In the grounds of this splendidly appointed country
hotel, health club and spa is an 18-hole golf course,
with its own Grade II-listed clubhouse. Like the
nearby Vineyard at Stockcross, the hotel is owned
by entrepreneur Sir Peter Michael and you can
expect similarly high standards in the elegantly
designed air-conditioned bedrooms and suites, all
with marble bathrooms, Egyptian cotton sheets,
Wi-fi and laptop-sized safes. The food here is of
an equally high standard. From the bedroom
windows, you can see golfing fairways and gently
rolling countryside. Now entering his third decade
here, Head Chef Kelvin Johnson offers diners in
the WinePress restaurant (with two AA Rosettes) a
choice of modern and traditional, locally sourced
dishes. Good examples include lamb rump with
braised shoulder faggot; veal cutlet with wild
mushroom, shallot and parmesan tart; pan-fried
fillet of brill with chive mash and broad bean salsa;
and goat's cheese and walnut ravioli. Lighter snacks,
coffees and pastries are served in the Bar + Mezz
during the day, cocktails are served at night. Over 30
of the 300 wines are served by the glass. Regarded
as one of the country's best, the spa includes
an 18-metre swimming pool, sauna, steam and
aromatherapy rooms, gym and dance studio.

Recommended in the area

Donnington Castle; The Watermill Theatre; Highclere
Castle

The Vineyard at Stockcross

★★★★★ ◉◉◉ HOTEL

Address: Stockcross, NEWBURY, RG20 8JU
Tel: 01635 528770
Fax: 01635 528398
E-mail: general@the-vineyard.co.uk
Website: www.the-vineyard.co.uk
Map ref: 3, SU36
Directions: From M4 take A34 towards Newbury, exit at 3rd junct for Speen. Right at rdbt then right again at 2nd rdbt
Rooms: 49
Facilities: Spa STV ⊙ Gym Treatment rooms ♫ Wi-fi
Parking: 100 **Notes:** ⊗

How better could entrepreneur owner Sir Peter Michael demonstrate his passion for fine food and wine than in this stylish hotel and spa in the heart of Berkshire? With the name inspired by his winery in California's Sonoma Valley, it offers a variety of luxurious, air-conditioned suites, from traditional with a four-poster, to contemporary with an open-plan seating area, and patio or balcony. You can be sure that the iconic wines these rooms are named after feature among Sir Peter's impressive 2,500-bin selection. Italian marble graces the bathrooms, some of which have free-standing baths and separate showers. At the heart of the hotel is the dining room, where a mere glance tells you that everything has been meticulously put in place, from the bespoke linen and chinaware to the original sculpture and art. Awarded three AA Rosettes, Daniel Galmiche's modern French cuisine, with Mediterranean and Far Eastern influences, is illustrated by pan-fried brill with spiced bread crust, glazed carrot, crab and chicken jus; and roasted squab breasts and confit leg rolled in pistachio, with couscous, peach and spices. Light refreshments are also served by the poolside and in the garden. In addition to the spa, there's a small fitness suite.

Recommended in the area

Highclere Castle; The Watermill Theatre; Newbury Racecourse

Buckinghamshire

All Saints Church, Marlow

Danesfield House Hotel & Spa

★★★★ 81% ◉◉◉◉ HOTEL

Address: Henley Rd, MARLOW-ON-THAMES,
SL7 2EY
Tel: 01628 891010
E-mail: reservations@danesfieldhouse.co.uk
Website: www.danesfieldhouse.co.uk
Map ref: 3, SU88 **Directions:** 2m from Marlow on
A4155 towards Henley
Rooms: 86 (3 fmly) (27 GF) **S** £134-£199;
D £159-£349 (incl. bkfst) **Facilities:** Spa STV ⊙
⛳ Putt green 🏌 Gym Jogging trail Steam room
Hydrotherapy room Treatment rooms Wi-fi
Parking: 100 **Notes:** ⊗

This magnificent Tudor-style mansion is matched
only by its remarkable setting, located as it is in 65
acres of landscaped gardens overlooking the River
Thames and beyond towards the Chiltern Hills.
The third building since 1664 to have occupied this
site, the current house and gardens were designed
and built at the end of the 19th century. Today,
visitors can begin their stay by taking afternoon tea
on the south-facing terrace or in the impressive
Grand Hall, before retiring to one of the individually
furnished en suite bedrooms, where comfort is of
the essence. All the rooms come well equipped
with luxury bathrobes and L'Occitane amenities,
and valet service is also available. Danesfield Spa,
reached by a connecting bridge and with specially
commissioned artwork, has a 20-metre ozone-
cleansed pool, sauna, steam room, spa bath and
eight treatment rooms featuring Aromatherapy
Associates. The award-winning Adam Simmonds
restaurant offers stylish, intimate dining and an
extensive and far-reaching wine list. Those seeking
a more informal atmosphere should head for The
Orangery, where the first-class service continues
and diners can enjoy beautiful views of the River
Thames through a stunning full-height glass wall.

Recommended in the area

Windsor Castle; Boutique shopping in Marlow and
Henley; Legoland; River Thames trips

Stoke Park

★★★★★ 85% ◉◉ HOTEL

Address: Park Rd, STOKE POGES, SL2 4PG
Tel: 01753 717171
Fax: 01753 717181
E-mail: info@stokepark.com
Website: www.stokepark.com
Map ref: 3, SU98
Directions: M4 junct 6, A355 towards Slough,
B416 (Park Rd). Hotel 1.25m on right
Rooms: 49 (28 annexe) (14 fmly)
Facilities: Spa STV FTV ⊕ ↕ 27 ⏚ Putt green
Fishing ⛳ Gym Wi-fi
Parking: 460 **Notes:** ⊛

For luxury accommodation in 18th-century parkland, yet within easy reach of London, this Palladian mansion ticks both boxes, and plenty more too. Originally the private home of the Penn family, founders of Pennsylvania, USA, its rooms in The Mansion are exquisitely furnished in traditional style, and in contemporary boutique-style in the Pavilion. A high degree of care lies behind the choice of furnishings and fabrics, and, needless to say, all rooms have the most up-to-date technology, including plasma TV, Wi-fi and iPod docking station. Three contrasting restaurants offer plenty of variety: the Dining Room, holder of two AA Rosettes, serves modern British food, typically pan-fried pavé of halibut, with leek, pumpkin and sorrel risotto; and cannon of new season lamb with slow-braised osso buco. For Italian cuisine, head for San Marco; or, for summer lunching and afternoon teas there's the Orangery, which is even more laid-back and has delightful views of the estate. Given these gastronomic temptations, thank goodness for the sporting and exercise facilities, including the grass, all-weather and indoor tennis courts, 27-hole championship golf course, technology-led gym, award-winning spa and indoor pool. Parents with youngsters will appreciate the supervised crèche and under-eights' playroom.

Recommended in the area

Windsor Castle; River Thames trips; Marlow; Henley

Cambridgeshire

Trinity College, Cambridge

Slepe Hall Hotel

★★★ 79% HOTEL

Address: Ramsey Rd, ST IVES, PE27 5RB
Tel: 01480 463122
Fax: 01480 300706
E-mail: reception@slepehallhotel.co.uk
Website: www.slepehallhotel.co.uk
Map ref: 3, TL37
Directions: A14 junct 26 onto A1096, left at Toyota car showroom into Ramsey Rd
Rooms: 16 (5 fmly) **S** £82-£92; **D** £92-£112 (incl. bkfst)
Facilities: STV FTV ♫ Wi-fi **Parking:** 60
Notes: ⊗

Completely refurbished during 2011, this hotel's luxury and comfort take some beating. Built in 1850 on the site of an earlier hall, it was a school for many years until, in the mid-Sixties, it was converted into a hotel. The bedrooms all have swish en suite bathrooms featuring a Jacuzzi and Monsoon shower, while the executive and bridal suites both have four-posters. In the restaurant, weekly menus and daily specials offer ravioli and noisettes of lamb; turbot poached in red wine; and beetroot risotto, while the Sunday carvery offers a good choice of roasts. Part of the restaurant can be closed off for a private party. Children will probably prefer to beat a path to AJ's American-style diner, to feast on a burger, salad, sausages or pizza, while being entertained by films and cartoons on wall-mounted plasma TVs. The delights go further, with milkshakes, children's cocktails, ice cream and 'healthy smoothies', to which children can add a variety of 'tops and bottoms', and even make their own fruit dessert. Adults will no doubt prefer their own menu, which offers Thai green chicken curry; wholetail scampi; and broccoli, mint and cheese frittata. Light meals, morning coffee and afternoon tea are served in the bar.

Recommended in the area

Chapel of St Ledger (Chapel on the Bridge); Paxton Pits Nature Reserve; Cambridge

Swynford Hotel

★★★ 79% ⊕ HOTEL

Address: SIX MILE BOTTOM, Newmarket, CB8 0UE
Tel: 01638 570234
Fax: 01638 570283
E-mail: reception@swynfordhotel.com
Website: www.swynfordhotel.com
Map ref: 4, TL55
Rooms: 15 **S** £90; **D** £90–£185
Facilities: Bar Restuarant Complimentary Wi-fi
Complimentary parking Function facilities

Fine trees flank the meandering approach to this historic, gabled country house hotel, which stands in over five acres of open parkland. These are the lovely grounds that can be seen from many of the spacious, individually styled, en suite bedrooms, each well equipped with direct-dial phone, trouser press, hairdryer, flat-screen digital TV, coffee machine and iPod dock with integrated clock radio. Free wireless broadband is available throughout the hotel. The colonial-style conservatory restaurant is where Head Chef Daniel Livesey describes the cooking style as 'fine dining with substance'. On the menu this might appear as strip loin and braised shoulder of Balmoral venison with cherry cannelloni and caramelised chicory; seared king Scottish hand-dived scallops with curry beignets, butternut squash purée and red vein sorrel; and risotto of girolles, ceps, chanterelles, Perigord black truffles, mushroom and truffle foam, and tarragon caviar. If you fancy a morning coffee or afternoon tea, head for the lounge, where you can sit on the terrace with a cuppa and enjoy sandwiches made with home-baked bread, scones with clotted cream and jam or tuck in to home-made cakes.

Recommended in the area

National Horse Racing Museum; Cambridge; Anglesey Abbey

Crown Lodge Hotel

★★★ 83% ◉ HOTEL

Address: Downham Rd, Outwell, WISBECH,
PE14 8SE
Tel: 01945 773391 & 772206
Fax: 01945 772668
E-mail: office@thecrownlodgehotel.co.uk
Website: www.thecrownlodgehotel.co.uk
Map ref: 4, TF40
Directions: On A1122, approx 5m from Wisbech
Rooms: 10 (1 fmly) (10 GF) **S** £79; **D** £99
(incl. bkfst)
Facilities: FTV Squash Wi-fi
Parking: 55

A little off the beaten track in a Fenland village, this privately owned hotel is a mere stone's throw from the Cambridgeshire border. It stands on the banks of meandering Well Creek, a mile from where it crosses on an aqueduct – the prosaically named Middle Level Main Drain, which is used by canal boats. Stylish public areas in the hotel include a lounge bar with leather sofas, an open-plan bar and a brasserie restaurant. The bedrooms are pleasingly decorated, with co-ordinated fabrics, and facilities that include TV, radio, trouser press, iron and ironing board, hot drinks tray and hairdryer. In the AA Rosette restaurant, the evening menu has choices covering a lot of culinary ground: sage and thyme sausages with bubble and squeak; rack of ribs with barbecue sauce; pan-fried, saffron-marinated sea bream; and leek and mango tart. Everything meets the same high standards because it comes from the best local sources, like the butcher who raises his own cattle and sheep, and the fishmonger who also supplies Sandringham, the Queen and Prince Philip's much-loved country retreat near King's Lynn. Squash is an important part of hotel life, with teams competing in the Cambridgeshire and Peterborough leagues.

Recommended in the area

Ely Cathedral; Welney Wildfowl and Wetlands Trust; Wicken Fen National Nature Reserve

Cheshire

The ornate Diamond Jubilee Clock in Eastgate, Chester

Alderley Edge

★★★★ 75% ◉◉◉ HOTEL

Address: Macclesfield Rd, ALDERLEY EDGE, SK9 7BJ
Tel: 01625 583033
Fax: 01625 586343
E-mail: sales@alderleyedgehotel.com
Website: www.alderleyedgehotel.com
Map ref: 6, SJ87
Directions: Off A34 in Alderley Edge onto B5087 towards Macclesfield. Hotel 200yds on right
Rooms: 50 (4 fmly) (6 GF) **S** £89.50-£260; **D** £130-£400
Facilities: STV ♫ Wi-fi
Parking: 90 **Notes:** ⊗

Standing in charming, wooded grounds in a commanding position with panoramic views over the Cheshire Plain and Derbyshire countryside, this hotel offers a relaxed and inviting atmosphere. It was built in 1850 for one of the region's wealthy 'cotton kings' and was very much considered to be a grand mansion. Since that time it has been home to a doctor and then to American servicemen in the Second World War. Today there is easy access to central Manchester and transport networks, and the hotel makes a great base for exploring this interesting area. The attractively furnished bedrooms and suites offer excellent quality and comfort; all have good facilities including internet access and some have splendid views.

The Presidential Suite also has a lounge, dressing room and en suite bathroom with walk-in shower. The welcoming bar and adjacent lounge lead into the light and airy, award-winning conservatory restaurant where imaginative and memorable food is showcased on menus of modern British dishes. The six-course Gourmet Tasting menu demonstrates the chef's talents perfectly and, for a real treat, should not be missed. Throughout the hotel the friendly, attentive service is noteworthy and makes any stay one to remember.

Recommended in the area

Jodrell Bank; Tatton Park; Gawsworth Hall

Mere Court Hotel & Conference Centre

★★★★ 77% ◉ HOTEL

Address: Warrington Rd, Mere, KNUTSFORD,
WA16 0RW
Tel: 01565 831000
Fax: 01565 831001
E-mail: sales@merecourt.co.uk
Website: www.merecourt.co.uk
Map ref: 6, SJ77
Directions: A50, 1m W of junct with A556, on right
Rooms: 34 (24 fmly) (12 GF) **S** £80; **D** £100
(incl. bkfst)
Facilities: STV Wi-fi
Parking: 150 **Notes:** ⊗

Originally built in 1903 as a wedding present for the marriage of William Dunkerley and Amy Constance, this outstanding example of the Arts and Crafts style of architecture stands in seven acres of well-tended grounds in a very desirable part of Cheshire. In the late 1950s it was occupied by the North Western Gas Board, who renamed it Mere College; in 1998, following careful restoration, it reopened as a country house hotel. Its architectural heritage survived and is demonstrated throughout by fine metalwork, woodcarving, carpentry and stained glass. In the original house are individually designed and furnished executive bedrooms that look out to the ornamental lake and gardens; two have four-posters. Separate from the main house and furnished to the same high standard, are the Lakeside Rooms, with king-size bed, Jacuzzi spa bath and a host of extras. Lunch (including Sunday) and dinner are taken in the beamed, oak-panelled Arboreum Restaurant, again looking out over the lake. A menu of traditional English cooking with Mediterranean influences uses only the very best ingredients, for which it has an AA Rosette. Quality wines come from around the world. Conference facilities are particularly impressive and there is a large, self-contained, conservatory function suite.

Recommended in the area

Tatton Park; Peover Hall Gardens; Manchester

Cornwall

Towanroath Engine House at Wheal Coates Tin Mine, St Agnes

Falcon

★★★ 79% HOTEL

Address: Breakwater Rd, BUDE, EX23 8SD
Tel: 01288 352005
Fax: 01288 356359
E-mail: reception@falconhotel.com
Website: www.falconhotel.com
Map ref: 1, SS20
Directions: Exit A39 to Bude, then Widemouth Bay.
Hotel on right over canal bridge
Rooms: 29 (7 fmly) **S** £57-£70; **D** £114-£140
(incl. bkfst)
Facilities: STV FTV ❸ ♫ Wi-fi
Parking: 40 **Notes:** ⊗

The Falcon, the oldest coaching house in north Cornwall, was once the headquarters for the four-horse coaches running between Bideford, Bude, Boscastle, Tintagel and Newquay. Travellers have been welcomed here for more than 200 years and the warm and friendly atmosphere is still apparent as you walk through the front door. Overlooking the picturesque and historic Bude Canal, and with beautiful walled gardens, the hotel occupies a delightful setting. The well-appointed bedrooms are traditionally furnished with co-ordinated fabrics and have spacious modern bathrooms, irons, trouser presses, hairdryers, direct dial telephones, tea- and coffee-making facilities, guest controlled heating and flat-screen TVs with Freeview and Sky. Guests can also choose one of the four-poster bedrooms with a luxury spa bath, or the Summerleaze Suite, for a memorable occasion. The informal Coachman's Bar and elegant Tennyson's Restaurant offer a wide range of quality, modern dishes using the best of local produce complemented by a carefully chosen wine list and range of beers. The Garden Room, residents' lounge, Carriage Room and Acland Suite are all licensed for civil ceremonies so the hotel can easily cater for both small and large wedding parties. Wi-fi is freely available throughout.

Recommended in the area

Clovelly; Tintagel; Boscastle; Port Isaac; Padstow

Royal Duchy

★★★★ 79% ◎◎ HOTEL

Address: Cliff Rd, FALMOUTH, TR11 4NX
Tel: 01326 313042 & 214001
Fax: 01326 319420
E-mail: reservations@royalduchy.com
Website: www.royalduchy.com
Map ref: 1, SW83
Directions: On Cliff Rd, along Falmouth seafront
Rooms: 43 (6 fmly) (1 GF) **S** £80–£120; **D** £140–£290 (incl. bkfst)
Facilities: FTV ◎ Games room Beauty salon Sauna ♫ Wi-fi Child facilities
Parking: 50 **Notes:** ⊗

It could so easily be the Med. Stretching away to the horizon is an azure bay, to the left a castle stands high on a headland, above your head palm fronds quiver in the gentle breeze, while on the umbrella shaded table your chilled cocktails await. Actually, this is the Gulf Stream-warmed English Channel on Cornwall's southern coast, and the view is that from the hotel terrace. A short stroll away are the beaches, alleyways and quaint streets of Falmouth, a town that seems content to run at a gentler pace than most, and where you can lose yourself in centuries of maritime history. With so much to see, how useful it is to have binoculars provided in the bedrooms, along with bathrobes, slippers, hairdryer, TV, radio, telephone, and tea and coffee tray. In the Terrace Restaurant a talented team of chefs brings diners an appealing variety of AA Rosette-awarded, classical signature dishes, such as seared calves liver with mashed potato, wild mushrooms, onion confit and sherry vinegar sauce or sirloin of beef with potato rösti and shallots, followed by a selection of sumptuous desserts, all created from top Cornish produce. And from the bar it's but a few steps to the sun lounge where light snacks, lunches and delicious cream teas are served.

Recommended in the area

Lizard Peninsula; Trelissick Garden; St Michael's Mount

The Lugger Hotel

★★★ 82% ◉ HOTEL

Address: PORTLOE, Truro, TR2 5RD
Tel: 01872 501322
Fax: 01872 501691
E-mail: reservations.lugger@ohiml.com
Website: www.oxfordhotelsandinns.com
Map ref: 1, SW93
Directions: A390 to Truro, take B3287 to Tregony, then A3078 (St Mawes Rd), turn left for Veryan, then left for Portloe
Rooms: 22 (17 annexe) (1 GF)
Facilities: FTV Wi-fi
Parking: 26

The very Cornish harbour of Portloe, its picturesque cove familiar perhaps from that childhood jigsaw puzzle, was once popular with smugglers. They would meet in this 17th-century inn to share out their contraband, but it all came to an end in the 1890s, when the landlord was hanged for complicity, the liquor licence was withdrawn and a boat builder used it as a shed for the next half century. Today's bijou luxury hotel has spread into adjoining cottages with modern, en suite bedrooms featuring bleached Portuguese woods and crisp white linens. A sun terrace overlooking the harbour and the ocean is the perfect place for a morning coffee or an evening drink, but when the waves are crashing against the rocks the open fireplaces in the beamed sitting room may become a more appealing proposition. Taking full advantage of its location, the restaurant specialises in locally sourced produce, particularly straight-off-the boat seafood, such as megrim sole served lightly grilled with crab and shellfish linguine; and baked fillet of hake that comes with a lemon and herb crust. Other options include roasted duck breast with root vegetable casserole; roasted rump of Cornish lamb; and Mediterranean vegetable gateau topped with Cornish cheese.

Recommended in the area

The Eden Project; Lost Gardens of Heligan; National Maritime Museum Cornwall

Driftwood

★ ★ ★ ◉◉◉ HOTEL

Address: Rosevine, PORTSCATHO, TR2 5EW
Tel: 01872 580644
Fax: 01872 580801
E-mail: info@driftwoodhotel.co.uk
Website: www.driftwoodhotel.co.uk
Map ref: 1, SW83
Directions: A390 towards St Mawes. On A3078
turn left to Rosevine at Trewithian
Rooms: 15 (1 annexe) (3 fmly) (1 GF) **S** £157-£221;
D £165-£260 (incl. bkfst)
Facilities: FTV Private beach Treatments on request
Wi-fi **Parking:** 30 **Notes:** ⊛

In seven acres of cliffside gardens, with panoramic views of Gerrans Bay, stands this peaceful and secluded hotel. Walk down a wooded path to your own little cove and look out across the very waters that will provide your dinner lobster or crab. Head indoors to find stylishly contemporary sitting rooms stocked with books, magazines and board games. There's even a small games room for the children. Comfortable, uncluttered bedrooms are decorated in soft shades reminiscent of the seashore. Ground floor rooms have their own decked terrace, while tucked away, overlooking the sea, is a restored weatherboarded cabin with two bedrooms and a sitting room. A large deck in the sheltered terraced garden is strewn with steamer chairs for taking in the unbroken sea view. On warm evenings hurricane lamps are lit for pre-dinner drinks and after-dinner coffee. The three AA Rosette awarded restaurant (from which, no surprise, you can again see the sea) serves fresh, locally sourced food – and not just fish. Yes, there's John Dory or monkfish, for example, but the menu will also feature dishes such as roasted Terras Farm duck breast, pastilla of duck leg, endives and orange and port jus.

Recommended in the area
Falmouth Maritime Museum; Lost Gardens of Heligan; Tate Gallery St Ives

The Carlyon Bay Hotel

★★★★ 76% HOTEL

Address: Sea Rd, Carlyon Bay, ST AUSTELL,
PL25 3RD
Tel: 01726 812304 & 811006   **Fax:** 01726 814938
E-mail: reservations@carlyonbay.com
Website: www.carlyonbay.com
Map ref: 1, SX05 **Directions:** From St Austell,
follow signs for Charlestown. Carlyon Bay signed on
left, hotel at end of Sea Rd
Rooms: 86 (14 fmly) **S** £90-£310; **D** £140-£310
Facilities: Spa FTV ⊙ ↳ ↕ 18 ♨ Putt green Gym
9-hole approach course Snooker room Sauna Steam
room ♫ Wi-fi Child facilities **Parking:** 100 **Notes:** ⊛

From the air, this sprawling, creeper-covered hotel points like an arrowhead across some of its 250 clifftop acres of secluded gardens and grounds, part of which is taken up by a championship 18-hole golf course. Nearby, you'll find a 10-acre practice ground, putting lawns and a nine-hole approach course. If none of that appeals, you can swim in both outdoor and indoor pools, play tennis, enjoy all the benefits of the spa, or take it relatively easy with a game of snooker. Bedrooms are well equipped and maintained, and many have marvellous views across St Austell Bay. So too, as the name rather suggests, does the Bay View restaurant, where a four-course dinner menu makes full use of the best local produce, including fresh day-boat fish and seafood. Must-eat main courses to try include saddle of spring lamb with crushed peas and fève beans; English Rose veal with white truffle pumpkin and golden raisins; pan-fried bass with lobster fumet; or mascarpone tart with tomato and cardamom. Alternative dining options are Fusion, which offers Asian cuisine, and the Green Bar and Terrace for traditional grills and light bar snacks in the evening. During school holidays there's a supervised nursery.

Recommended in the area

The Eden Project; Georgian Charlestown;
Lanhydrock (NT)

The Cornwall Hotel Spa & Estate

★★★★ 78% ◉◉ COUNTRY HOUSE HOTEL

Address: Pentewan Rd, Tregorrick, ST AUSTELL,
PL26 7AB
Tel: 01726 874050
Fax: 01726 874056
E-mail: enquiries@thecornwall.com
Website: www.thecornwall.com
Map ref: 1, SW05
Directions: A391 to St Austell then B3273 towards
Mevagissey. Hotel approx 0.5m on right
Rooms: 65 (4 fmly)
Facilities: Spa STV FTV ◔ ⓢ ⓨ Gym Wi-fi Child
facilities **Parking:** 200

Standing in 43 acres of wooded parkland, this newly renovated mansion was built in 1834 for a wealthy St Austell banker. In 2005, specialists set about restoring the estate from the overgrown wilderness it had become, painstakingly conserving its historical and architectural integrity, not least by restoring a medieval wayside cross, Victorian vinery, walled garden and a quirky wine cellar. The park itself contains beautiful oak, sycamore, beech, poplar and chestnut trees, and is home to woodpeckers, ducks, geese, owls and rare bats. Suites and traditionally styled bedrooms are in The White House; adjacent are the contemporary Woodland rooms, which overlook the Pentewan Valley. Places to eat are the two-AA Rosette Arboretum restaurant for dishes

such as poached and roasted saddle of rabbit with carrot purée and sautéed spinach; baked fillets of local plaice with creamy pepper sauce and crab-crushed potatoes; and platter of vegetarian dishes. For less formality, try Acorns Brasserie for hearty breakfasts and evening meals of braised local steak; St Austell Bay mussels; and honey-roasted pork loin. Light lunches, Cornish cream teas and cocktails are served in, and outside, the Parkland Terrace, which too looks across the valley. Leisure facilities include a spa, infinity pool and fitness centre.

Recommended in the area

The Eden Project; Lanhydrock Park (NT); Georgian Charlestown

Carbis Bay Hotel & Apartments

★★★ 74% ◉ HOTEL

Address: Carbis Bay, ST IVES, TR26 2NP
Tel: 01736 795311
Fax: 01736 797677
E-mail: info@carbisbayhotel.co.uk
Website: www.carbisbayhotel.co.uk
Map ref: 1, SW54
Directions: A3074, through Lelant. 1m, at
Carbis Bay 30yds before lights, right into
Porthrepta Rd to hotel
Rooms: 47 (16 fmly) **Facilities:** ⌁ (seasonal)
Games room Fishing Private beach ♫ Private motor
yacht Sub-tropical gardens **Parking:** 200 **Notes:** ⊗

In a wonderful location above 25 acres of stunning golden sands, this is Britain's only hotel with a private Blue Flag beach, awarded for its high environmental standards. Individually decorated bedrooms, waterfront beach houses, cosy cottages and chic apartments all lie within the grounds. From the hotel's main entrance, elegant hallways lead to terraced gardens from where the views over the grounds and Carbis Bay must rank up there with the world's best. Day boats out of St Ives supply the fresh fish and shellfish that appear on the The Conservatory lunch menu, and on the dinner menu in Sands Restaurant, which has held an AA Rosette for 11 years. Fish dishes to expect here include grilled local sole with crayfish; and pan-fried sea bass on crab and spring onion mash, while others might be tenderloin of pork in smoked ham; and vegetable rocket risotto. The Conservatory is also open for morning coffee, lunch, afternoon tea and evening tapas, while both restaurants are open for Sunday lunch. The bar offers lunchtime snacks as well. Relax in one of the spacious lounges, enjoy a stroll on the beach or be entertained by the resident pianist. The open-air pool is open from May to September.

Recommended in the area

Tate Gallery St Ives; Eden Project; Land's End

The Nare Hotel

★★★★ ◎ COUNTRY HOUSE HOTEL

Address: Carne Beach, VERYAN-IN-ROSELAND, TR2 5PF
Tel: 01872 501111
Fax: 01872 501856
E-mail: stay@narehotel.co.uk
Website: www.narehotel.co.uk
Map ref: 1, SW93 **Directions:** From Tregony follow A3078 for 1.5m. Left at Veryan sign, through village
Rooms: 37 (7 fmly) (7 GF) **S** £140-£268; **D** £270-£768 (incl. bkfst) **Facilities:** Spa FTV ⊕ ↘ ⛱ ✤ Gym Health & beauty clinic Sauna Steam room Hotel sailing boat Shooting Wi-fi **Parking:** 80

Overlooking a superb beach, The Nare is the only four-red-star hotel in Cornwall. It has a delightful country-house ambience and is now in its third generation of family ownership. Those guests looking for total relaxation will certainly find it here, from the comfy sofas in the lounge to the spa treatments and hot tub overlooking the sea. More active types can enjoy a good range of leisure activities including tennis courts, croquet, billiards, two swimming pools, a gym and even a 22-foot yacht for charter. The owners have shied away from the trend for designer hotels, preferring to individually style their rooms in a more traditional but equally luxurious style. Most are spacious and many have a balcony or terrace with wonderful sea views. Suites have a separate lounge and one has a kitchen, too. All rooms enjoy the valet service, including 24-hour room service. For dinner there's a choice of two excellent eating options – the more formal Dining Room and the casual Quarterdeck. Whichever you go for, expect to enjoy plenty of first-class Cornish ingredients, including locally reared beef, seafood from local fishermen, and lots of fresh seasonal vegetables and fruit. The Nare also boasts an extensive wine cellar.

Recommended in the area

Eden Project; Lost Gardens of Heligan; Caerhays Castle

Cumbria

Wasdale Head and Wast Water, Lake District National Park

Rothay Manor

★★★ 83% ◎ HOTEL

Address: Rothay Bridge, AMBLESIDE, LA22 0EH
Tel: 015394 33605
Fax: 015394 33607
E-mail: hotel@rothaymanor.co.uk
Website: www.rothaymanor.co.uk/aa
Map ref: 6, NY30
Directions: In Ambleside follow signs for Coniston
(A593). Hotel is situated 0.25m SW of Ambleside
opposite rugby pitch
Rooms: 19 (2 annexe) (7 fmly) (3 GF) **S** from £105;
D £175-£235 (incl. bkfst) **Facilities:** STV Free fishing
permit Wi-fi **Parking:** 45 **Notes:** ⊛

This traditional Regency country house hotel was built in 1825 and lies in the heart of the Lake District, just a quarter of a mile from Lake Windermere, making it ideally situated for walking, cycling or exploring the local towns and villages. Set in its own landscaped gardens, it offers guests the perfect opportunity to relax and recharge their batteries. Owned and run by the Nixon family for over 40 years, it has a long-standing reputation for its relaxed, comfortable and friendly atmosphere, as well as its excellent food and wine. All the bedrooms are en suite and include a number of suites, family rooms and rooms with balconies, from which to enjoy fine views of the fells. For added privacy, two suites are located in a separate building close to the main hotel. All the guest rooms are comfortably equipped and furnished to a very high standard, with TV and tea- and coffee-making facilities supplied. Public areas include a choice of lounges, a spacious restaurant with an imaginative menu making much use of fresh, local produce, and conference facilities. Guests can also enjoy free use of the Low Wood leisure club, which has an indoor heated pool and is located 1.5 miles from the hotel.

Recommended in the area

Cruises on the Lakes; Hill Top (Beatrix Potter); Holker Hall and Gardens

The Pheasant

★★★ 86% ◉ HOTEL

Address: BASSENTHWAITE, Cockermouth,
CA13 9YE
Tel: 017687 76234
Fax: 017687 76002
E-mail: info@the-pheasant.co.uk
Website: www.the-pheasant.co.uk
Map ref: 10, NY23
Directions: Midway between Keswick &
Cockermouth, signed from A66
Rooms: 15 (2 annexe) (2 GF) **S** £90-£110;
D £140-£200 (incl. bkfst) **Facilities:** Wi-fi
Parking: 40 **Notes:** 🧒 under 12yrs

Dating back over 500 years, this historic coaching inn, in the unspoilt northern end of the Lake District, was further enhanced in 2010 by the creation of a fine-dining restaurant that overlooks the well-tended gardens and the fells beyond. One 19th-century regular was the famous huntsman John ("With his hounds and his horn in the morning") Peel, who recounted his exploits in the tap room, now the hotel bar. This oak-panelled room, with exposed beams, polished parquet flooring and log fire remains more or less as it was then, although it now offers 60 malt whiskies, 12 vodkas, 12 gins, 12 wines by the glass and three draught ales on hand pump; it also displays two watercolours by renowned Cumbrian artist Edward W Thompson who exchanged them for beer. The Pheasant has a reputation for high quality cuisine, using the best local produce whether in the restaurant or the more informal bistro; lighter lunches and afternoon teas are served in the lounges and bar. The individually decorated bedrooms have been appointed to a high standard with en suite bathrooms offering both bath and power shower, and all equipped with phone, tea tray and flat-screen TV.

Recommended in the area

Muncaster Castle; Wordsworth House; Rheged Discovery Centre

Crooklands Hotel

★★★ 78% HOTEL

Address: CROOKLANDS, Kendal, LA7 7NW
Tel: 015395 67432
Fax: 015395 67525
E-mail: reception@crooklands.com
Website: www.crooklands.com
Map ref: 6, SD58
Directions: M6 junct 36 onto A65. Left at rdbt.
Hotel 1.5m on right past garage
Rooms: 30 (3 fmly) (14 GF) **S** £70-£95; **D** £88-£130
(incl. bkfst)
Facilities: FTV Wi-fi **Parking:** 80
Notes: ⊗

The tranquil, winding Lancaster Canal, which links
Kendal and Preston, runs right past this early-
18th-century former farmhouse. After supplying
refreshments to canal users for many years, it finally
became a fully-fledged hotel in the 1970s. Today's
owners, Charles and June Horrax, continue to
enhance and modernise the property, while taking
care to maintain its original character and charm.
Their most recent additions are a new reception
area, restaurant and residents' lounge, although
they've also upgraded the bedrooms too. These
provide luxury toiletries in the en suite bathroom,
free Wi-fi, Freeview TV, radio, writing desk, direct-dial
phone, hairdryer, hot drinks tray and room service;
a king-size bed in the Executive Suite is fitted with
Egyptian cotton linen. Food in Jules Restaurant
tends towards traditional English, although other
ideas from around the world also get a look in; thus,
on the menu might be roast half-duck with sweet
black cherry and brandy sauce; Fleetwood haddock
in beer batter; and vegetable balti. In CJ's Bar, the
evening options typically include suet pudding
of the day; bangers and mash, and minted lamb
Henry. In winter, CJ's coal fire keeps it warm, while
in summer the thick stone walls keep the place
pleasantly cool.

Recommended in the area

Levens Heritage; Lake Windermere; Sizergh Castle

Borrowdale Gates Country House Hotel

★★★ 81% COUNTRY HOUSE HOTEL

Address: GRANGE-IN-BORROWDALE, Keswick,
CA12 5UQ
Tel: 017687 77204
Fax: 017687 77195
E-mail: hotel@borrowdale-gates.com
Website: www.borrowdale-gates.com
Map ref: 10, NY21
Directions: From A66 follow B5289 for approx 4m.
Turn right over bridge, hotel 0.25m beyond village
Rooms: 27 (10 GF)
Facilities: FTV Wi-fi
Parking: 29

Surrounded by first-class fell-walking country and set in two acres of peaceful, wooded grounds, this delightful hotel, is close to the shores of Derwentwater, with the many attractions of Keswick nearby. This Victorian country house is a real home-from-home with log fires, Lakeland-inspired cooking and updated and stylish accommodation. Rooms with views might be considered a speciality here – the cosy bar and beamed lounges look out over the gardens to the valley beyond and each bedroom has picture-perfect views whether bathed in glorious sunshine or shimmering with a wintery frost. The dining room looks onto green pastures where Herdwick sheep graze, and is a wonderful place to linger over a hearty Cumbrian breakfast or delicious candlelit dinner. Each of the bedrooms comes complete with crisp cotton sheets, feather pillows (unless you prefer a different kind), fluffy white towels and a tray of morning tea and coffee. All the bedrooms are individually designed and some boast a decked balcony or French doors opening onto the gardens. Contemporary country-house cooking with a lightness of touch is the mainstay of the kitchen, with menus making the most of superb Lake District produce.

Recommended in the area

Keswick's Theatre by the Lake; Honister Slate Mine; lakeside and fell walks

Rothay Garden

★★★★ 84% ◉◉ HOTEL

Address: Broadgate, GRASMERE, LA22 9RJ
Tel: 015394 35334 **Fax:** 015394 35723
E-mail: stay@rothaygarden.com
Website: www.rothaygarden.com
Map ref: 10, NY31 **Directions:** Off A591,
opposite Swan Hotel, into Grasmere, 300yds on
left **Rooms:** 30 (3 fmly) (8 GF) **S** from £109; **D** from
£125 (incl. bkfst) **Facilities:** FTV HydroSpa Sauna
Aromatherapy room Infrared loungers Reflexology
walk Wi-fi **Parking:** 38
Notes: ⚑ under 5yrs

Situated on the edge of picturesque Grasmere village, and nestling in two acres of riverside gardens, Rothay Garden is the perfect choice for a relaxing break in the Lake District. The hotel has benefitted from a £3 million redevelopment programme and the stylish two-AA Rosette awarded Garden Restaurant, chic lounge bars and the new Riverside Spa all combine to ensure that guests have a memorable stay. The 30 beautiful bedrooms, including 12 suites, provide comfort and luxury. All the rooms have excellent views over the nearby fells, and many have their own patios or balconies overlooking the gardens or the babbling river Rothay. The new Riverside Spa offers hotel guests exclusive facilities including Hydrospa, Herbal Pine Sauna, Infrared Loungers and an amazing Reflexology Walk. It's the ideal place to chill out and relax – or enjoy a chilled glass of wine or a cold beer before dinner. The beauty of the Lake District is right on the doorstep and Wordsworth's Grasmere really is the "jewel of the Lakes"; the hotel is ideally situated for visiting Ambleside, Windermere, Keswick and Kendal. Special short breaks are offered all year, as are Christmas, New Year and specialist Food & Wine breaks.

Recommended in the area

Dove Cottage and Wordsworth Museum; Grasmere Gingerbread Shop; Lake Windermere Steamers

Wordsworth Hotel & Spa

★★★★ 80% ◉◉ HOTEL

Address: GRASMERE, LA22 9SW
Tel: 015394 35592
Fax: 015394 35765
E-mail: enquiry@thewordsworthhotel.co.uk
Website: www.thewordsworthhotel.co.uk
Map ref: 10, NY30
Directions: Off A591 centre of village adjacent to
St Oswald's Church
Rooms: 39 (2 fmly) (2 GF) **S** £40-£175; **D** £120-£375
(incl. bkfst) **Facilities:** Spa FTV ⏱ ⚓ Gym Treatment
room Mixed sauna Whirlpool Nail bar Wi-fi
Parking: 60

This historic, family-owned and operated hotel is situated in two acres of riverside gardens, with terrific views of Grasmere Vale and the surrounding mountains. A complete internal refurbishment has left it providing even higher levels of style and luxury, amply illustrated by the smartly furnished en suite bedrooms, bathrooms with bathrobes and luxury toiletries, and Egyptian cottons on the beds. The rooms also contain a flat-screen TV, direct-dial phone, Wi-fi internet access, hot drinks tray and the hotel's own specially bottled mineral water. It seems that honeymooners and old romantics tend to go for a four-poster room or a suite. Those with mobility difficulties, or those who simply prefer this bathing option, can ask for a room with a walk-in shower. While they are accompanying their owners within the hotel, dogs are allowed in ground floor bedrooms, Garden Room and Dove Bar, but nowhere else. For fine-dining, there's Signature restaurant, holder of two AA Rosettes; Dove Bistro for somewhere less formal; one of the lounges for a cream tea; and the bar for a snack. Next door to the hotel is Grasmere Gingerbread Shop, from where it's a brisk walk to Wordsworth's home and Dove Cottage. After a long day a dip in the heated pool, or time in the new sauna and spa is recommended.

Recommended in the area

Dove Cottage and Wordsworth Museum; Lake Windermere Steamers; Grasmere Gingerbread Shop

Highfield Hotel

★★★ 79% ◉◉ SMALL HOTEL

Address: The Heads, KESWICK, CA12 5ER
Tel: 017687 72508
Fax: 017687 80837
E-mail: info@highfieldkeswick.co.uk
Website: www.highfieldkeswick.co.uk
Map ref: 10, NY22
Directions: M6 junct 40, A66, 2nd exit at rdbt. Left to T-junct, left again. Right at mini-rdbt. Take 4th right
Rooms: 18 (1 fmly) (2 GF) **S** £95| **D** £170-£220 (incl. bkfst & dinner)
Facilities: STV Wi-fi
Parking: 20 **Notes:** ⊗

For that country-house feel in the heart of town, this turreted, late-Victorian villa, close to Derwent Water, and surrounded by magnificent mountains, is surely the answer. Indeed, with the centre of Keswick only a few minutes' walk away, even a hotel guest who detests shopping might find compensation in the views from Main Street. The hotel incorporates many original features – balconies, bay windows, a veranda for that pre-dinner drink, and a converted chapel, now a guest room. The en suite bedrooms, all carefully restored by owners Howard and Caroline Speck, are decorated to a high standard and equipped with colour TV and DVD, radio alarm clock, phone and hot drinks tray. Most enjoy panoramic views, some of the lake, Borrowdale or maybe Skiddaw. The clean lines of the restaurant give it a very different look from Victorian times, but the design and decor work well and it's the only hotel/restaurant in town to hold two AA Rosettes. The daily changing menu makes use of the best fresh local produce for roast loin and cutlet of Cumbrian lamb; tempura of monkfish with fresh egg pasta; sweet and sour vegetable stir-fry; and crisp spiced vegetable strudel with minted cucumber yoghurt.

Recommended in the area

Honister Slate Mine; Cumberland Pencil Museum; Derwent Water

Scafell Hotel

★★★ 79% HOTEL
Address: ROSTHWAITE, Borrowdale, CA12 5XB
Tel: 017687 77208
Fax: 017687 77280
E-mail: info@scafell.co.uk
Website: www.scafell.co.uk
Map ref: 10, NY21
Directions: M6 junct 40 to Keswick on A66. Take B5289 to Rosthwaite
Rooms: 23 (2 fmly) (8 GF) **S** £45-£75; **D** £90-£150 (incl. bkfst)
Facilities: FTV Guided walks
Parking: 50

The Scafell Hotel is a wonderful country house hotel located in the very heart of Borrowdale, considered by many as England's finest valley, surrounded by mighty fells, tranquil meadows and crystal-clear waters. Situated almost at the foot of Great Gable and the Scafell Massif, the hotel is regarded as one of the Lake District's headquarters for climbers and hill walkers. Those who prefer gentle rambling or just lazing on lawns fringed by trees amidst imposing scenery will be equally happy staying here. Rooms were fully refurbished in 2009 in a warm and rich country house style with a 'contemporary twist'. It's the perfect setting for a peaceful and relaxing break in the beautiful Borrowdale Valley. The restaurant, lounges and bar have been tastefully decorated and furnished to retain that all-important country house warmth, allowing for complete relaxation after a great day's walking on the Fells, and maybe even a little nap by the fire after a delicious five-course dinner. Under the constant direction of owners Miles Jessop MBE (Chairman) and Andrew Nelson (Managing Director), the management and team of Scafell Hotel offer truly warm and friendly service.

Recommended in the area

Keswick Museum and Art Gallery; Rydal Mount and Gardens; Muncaster Castle

Sella Park House Hotel

★★★ 85% COUNTRY HOUSE HOTEL

Address: Calderbridge, SEASCALE, CA20 1DW

Tel: 0845 450 6445 & 01946 841601

Fax: 01946 841339

E-mail: info@penningtonhotels.com

Website: www.penningtonhotels.com

Map ref: 5, SC00

Directions: From A595 at Calderbridge, follow sign for North Gate. Hotel 0.5m on left

Rooms: 16 (5 annexe) (2 GF) **S** £90-£120; **D** £110-£160 (incl. bkfst)

Facilities: FTV Fishing Wi-fi

Parking: 30

Standing in six acres of quiet, mature gardens sweeping down to the River Calder, this historic property can trace its origins back to the 16th century. One theory is that it was a pele, or watch tower, built to spot marauding Scottish raiders, but nobody's really sure. Whatever it was, it's a fine building, whose individual, en suite bedrooms are all equipped with a power shower, flat-screen TV, DVD player, phone and free Wi-fi, and one has a four-poster. There are plenty of places to unwind. Outside, of course, are the spacious grounds in which one can wander; inside, there's the bar and snug room for a morning coffee, light lunch, or afternoon tea with home-baked cakes and scones. The candlelit, wood-panelled Priory Restaurant offers a fine-dining menu with an emphasis on seasonal, high-quality Cumbrian produce. Employing local vernacular, the menu invites you to 'Fill yer boots' with a starter such as Whitehaven line-caught mackerel, followed by Goosnargh duck breast, or rump of Lakeland lamb, then whisky jelly for dessert. Many of the vegetables, fruits and herbs come from the kitchen gardens at nearby Muncaster Castle. The hotel's own luxury marquee is often used for weddings and corporate events. Residents may fish in the river.

Recommended in the area

Muncaster Castle and Gardens; Railway Museum, Ravenglass; Ravenglass Roman Bath House

Westmorland Hotel

★★★ 83% ◉ HOTEL

Address: Westmorland Place, Orton, TEBAY, CA10 3SB
Tel: 015396 24351
Fax: 015396 24354
E-mail: reservations@westmorlandhotel.com
Website: www.westmorlandhotel.com
Map ref: 6, NY60
Directions: Signed from Westmorland Services between M6 junct 38 & 39 N'bound & S'bound
Rooms: 50 (5 fmly) (12 GF) **S** £87-£113; **D** £104-£124 (incl. bkfst) **Facilities:** FTV Wi-fi
Parking: 60

To its west is the Lake District, to the southeast are the Yorkshire Dales, while all around are the Cumbrian fells. Tranquil is the word for the setting of this farming, family-owned hotel, yet at the same time it's very convenient for the M6. Natural materials have been used throughout the interior to create a contemporary appearance, although there's a good old-fashioned log fire in the lounge. The suites and rooms are all en suite and, depending on their grade, offer an increasingly wide range of complimentary extras, from fluffy bathrobes to world-famous Kendal mint cake. Most look out to the surrounding countryside. The restaurant, which has held an AA Rosette for more than 10 years, has floor-to-ceiling windows that overlook a water feature and those ever-present hills. Mostly traditional dishes are on the menus, such as five-hour roasted Herdwick lamb with pearl barley risotto; and shin of Galloway beef with root vegetable mash and mini kidney pudding. The hotel is committed to local sourcing and, in fact, the lamb and beef come from its own farm less than a mile away. Further evidence of its commitment to local produce is its farm shop only a short walk away, and its butcher's counter, the only one on a British motorway (the M6).

Recommended in the area

Holker Hall; Trip on an Ullswater Steamer; Mirehouse Historic House and Gardens

Cedar Manor Hotel & Restaurant

★★ 85% ◉◉ HOTEL

Address: Ambleside Rd, WINDERMERE, LA23 1AX
Tel: 015394 43192 & 015394 45970
Fax: 015394 45970
E-mail: info@cedarmanor.co.uk
Website: www.cedarmanor.co.uk
Map ref: 6, SD49
Directions: From A591 follow signs to Windermere.
Hotel on left just beyond St Mary's Church
Rooms: 10 (1 annexe) (1 fmly) (3 GF) **S** £80-£180;
D £120-£350 (incl. bkfst)
Facilities: FTV Wi-fi
Parking: 11 **Notes:** ⊗

In the 19th century, the seriously wealthy often built themselves sumptuous houses in the Lake District – this was one. Now a boutique hotel, it stands in secluded walled gardens, dominated by the ancient cedar from which it takes its name, and is a short stroll from Lake Windermere and the village. The variously styled bedrooms are all equipped with flat-screen TV and DVD player, and some have been fitted with a spa bath. From both the Coniston and Langdale rooms there's a fine panorama of the lake and the Langdale Pikes; the Crinkle Crag and Wansfell rooms are furnished with locally hand-crafted, four-poster finial beds. The recently extended, two-floor Coach House Suite features a super-king-size bed, stunning bathroom, lounge, dining area and french doors to an outside seating area. Guests and non-residents may eat in the two-AA Rosette awarded candlelit restaurant. Local sourcing of ingredients may be taken as read for seasonal menus that might offer starters of Breton-style mussels; or roast fennel and butternut squash salad; main courses of linguine in wild mushroom sauce; or lamb, rosemary and olive casserole; and, for dessert, steamed marmalade sponge pudding. The descriptions on the wine list are admirably brief, yet sufficiently informative.

Recommended in the area

Lake Windermere; Beatrix Potter Gallery; Dove Cottage and Wordsworth Museum

Gilpin Hotel & Lake House

★ ★ ★ ★ ⊚ ⊚ ⊚ HOTEL

Address: Crook Rd, WINDERMERE, LA23 3NE
Tel: 015394 88818
Fax: 015394 88058
E-mail: hotel@gilpinlodge.co.uk
Website: www.gilpinlodge.co.uk
Map ref: 6, SD49
Directions: M6 junct 36, A590, A591 to rdbt N of
Kendal, onto B5284, hotel 5m on right
Rooms: 26 (12 annexe) (12 GF) **S** £180-£510;
D £290-£550 (incl. bkfst & dinner)
Facilities: ⤸ **Parking:** 40
Notes: ⊗ ⋈ under 7yrs

Along a quiet country lane, two miles from
Windermere but hidden from the crowds, enter
through the electric gates to discover a Lake District
sanctuary. With six stunning suites, the Lake House
is set on a stunningly beautiful four acre private
lake with boat-house and boat. Facilities include
in-room spa treatments, traditional sauna, indoor
swimming pool leading onto the lakeshore, and
an outdoor cedarwood hot tub – all exclusively
for the enjoyment of Lake House guests. The 100
acres of private gardens, craggy green countryside
and woodland includes a summerhouse, kitchen
gardens, druids circle, lake walk and other walks
leading to panoramic views of the Lake District
mountain ranges. Enjoy breakfast and afternoon
tea from the fire-lit lounge and conservatory whilst
watching wild ducks and geese frolicking on the
lake. For dinner, a chauffeur will take you to the
main hotel, just a mile away. Enjoy pre-dinner
drinks either at the Lake House or in the hotel's
stylish bar and wine cellars. The hotel's three AA
Rosette restaurant has four intimate dining rooms;
the five-course dinner has plenty of choice and is
a celebration of some of the finest Lake District
produce and West Coast seafood.

Recommended in the area

Lake Windermere; Beatrix Potter Gallery; Dove
Cottage and Wordsworth Museum

Holbeck Ghyll Country House Hotel

★ ★ ★ ★ ◎◎◎ COUNTRY HOUSE HOTEL

Address: Holbeck Ln, WINDERMERE, LA23 1LU
Tel: 015394 32375
Fax: 015394 34743
E-mail: stay@holbeckghyll.com
Website: www.holbeckghyll.com
Map ref: 6, SD49
Directions: 3m N of Windermere on A591, right into
Holbeck Lane (signed Troutbeck), hotel 0.5m on left
Rooms: 26 (12 annexe) (5 fmly) (11 GF) **D** £250-£570
(incl. bkfst & dinner)
Facilities: Spa STV ⌁ ⌁ Gym Sauna Steam room
Treatment rooms Beauty massage Wi-fi **Parking:** 34

It so happens that the first president of the AA was the fifth Earl of Lonsdale (he of boxing's famous belt fame). In 1888, he decided he wanted Holbeck Ghyll as a hunting lodge, so bought it, moved in and proceeded to give it an Arts and Crafts makeover. The alterations he commissioned are still very much in evidence, as the stained glass, fine plasterwork and carved wooden panelling testify. A hotel since 1973, it stands in woodland high above Lake Windermere, with views of some of the Lake District's most famous peaks – Coniston Old Man, the Langdale Pikes and Scafell Pike. No wonder the views from the richly appointed rooms have been called intoxicating (and that's without help from the complimentary decanter of locally distilled damson

gin). Hollywood star Renée Zellweger lived in the Miss Potter Suite during filming of a 2006 movie about Beatrix Potter. A further six rooms are in The Lodge, and there are two luxury cottages. Head chef David McLaughlin sources local produce for daily menus that may initially vie for attention with the views through the windows of the oak-panelled dining room. But with dishes like *poulet de Bresse*, truffle risotto and cep purée; and roasted brill with apple, potato, celery and cider foam, the menu always wins.

Recommended in the area

Lake Windermere; Beatrix Potter Gallery;
Dove Cottage and Wordsworth Museum

Washington Central

★★★★ 74% HOTEL

Address: Washington St, WORKINGTON, CA14 3AY

Tel: 01900 65772

Fax: 01900 68770

E-mail: kawildwchotel@aol.com

Website:
www.washingtoncentralhotelworkington.com

Map ref: 10, NX02 **Directions:** M6 junct 40, A66
to Workington. Left at lights, hotel on right

Rooms: 46 (4 fmly) **S** £95-£115; **D** £140-£220
(incl. bkfst) **Facilities:** FTV ⊛ Supervised gym Sauna
Steam room Sunbed Free Wi-fi

Parking: 25 **Notes:** ⊗

Enjoying a prominent town centre location, this
distinctive red-brick hotel is within walking distance
of most amenities, including shops, cinema and
parks, while only a little further afield are the
delights of the Lake District National Park. Public
areas include several lounges, a spacious bar, a
popular coffee shop and Caesar's leisure club,
which has a 20-metre swimming pool surrounded
by frescoes. The well-maintained, comfortable
and recently refurbished en suite bedrooms are
equipped with TV (freeview), complimentary Wi-
fi, safe, hairdryer, trouser press, work desk, and
tea- and coffee-making facilities. The executive
accommodation includes a four-poster suite with
hi-fi system, luxurious lounge, and complimentary
bath robes. In the wood-panelled Carlton Restaurant
the best local ingredients are used in dishes such
as rump of Cumbrian fell-bred lamb on crushed
herb potatoes, and Solway sea bass with scallops
and roasted beetroot. For special occasions, book
the eight-cover Clock Tower Restaurant on the sixth
floor, not just for the food, but for views towards
Scotland, The Isle of Man and the Western Lake
District Fells. The Bar Lounge serves a choice of
lighter bites.

Recommended in the area

Western Lakes; Scafell and Wasdale; Keswick;
Solway Firth; Cockermouth

Derbyshire

Curbar Edge, Peak District National Park

Casa Hotel

★★★★ 81% ◉ HOTEL

Address: Lockoford Ln, CHESTERFIELD, S41 7JB

Tel: 01246 245999

Fax: 01246 245998

E-mail: enquiries@casahotels.co.uk

Website: www.casahotels.co.uk

Map ref: 7, SK37

Directions: M1 junct 29 to A617 Chesterfield/A61
Sheffield, 1st exit at rdbt, hotel on left

Rooms: 100 (6 fmly) **S** £90-£125; **D** £99-£140
(incl. bkfst)

Facilities: FTV Gym Wi-fi **Parking:** 200

Notes: ⊛

Situated a little to the north of the town's famous twisted church spire, this architecturally striking new hotel is part of a massive regeneration scheme to transform the run-down River Rother corridor into a modern and vibrant urban village. Shops, a large traditional market and a full range of restaurants and bars are not far away. Further afield, but still easy to reach by car, are the Peak District National Park, Chatsworth, Bolsover Castle and the neighbouring towns of Matlock Bath and Buxton. The air-conditioned rooms are finished in warm, autumnal tones, and incorporate a super-king-size bed, rain shower, 32" flat-screen TV, Wi-fi, laptop safe and mini-bar. Suites have south-facing balconies, and two have private hot tubs. The menu in the one-AA Rosette Cocina restaurant displays some of the Spanish influences that run through the hotel – tapas, for example, are served as a starter. Mains on the same menu include 10oz sirloin steak from organic Belted Galloways reared just four miles away; pan-fried salmon; and vegetable risotto. Barça, one of the bars, offers light meals, including traditional favourites. Eleven purpose-built conference rooms seat from two up to 280 people, and the hotel is licensed for civil weddings.

Recommended in the area

'Crooked Spire' Church, Chesterfield; Hardwick Hall; Balsover Castle

Horsley Lodge Hotel & Golf Club

★★★ 79% HOTEL

Address: Smalley Mill Rd, HORSLEY, DE21 5BL
Tel: 01332 780838
Fax: 01332 781118
E-mail: reception@horsleylodge.co.uk
Website: www.horsleylodge.co.uk
Map ref: 7, SK34
Directions: A61 N, A38 signed Ripley. Right at
Coxbench. Follow to end, turn right, hotel 1m on left
Rooms: 11 (1 annexe) (2 fmly) **S** £80-£120;
D £100-£150 (incl. bkfst)
Facilities: STV FTV ↓ 18 Putt green Fishing Golf
driving range Wi-fi **Parking:** 100

The Earl of Stainsby built this fine country house
for his son in 1850. In 1986 the Salt family, today's
proprietors, fell in love with it and bought it at
auction. Since then they have restored it, created
bedrooms in the older part, turned some of the 180
acres of undulating land into an award-winning,
18-hole golf course, and built the brasserie-style
Highlander restaurant. Recently, they embarked on
a total renovation of the original bedrooms, so that
guests now have a choice of staying in a luxury,
executive or family room, a four-poster suite, or the
three-storey Barn Cottage, featuring a whirlpool
bath and an original inglenook fireplace. All rooms
have super-king-size beds, fine fabrics and wall
coverings, and quality bathroom toiletries. The
restaurant depends on freshly delivered produce,
with beef and lamb from stock reared on naturally
fresh grass in Derbyshire and Staffordshire, fresh
fish from the south coast, and vegetables from the
rich loamy soil of Lincolnshire. Typically, a menu
might feature pear, chicory and blue cheese tart;
pork belly stuffed with black pudding and apple; and
baked halibut with leek and mussel chowder. For
golfers, there are golf days and breaks, a pro shop
and a driving range.

Recommended in the area

Derby Cathedral; Strutt's North Mill, Belper;
Derby Museum & Art Gallery

The Peacock at Rowsley

★★★ ◎◎◎ HOTEL

Address: Bakewell Rd, ROWSLEY, DE4 2EB
Tel: 01629 733518
Fax: 01629 732671
E-mail: reception@thepeacockatrowsley.com
Website: www.thepeacockatrowsley.com
Map ref: 7, SK26
Directions: A6, 3m before Bakewell, 6m from Matlock towards Bakewell
Rooms: 16 (5 fmly) **S** £85-£140; **D** £150-£257.50
Facilities: Fishing ↩ Free use of Woodlands Fitness Centre Free membership to Bakewell Golf Club ♫ Wi-fi **Parking:** 25 **Notes:** ⚡ under 10yrs

Within Britain's oldest national park, this is a perfect base for taking exhilarating walks across lonely moorland, for exploring beautiful secluded valleys and pretty villages, and for fishing – the hotel owns fly fishing rights on the Wye and Derwent, the latter flowing through the garden. Some years ago Keira Knightley, Matthew Macfadyen and other actors and crew stayed here while filming *Pride and Prejudice* at Haddon Hall. The bedrooms are luxurious, most with king or super-king-size beds, and each has been styled by the international designer, India Mahdavi, who has blended antique furniture with contemporary decor. One room has a four-poster bed, another has an antique bed from Belvoir Castle. Modern facilities include Wi-fi, and there are soft drinks as well as tea- and coffee-making supplies. The main restaurant overlooks the garden and has an interesting menu that might include starters like duck liver ballotine with hazelnuts and figs; or smoked eel with apple purée, celeriac remoulade and a quail's egg. Main courses are equally imaginative, perhaps shoulder of lamb with roast sweetbread, black olive gnocchi, fennel and goats' cheese. There's also a cosy bar, with an open fire and stone walls, serving real ales, cocktails and simple dishes.

Recommended in the area

Haddon Hall; Chatsworth House; Peak District National Park

Devon

Lynmouth, Exmoor National Park

The Imperial

★★★★ 75% HOTEL

Address: Taw Vale Pde, BARNSTAPLE, EX32 8NB
Tel: 01271 345861
Fax: 01271 324448
E-mail: reservations@brend-imperial.co.uk
Website: www.brend-imperial.co.uk
Map ref: 1, SS53
Directions: M5 junct 27/A361 to Barnstaple. Follow town centre signs, passing Tesco. Straight on at next 2 rdbts. Hotel on right
Rooms: 63 (9 fmly) (4 GF) **S** £87-£185; **D** £97-£185
Facilities: FTV Leisure facilities at sister hotel ♪
Wi-fi **Parking:** 80 **Notes:** ⊗

In the heart of Barnstaple, the River Taw runs right past the manicured gardens and sun terrace of this traditional Victorian hotel. Public areas feature specially commissioned paintings by local artists of North Devon scenes, and pieces from the town's Brannam Pottery. The en suite bedrooms, many overlooking the river and some with balconies, are furnished and equipped to a high standard, perhaps none more so than the State Rooms, offering fresh flowers and 42" digital plasma TV. Both traditional and contemporary food is served in the air-conditioned Arlington restaurant, whose set menu offers duo of haddock with Parma ham, creamed cabbage and fennel; Dover sole meunière with herb butter and garlic prawns; galette of pork medallions, black pudding, caramelised peach and scrumpy cider reduction; and Moroccan spiced vegetable and feta b'stilla with mango, pawpaw and mint chutney. For a lighter meal, Colours Lounge Bar has an appetising snack menu and is also good for an aperitif or after-dinner port. Guests may use the heated indoor and outdoor pools free at sister hotel, the Barnstaple; normal member rates apply to the solarium, sauna and other facilities. Banqueting and conference suites are available for businesses.

Recommended in the area

Clovelly; Arlington Court (NT); RHS Garden Rosemoor

Northcote Manor

★★★ ⊚⊚ COUNTRY HOUSE HOTEL

Address: BURRINGTON, Umberleigh, EX37 9LZ
Tel: 01769 560501
Fax: 01769 560770
E-mail: rest@northcotemanor.co.uk
Website: www.northcotemanor.co.uk
Map ref: 2, SS61
Directions: Off A377 opposite the Portsmouth Arms, into hotel drive. (NB do not enter Burrington village)
Rooms: 11 **S** £110-£170; **D** £160-£260 (incl. bkfst)
Facilities: FTV ⊜ ⊜ Wi-fi
Parking: 30

From this beautiful country house hotel, surrounded by 20 acres of grounds and woodlands, you can enjoy wonderful views over the Taw Valley. The oldest part was built in 1716 on the site of an earlier manor, then the north-east wing was added in the mid-19th century. Spacious, newly refurbished bedrooms and suites exude comfort and style, with special touches like designer bath products and fluffy bath robes. Murals in the Drawing Room and two-AA Rosette Manor House Restaurant are the work of Barrington Barber, a London art teacher and illustrator, who was commissioned to depict three periods in the life of Northcote. An evening meal starts with a complimentary amuse bouche, followed perhaps by a starter of chicken and duck liver parfait, then lightly chilli-seasoned, pan-fried Cornish grey mullet; or marinated rump of free-range Red Ruby Devon beef. For something simpler, the less formal Walled Garden restaurant serves beer-battered, line-caught fish with chips and mushy peas served in newspaper; and, for vegetarians, butternut squash and rosemary ravioli. Outdoor facilities include a croquet lawn and hard tennis court, while golf, game-fishing, horse-riding and cycling can be arranged. The hotel's setting makes it ideal for weddings and conferences.

Recommended in the area

Rosemoor RHS garden; Dartington Crystal; North Devon coast

Combe House - Devon

★★★★ 77% ◎◎ COUNTRY HOUSE
HOTEL AND RESTAURANT
Address: Gittisham, NR HONITON, Exeter EX14 3AD
Tel: 01404 540400
E-mail: stay@combehousedevon.com
Website: www.combehousedevon.com
Map ref: 2, ST10
Directions: Off A30 1m S of Honiton, follow
Gittisham Heathpark signs. From M5 exit 29 for A30,
airport and Honiton. Exit Pattesons Cross
Rooms: 16 (1 cottage) **S** £169-£379; **D** £199-£399
(incl. bkfst) **Facilities:** Wi-fi
Parking: 39+ **Notes:** Dogs welcome

This elegant, privately-run Elizabethan Manor, Restaurant and Gardens with stunning views is set in 3,500 acres of Devon's finest countryside, all located within an easy drive to the South West Coast. A unique English venue, Combe House has a relaxed atmosphere with a spirit of times gone by, almost like staying in the home of big-hearted country cousins. The reception rooms are warm and welcoming, as are the staff. The Great Hall has a huge open fireplace, oak paneling and beautiful mullioned windows, whilst the spacious bedrooms offer a combination of contemporary elegance and comfortable charm. There is also a luxury thatched cottage with large secluded walled garden tucked away at the entrance to the winding drive and on the edge of the picturesque village of Gittisham. Combe House has a reputation for high quality food and generous hospitality, whether in the restaurant for lunches, dinners and afternoon cream teas, or for special celebrations including weddings with exclusive use of the House and handsome gardens. The two talented Master Chefs of Great Britain and their team create dishes from produce grown from their restored Victorian kitchen gardens. Here they talk food metres not miles! All of which makes Combe 'somewhere different, somewhere special'.

Recommended in the area

Southwest coast (Sidmouth to Lyme Regis); National Trust houses and gardens; Honiton Antiques

Tides Reach

★★★ 82% ◎ HOTEL

Address: South Sands, SALCOMBE, TQ8 8LJ
Tel: 01548 843466
Fax: 01548 843954
E-mail: enquire@tidesreach.com
Website: www.tidesreach.com
Map ref: 2, SX73 **Directions:** Off A38 at
Buckfastleigh to Totnes. Then A381 to Salcombe,
follow signs to South Sands **Rooms:** 32 (5 fmly)
S £85-£144; **D** £140-£332 (incl. bkfst & dinner)
Facilities: Spa STV FTV ◎ supervised Gym Squash
Watersports Scuba diving Hair & beauty treatment
Wi-fi **Parking:** 100 **Notes:** ↰ under 8yrs

This hotel sits in an idyllic spot overlooking a quiet, sandy cove on the shores of the beautiful Salcombe Estuary. The views from the public rooms and the bedrooms are fabulous, but you needn't merely look out across the water – there are plenty of opportunities to get out on the water. A short walk or ferry ride along the estuary will bring you to the picturesque sailing resort of Salcombe, while right in front of the hotel you can enjoy safe swimming and various watersports. The hotel has been owned by the Edwards family for three generations, which probably has a lot to do with its friendly, homely atmosphere. The accommodation is tastefully furnished and there are several different room types, including many with balconies. The conservatory-style Garden Room Restaurant offers a daily-changing modern British menu featuring top-quality Devon produce, especially fish and seafood. Expect the likes of hand-picked Salcombe crab or Bigbury Bay mussels to begin, followed by line-caught Salcombe sea bass or rib of prime South Devon beef. During your stay make sure you find time to visit the spa, take a dip in the indoor pool and relax in the peaceful garden with its centrepiece ornamental lake.

Recommended in the area

Overbeck's Museum & Gardens (NT); Dartmoor National Park; South West Coastal Path

Saunton Sands

★★★★ 79% ⊚ HOTEL

Address: SAUNTON, EX33 1LQ
Tel: 01271 890212 & 892001
Fax: 01271 890145
E-mail: reservations@sauntonsands.com
Website: www.sauntonsands.com
Map ref: 1, SS43 **Directions:** Off A361 at
Braunton, signed Croyde B3231, hotel 2m on left
Rooms: 92 (39 fmly) **S** £170; **D** £478 (incl. bkfst &
dinner) **Facilities:** Spa STV FTV ⊗ ﹖ ⠃ Putt green
Gym Squash Nursery Snooker room Games room ♫
Wi-fi Child facilities
Parking: 142 **Notes:** ⊗

From the front of this majestic hotel, high above
Braunton Burrows, three things account for what
you can see – sea, sand and sky, stretching far
into the distance. It's an inspiring view, probably
best savoured from a seat on the terrace, while
inside other moods may be satisfied in one of the
public rooms – a quiet corner in which to read or
snooze maybe, or the bar for freshly ground coffee,
or perhaps a peaty malt. Imagine then the views
from the many bedrooms that face the beach and
the sometimes gentle, sometimes roaring Atlantic
Ocean. Wherever your room, it will be equipped to
the standard expected from a luxury hotel. In the
restaurant, daily changing dinner menus make the
most of seasonal produce, offering locally sourced,
West Country delights such as Exmoor beef and
venison, and Combe Martin strawberries. Jacket
and tie is the preferred dress code in the restaurant
after 7pm. The more informal Terrace Lounge offers
snacks, hot and cold meals throughout the day,
and traditional afternoon cream teas. At night these
areas become the social heart of the hotel, with
live music and entertainment. Just below the hotel
is The Sands Café Bar, a more relaxed place for a
daytime drink or light bite, or freshly cooked pastas
and grills in the evening.

Recommended in the area

Exmoor National Park; Tarka Trail; Hartland Heritage
Coast

Belmont Hotel

★★★★ 75% HOTEL
Address: The Esplanade, SIDMOUTH, EX10 8RX
Tel: 01395 512555
Fax: 01395 579101
E-mail: reservations@belmont-hotel.co.uk
Website: www.belmont-hotel.co.uk
Map ref: 2, SY18
Directions: On seafront
Rooms: 50 (4 fmly) (2 GF) **S** £120-£160; **D** £150-£235
Facilities: STV Putt green Leisure facilities available
at sister hotel ♫ Wi-fi Child facilities
Parking: 45
Notes: ⊗

With plenty of land available, the Victorians cherry-picked the best building plots for their seafront houses and hotels. At the western end of Sidmouth's Regency esplanade, the Belmont is a case in point. Although just minutes from the town centre, you could be a world away as you enjoy a light lunch or cream tea on the hotel terrace. Fresh flowers greet guests on opening the door to their en suite bedroom, most of which have a sea view. Dinner is a formal occasion, with men expected to wear a jacket and tie in the lounges and dining rooms, where traditional and contemporary dishes are exemplified by carved fillet of beef Wellington with rich Madeira sauce; sautéed mignons of pork with port and sage jus; and poached délice of salmon with vermouth and scallop velouté. On hand is a sommelier to help you navigate the extensive wine list. For indoor relaxation there's a spa with sauna and hot stone therapy beds, while outdoor activities include swimming (children can use a smaller pool), an 18-hole putting green, tennis court and five acres of grounds in which to walk. A drink in the Pavilion Bar will then, no doubt, be most welcome.

Recommended in the area

Killerton House (NT); Powderham Castle; Lyme Regis

Riviera

★★★★ 82% ◉ HOTEL

Address: The Esplanade, SIDMOUTH, EX10 8AY
Tel: 01395 515201
Fax: 01395 577775
E-mail: enquiries@hotelriviera.co.uk
Website: www.hotelriviera.co.uk
Map ref: 2, SY18
Directions: Leave M5 at junction 30 and follow A3052 to Sidmouth
Rooms: 26 (6 fmly) **S** £132-£194; **D** £264-£368 (incl. bkfst & dinner)
Facilities: FTV ♬ Wi-fi
Parking: 26

The Riviera Hotel, with its fine Regency façade and alluring blend of old-fashioned service and present day comforts, is splendidly positioned at the centre of Sidmouth's esplanade, overlooking Lyme Bay. With its mild climate and the beach just on the doorstep, the setting echoes the south of France and is ideal for those in search of relaxation. Glorious sea views can be enjoyed from bedrooms, all of which are fully appointed and have many thoughtful extras. In the elegant bay-view dining room guests are offered a fine choice of dishes from extensive menus, with local seafood being a particular speciality. Starters may include crab and lobster cake with home made chilli mayonnaise and crispy leeks, while a tempting main could be a

fish dish or perhaps fillet of Devonshire beef with celeriac puree, baby vegetables and a red wine jus. Wedding parties and business conferences can be accommodated, and the hotel can arrange sporting activities in the area, including golfing with concessionary fees at the nearby Sidmouth Golf Club and Woodbury Park Golf and Country Club. Arrangements can also be made for riding, and pheasant and duck shooting on local estates. The hotel has a long tradition of hospitality and is perfect for holidays, weekends or a Christmas break.

Recommended in the area

Bicton Gardens; Killerton House and Gardens; Exeter Cathedral

Victoria

★★★★ 83% ⊛ HOTEL

Address: The Esplanade, SIDMOUTH, EX10 8RY
Tel: 01395 512651
Fax: 01395 579154
E-mail: reservations@victoriahotel.co.uk
Website: www.victoriahotel.co.uk
Map ref: 2, SY18
Directions: On seafront
Rooms: 65 (6 fmly) **S** £135-£155; **D** £175-£360
Facilities: FTV ⊛ ⊸ ⊸ Putt green Sauna Snooker
room Games room Spa bath Treatment room ♫
Wi-fi Child facilities
Parking: 104 **Notes:** ⊛

In its architectural sense the word 'imposing' can be a cliché; not, however, in this case, for here is a truly splendid pile built in the early 1900s that lords it not just over its five acres of landscaped grounds, but over Sidmouth and its bay too. Its dignified period style is just as evident inside, where high ceilings and fancy plasterwork provide just the right setting for a dress code that requires men to wear a jacket and tie for dinner in the elegant, AA Rosette restaurant, and where a resident orchestra or pianist may strike up. Equally in tune is the kitchen, devising menus that may well partner trout mousse and rillettes with horseradish cream, followed by guinea fowl breast with bacon, peas and fondant potato, and finally a more contemporary dessert which partners a trio of passion fruit jelly with sorbet and cheesecake. The en suite bedrooms, most facing the English Channel, and many with private balconies, are beautifully furnished. The sun lounge is the place for morning coffee, traditional Devonshire cream tea, and a fireside after-dinner liqueur. Other ways of passing the time include swimming in the indoor or outdoor heated pool, relaxing in the spa and playing tennis.

Recommended in the area

Exeter Cathedral; Crealy Adventure Park; Knightshayes Court (NT)

Watersmeet

★★★ 87% ⊛ HOTEL

Address: Mortehoe, WOOLACOMBE, EX34 7EB
Tel: 01271 870333
Fax: 01271 870890
E-mail: info@watersmeethotel.co.uk
Website: www.watersmeethotel.co.uk
Map ref: 1, SS44
Directions: Follow B3343 into Woolacombe, turn right onto esplanade, hotel 0.75m on left
Rooms: 25 (4 fmly) (3 GF)
Facilities: FTV ⊛ ✈ ✈ Steam room ♫ Wi-fi
Parking: 38
Notes: ⊛

In Edwardian times a private residence, this hotel stands in three acres of gardens above a quiet, sandy beach on North Devon's rugged Atlantic coast. Making the most of its beachside location, the lounge, restaurant, terrace and garden all offer uninterrupted sea views taking in Combesgate Beach, Baggy Point and distant Lundy Island, and all but three of the bedrooms offer similar coastal panoramas. Several have white-painted wooden balconies, which are perfect for watching the often-spectacular sunsets over Woolacombe Bay, and there are a few which, although they have no window, they do have a sun pipe, which allows sunlight to flood into the room. Classic English cooking tends to dominate the menus, although a few modern European influences can be detected. Local ingredients are used in the kitchen as much as possible, the venison and lamb, for example, coming from Exmoor, and the fish fresh from Brixham. On a menu featuring mostly classical English dishes, with occasional modern European influences, typical main courses might include whole grilled megrim sole; roast loin of lamb with devilled kidneys; and wild mushroom and tarragon risotto. Take time to relax in the indoor or heated outdoor pool, hot spa or steam room.

Recommended in the area

Woolacombe Bay; Arlington Court (NT); Ilfracombe Museum

Dorset

A view from Durdle Door to Bat's Head chalk promontory, Dorset

BridgeHouse

★★★ 81% ◉◉ HOTEL

Address: 3 Prout Bridge, BEAMINSTER,
DT8 3AY
Tel: 01308 862200
Fax: 01308 863700
E-mail: enquiries@bridge-house.co.uk
Website: www.bridge-house.co.uk
Map ref: 2, ST40
Directions: Off A3066, 100yds from town square
Rooms: 13 (4 annexe) (2 fmly) (4 GF) **S** £86-£120;
D £126-£215 (incl. bkfst)
Facilities: FTV Wi-fi Child facilities
Parking: 20

BridgeHouse Beauminster is a stylish, family run country town hotel, perfectly placed for guests to explore West Dorset's relatively undiscovered rolling hills, dramatic cliff-tops and fossil filled beaches. Nestled in Thomas Hardy country ('Emminster' in Hardy's *Tess*) and on the doorstep of the spectacular Jurassic Coast, it is no surprise that local food is always high on the agenda. 13th-century BridgeHouse has always enjoyed making the most of Dorset's wonderfully lush and abundant produce from land and sea. The hotel's two-AA Rosette Beauminster Brasserie (also Taste of the West Gold award winner) offers a choice of dining areas from Georgian panelled elegance to a lovely alfresco option overlooking the walled garden. While the origins of the hotel can be found in medieval times, every room has been brought up to the 21st century but without compromising the buildings inherent magic. Each room has its own distinct style and personality – a unique blend of historic and modern. Frette linen, Molton Brown toiletries, waffle robes, flat screen TVs and complimentary Wi-fi come as standard in the comfortable rooms.

Recommended in the area

The Jurassic Coast; Abbotsbury Swannery; Mapperton House and Gardens

Best Western Connaught Hotel

★★★ 85% ◎◎ HOTEL

Address: West Hill Rd, West Cliff, BOURNEMOUTH, BH2 5PH

Tel: 01202 298020

Fax: 01202 298028

E-mail: reception@theconnaught.co.uk

Website: www.theconnaught.co.uk

Map ref: 3, SZ09

Directions: Follow Town Centre West & BIC signs

Rooms: 56 **S** £45-£80; **D** £60-£130 (incl. bkfst)

Facilities: Spa FTV ⊗ supervised Gym Sauna Steam room Wi-fi Terraced garden Free parking

Parking: 66 **Notes:** ⊗

Built around 1850 as a gentleman's residence, this award-winning, environmentally friendly hotel is centrally located on the West Cliff in an acre of grounds. All of the attractions of the town centre are less than five minutes' walk away, as are the beach and the Bournemouth International Centre with its busy programme of concerts and events. Accommodation is stylish and well equipped, with a variety of rooms and suites, including family suites, available in the main hotel. All rooms are en suite, with complimentary Wi-fi; some rooms have their own private balcony or terrace overlooking the private garden. The Blue Water Spa with its 18-metre pool, sauna, aroma steam room and massage therapy suite adds to the relaxation factor, while for those feeling more energetic there are two gyms. The hotel was highly commended at the Bournemouth Tourism Awards 2010. It was the first hotel in the town to be awarded a silver shield through the Green Tourism Business Scheme for its commitment to the environment. 'Green' activities include recycling as much waste as possible, switching to low energy lighting and using local ingredients in the two-AA Rosette awarded Blakes restaurant. The restaurant now has a garden terrace for alfresco dining.

Recommended in the area

Bournemouth Pier; Lower Gardens; Bournemouth Oceanarium

The Green House

★★★★ 77% TOWN HOUSE HOTEL

Address: 4 Grove Rd, BOURNEMOUTH, BH1 3AX
Tel: 01202 498900
Fax: 01202 551559
E-mail: reception@thegreenhousehotel.com
Website: www.thegreenhousehotel.com
Map ref: 3, SZ19
Directions: On B3066. At Lansdowne roundabout
take Meyrick Rd exit. Straight over next roundabout
then right onto Grove Rd. Hotel on right.
Rooms: 32 (3 fmly) (6 GF) **D** £140-£240 (incl. bkfst)
Facilities: FTV Wi-fi
Parking: 32 **Notes:** ⊗

Privately owned, this eco-friendly boutique hotel in a Grade II Victorian villa in its own gardens is mere minutes from Bournemouth's famous sandy beaches. Sustainability is one of its driving forces: water is heated by the sun, electricity is generated on site, furniture is made from recycled wood, or from trees felled by storms, and the company car runs on used cooking oil. Staff are trained on green issues, and suppliers are assessed against recognised environmental standards. Styling throughout is contemporary, from the spacious reception area to the bedrooms, all of which have walk-in shower, organic goose-down duvet, 32-inch flat-screen TV, and Bose sound dock; in the larger ones, reclaimed Victorian roll-top baths stand in the rooms themselves. Sustainability is again the watchword in the kitchen, whose modern British cooking relies largely on organic or home-grown ingredients sourced from within a 30-mile radius. The slow-cooked venison, for example, comes from Salisbury Plain; accompanying the steaks are crisp Dorset snails and New Forest portobello mushrooms; and the turbot is line-caught offshore. Light meals are served throughout the day in the bar and garden. Organic and bio-dynamic wines are graded according to their carbon footprint.

Recommended in the area

New Forest National Park; Bournemouth beaches; Bournemouth Oceanarium

Hermitage Hotel

★★★ 85% ◎ HOTEL

Address: Exeter Rd, BOURNEMOUTH, BH2 5AH
Tel: 01202 557363
Fax: 01202 559173
E-mail: info@hermitage-hotel.co.uk
Website: www.hermitage-hotel.co.uk
Map ref: 3, SZ19
Directions: A338 Ringwood, follow signs for BIC &
pier. Hotel directly opposite
Rooms: 74 (11 annexe) (9 fmly) (7 GF) **S** £50.50-£77;
D £101-£154 (incl. bkfst)
Facilities: FTV Wi-fi
Parking: 58 **Notes:** ⊗

In motor racing terms, this hotel is in pole position. There are no roads to cross between it and Bournemouth's seven miles of golden sands, its famous pier, or the town centre. A near neighbour is the Bournemouth International Centre, which is an important venue for concerts, exhibitions and other big events, while the Pavilion Theatre and the pretty Lower Gardens are also close at hand. The bedrooms are modern, and most of them have good views of the sea through their floor-to-ceiling windows, and all are equipped with flat-screen TV, complimentary Wi-fi, hot drinks tray, and 24-hour room service. Superior rooms offer period furniture and sitting and dressing areas. The restaurant is proud to be one of only a few of the resort's hotels to hold an AA Rosette, for the quality of its regularly changing menus. Expect to find avocado and crab gâteau; confit duck leg; pan-seared Portland scallops; roasted rump of Hampshire lamb; goat's cheese, leek and red pepper tart; and ice creams and sorbets made at Barford Farm on the National Trust's Kingston Lacy Estate, near Wimborne. Lighter meals, snacks and afternoon tea are available in the lounge and bar. On-site parking is free to guests.

Recommended in the area

Bournemouth Pier; Lower Gardens; New Forest National Park

Captain's Club Hotel and Spa

★★★★ 81% ◉◉ HOTEL

Address: Wick Ferry, Wick Ln, CHRISTCHURCH,
BH23 1HU
Tel: 01202 475111
Fax: 01202 490111
E-mail: enquiries@captainsclubhotel.com
Website: www.captainsclubhotel.com
Map ref: 3, SZ19
Directions: B3073 to Christchurch. On Fountain
rdbt take 5th exit (Sopers Ln) 2nd left (St Margarets
Ave) 1st right onto Wick Ln
Rooms: 29 (12 fmly) **Facilities:** Spa STV FTV
Hydro-therapy pool Sauna ♫ Wi-fi **Parking:** 41

All bedrooms, suites and apartments in this ultra-modern, town-centre hotel on Christchurch Quay overlook the Stour and the ever-passing river craft. Designed in 'contemporary maritime' style, the rooms include air conditioning, flat-screen TV, DVD player and free high-speed wireless internet access. The hotel has an open-plan, level ground floor with lifts at both ends, which makes it wheelchair friendly. Dogs are allowed in some of the rooms, but guests should note that dogs will be allowed on local beaches only between September and May. Where to dine is a matter of choice between the lounge, outside on the terrace overlooking the river, or Tides Restaurant, with two AA Rosettes to its credit for a carte featuring plenty of fish and shellfish. Subject to catches, be won over by whole grilled Brixham sole; pan-fried skate wing; oysters; or a Sunday seafood buffet. Other options include New Forest venison casserole; roast half-rack of Dorset lamb; and vegetarian dishes. Musicians accompany diners in the evening. The lounge menu offers fish and chips, club sandwiches, fresh crab, lobster and mussels and afternoon tea. After enjoying a soothing spa treatment, take a cruise across the bay on the hotel's luxury motor yacht.

Recommended in the area

Christchurch Priory and harbour; Isle of Wight;
New Forest National Park

County Durham

Bishop Auckland Castle, ten miles from Durham

Headlam Hall

★★★★ 77% ⊚ HOTEL

Address: Headlam, Gainford, DARLINGTON,
DL2 3HA
Tel: 01325 730238
Fax: 01325 730790
E-mail: admin@headlamhall.co.uk
Website: www.headlamhall.co.uk
Map ref: 7, NZ21
Directions: 2m N of A67 between Piercebridge
& Gainford
Rooms: 40 (22 annexe) (4 fmly) (10 GF) **S** £95-£130;
D £120-£195 (incl. bkfst) **Facilities:** Spa STV FTV ⓣ ⚓
9 ⚑ Putt green Fishing ⚓ Gym Wi-fi **Parking:** 80

A fine 17th-century mansion set amid beautiful grounds and gardens in a tranquil part of Teesdale. A glorious haven for anyone conducting business in the Middlesbrough-Stockton-Darlington conurbation to the east, it is also perfect for exploring rural County Durham and the Yorkshire Dales. There is also the option of taking in a round of golf on the hotel's own nine-hole course, a dip in its spacious 14-metre indoor pool with water-jet feature, a work-out in the gym or a pampering spa treatment. The spa also has a sauna, steam room and air-conditioned exercise studio. The bedrooms come in a variety of sizes, some with elegant period furniture, others are more contemporary. All have modern facilities including Sky TV and free Wi-fi.

The public areas are richly decorated and include a cocktail bar and the elegant drawing room overlooking the main lawn. The restaurant, spread across four different dining areas, serves modern British cuisine along the lines of pan-fried rib-eye beef with roasted root vegetables, horseradish mash and red wine sauce; pan-seared sea bass with sautéed new potatoes, cauliflower purée, couscous and lemon butter sauce. There is a strong emphasis on locally sourced ingredients including produce from the hall's own gardens and farm.

Recommended in the area

Raby Castle; Bowes Museum; High Force waterfall

Rockliffe Hall

★★★★★ 86% ◉◉◉ HOTEL

Address: Hurworth on Tees, DARLINGTON, DL2 2DU
Tel: 01325 729999 **Fax:** 01325 720464
E-mail: enquiries@rockliffehall.com
Website: www.rockliffehall.com
Map ref: 7, NZ21
Directions: A1(M) junct 57, A66 (M), A66 towards
Darlington, A167, through Hurworth-on-Tees.
In Croft-on-Tees left into Hurworth Rd, follow
signs **Rooms:** 61 (5 fmly) (17 GF) **S** £140-£425;
D £165-£450 (incl. bkfst) **Facilities:** Spa STV FTV ⊙
↓ 18 Putt green Fishing Gym ♫ Wi-fi
Parking: 200 **Notes:** ⊗

In the midst of 375 acres of parkland bordered by the River Tees, this impressively restored, early 19th-century mansion was once the home of landscape painter, Thomas Surtees Raine. Later residents were the Backhouse family, renowned botanists who collected the estate's rare and exotic trees. After them came various occupants and then a period of neglect until 1996, when Middlesbrough Football Club rescued it and turned it into a team training facility. From this, today's luxury hotel, spa and championship golf course have evolved. The older public rooms retain their original stained-glass windows, marble pillars and ornate ceilings, while the bedrooms are big enough to accommodate king-and super-king-size beds;

even the twin beds are doubles. Modish colours and bold table lamps help to give rooms in the New Hall their contemporary look, and most have a patio or balcony. There are more rooms in Tiplady Lodge, and in Armstrong House are some one- and two-bedroom apartments. For dining, there are the glass-roofed Orangery, with daily-changing and multi-course tasting menus; the Brasserie, offering a simpler style of food, such as chef Kenny Atkinson's classic Craster fish pie; and slow-roasted pork loin with pease pudding; and The Clubhouse for snacks, steaks and Sunday lunch.

Recommended in the area

Raby Castle; Bowes Museum; High Force waterfall

Essex

Greensted Church, Greensted

Maison Talbooth

★ ★ ★ ◉◉ COUNTRY HOUSE HOTEL

Address: Stratford Rd, DEDHAM, CO7 6HN
Tel: 01206 322367
Fax: 01206 322752
E-mail: maison@milsomhotels.co.uk
Website: www.milsomhotels.com
Map ref: 4, TM03
Directions: A12 towards Ipswich, 1st turn signed
Dedham, follow to a left bend, turn right. The hotel is
one mile on right
Rooms: 12 (1 fmly) (5 GF) **S** £165-£290;
D £200-£405 (incl. bkfst)
Facilities: Spa STV ⚬ ⚬ Wi-fi **Parking:** 40

This impressive Victorian country house sits in a
peaceful rural location in the heart of Constable
country, amid pretty landscaped grounds
overlooking the River Stour. It boasts three principal
suites, each with its own hot tub on a private
terrace. All the spacious en suite bedrooms are
individually decorated, with tasteful furnishings,
co-ordinated fabrics and thoughtful extras such as
super-king-size beds, goose-feather duvets, fluffy
towels and mini-bars; many rooms have fine views
over Dedham Vale. The hotel features a day spa with
three treatment rooms, plus an outdoor hot tub.
In the Pool House there's a dining area complete
with kitchen, which can be used for house parties
and meetings, while other public areas include
a comfortable drawing room where guests may
stop for a snack or enjoy a leisurely afternoon tea,
maybe accompanied by a glass of Champagne
for that extra touch of luxury. The Garden Room
Restaurant is a light and airy room with a high-
vaulted ceiling and large windows. Here, guests can
enjoy everything from breakfast to a light lunch
through to dinner, and even dancing if the house is
booked for exclusive use. It's no wonder the hotel is
a popular venue for weddings.

Recommended in the area

Sir Alfred Munnings Museum; Beth Chatto Gardens;
Colchester Castle

milsoms

★★★ 81% ◎ SMALL HOTEL
Address: Stratford Rd, Dedham, DEDHAM,
CO7 6HW
Tel: 01206 322795
Fax: 01206 323689
E-mail: milsoms@milsomhotels.com
Website: www.milsomhotels.com
Map ref: 4, TM03 **Directions:** 6m N of Colchester
off A12, follow Stratford St Mary/Dedham signs. Turn
right over A12, hotel on left
Rooms: 15 (3 fmly) (4 GF) **S** £97-£133; **D** £117-£184
Facilities: STV Use of spa at nearby sister hotel ♫
Wi-fi **Parking:** 90

Dedham Vale, popularly known as Constable Country, is an Area of Outstanding Natural Beauty, and this delightful hotel makes a good base from which to explore it. Although it's an old building, Geraldine Milsom's contemporary interior design has transformed it by bringing the best out of its original features. Stylish, en suite bedrooms all have crisp white linen and fluffy towels, and are provided with a mini-bar, satellite TV and hot drinks tray. One room is set up for the disabled. The hotel's hub is the bar and two-tiered, brasserie-style restaurant that extends on to a terrace, covered with a huge architectural 'sail', overlooking the gardens. Globally inspired cooking, which has earned one AA Rosette, takes full advantage of locally sourced, seasonal produce, so sit down to tandoori lamb pizza with okra and goat's cheese; baked eggplant cannelloni with pine-nuts, feta, bulgar wheat and vine tomato sauce; or braised shin of Suffolk pork with bubble and squeak and caraway carrots. More traditional items include deep-fried, line-caught Icelandic haddock in beer batter with chips; and grilled rump and sirloin steaks. Children can choose from their own menu. Although tables can't be booked, all-day dining guarantees that you get one.

Recommended in the area

The Painters Trail – Constable, Gainsborough & Munnings; Suffolk Heritage Coast; Stour Valley

The Pier at Harwich

★★★ 87% ◉◉ HOTEL

Address: The Quay, HARWICH, CO12 3HH
Tel: 01255 241212
Fax: 01255 551922
E-mail: pier@milsomhotels.com
Website: www.milsomhotels.com
Map ref: 4, TM23 **Directions:** From A12, take
A120 to Quay. Hotel opposite lifeboat station
Rooms: 14 (7 annexe) (5 fmly) (1 GF) **S** £87-£142;
D £112-£192 (incl. bkfst)
Facilities: STV Day cruises on yachts Golf breaks
arranged with nearby course Sea bass fishing Wi-fi
Parking: 10 **Notes:** ⊗

Situated on the quay by the historic Ha'penny Pier, and overlooking the twin ports of Harwich and Felixstowe, this distinctive waterfront hotel was built in the 1850s for boat passengers travelling to Holland. The former Angel pub next door, dating from the 1700s, was acquired in 2000 to create more accommodation. The bedrooms all have private bathrooms and are tastefully decorated, thoughtfully equipped, and furnished in a contemporary style; many have terrific views. The public rooms include a smart lounge bar, plush residents' lounge, the all-day Ha'Penny Bistro, and the first-floor Harbourside Restaurant, with two AA Rosettes, where you can enjoy views of the Stour and Orwell estuaries. Much of the seafood in which

it specialises is landed in the harbour below. Begin with Mersea rock oysters or dressed Harwich crab, then follow with roast fillet of monkfish in pancetta with wild mushroom and pea risotto; or chargrilled Dedham Vale sirloin steak with hand-cut chips. During decent weather, you can eat outside on the terrace, if you wish. Have lunch or dinner before a visit to the town's Electric Palace cinema, one of the oldest in the UK to survive complete with its ornamental frontage, silent screen and original projection room.

Recommended in the area

Sailing; Ha'penny Pier and Museum; Redoubt Fort; Martello Tower

Roslin Beach Hotel

★★★ 80% HOTEL
Address: Thorpe Esplanade, Thorpe Bay,
SOUTHEND-ON-SEA, SS1 3BG
Tel: 01702 586375
Fax: 01702 586663
E-mail: info@roslinhotel.com
Website: www.roslinhotel.com
Map ref: 4, TQ88
Directions: A127, follow Southend-on-Sea signs.
Hotel between Walton Rd & Clieveden Rd on seafront
Rooms: 57 (5 fmly) (7 GF)
Facilities: FTV Wi-fi
Parking: 40 **Notes:** ⊗

Facing one of Southend's award-winning beaches, this hotel is in Thorpe Bay, a little way east of the pier that stretches 1.34 miles out into the wide Thames Estuary, making it the longest pleasure pier in the world. This is the view that awaits guests in many of the New England-style en suite bedrooms, whose luxury bathrooms are well provided with thick fluffy towels, and in which flat-screen digital TV, hot drinks tray and free Wi-fi are standard. Nor must the complimentary, home-made shortbread starfish be forgotten! Individually styled Executive rooms are in the newly refurbished beach house, all with either a king- or a super-king-size bed. Food is freshly, ethically and locally sourced. Indeed, some of the meats and poultry are from the hotel's own free-range farm, thus the carte may well offer cottage pie; cider-cooked ham; rare-breed Berkshire pork; and estuary-caught fish and chips. The fish bar offers fresh lobster, king prawns, wolf fish and a whole lot more seafood on Friday evenings. A traditional three-course lunch is available on Sundays. Snacks and afternoon tea, with sandwiches, scones, clotted cream, cakes and biscuits, are served in the Terrace and Lounge; or you can take it outdoors and watch the ships go by.

Recommended in the area
Southend Pier; Pier Museum; Heritage Centre, Leigh on Sea

Gloucestershire

Picturesque Church Street beyond the Abbey gates, Tewkesbury

Bibury Court Hotel

★★★ 85% ◎◎ COUNTRY HOUSE HOTEL

Address: BIBURY, Cirencester, GL7 5NT
Tel: 01285 740337 & 741171
Fax: 01285 740660
E-mail: info@biburycourt.com
Website: www.biburycourt.com
Map ref: 3, SP10
Directions: On B4425, 6m N of Cirencester (A4179).
8m S of Burford (A40), entrance by River Coln
Rooms: 18 (3 fmly) (1 GF) **S** £150-£410; **D** £150-£425
(incl. bkfst)
Facilities: FTV Fishing ⛵ Wi-fi
Parking: 40

The River Coln runs gently through the six acres of rolling Cotswold countryside that surround this lovely Jacobean mansion, whose interior cleverly mixes the old with the new. The bedrooms, for example, display a range of styles, some deliberately very much in keeping with the hotel's period charm, others, equally deliberately, successfully incorporating modern furniture and designer bathroom fittings. Tea and coffee-making facilities are provided, as well as a hairdryer, LCD TV, Wi-fi and a room service menu that includes regional dishes and light snacks. Newly appointed head chef Nigel Godwin has introduced a new carte and a seven-course tasting menu for the fine-dining Oak Room, which looks out over the grounds and distant hills. The walls are covered in handmade silk and embroidery, which gives diners with their backs to the windows plenty to admire. You can see the Saxon church of St Mary from the Conservatory, where the menu typically offers rib-eye steak and fries; and wild mushroom and truffle risotto. There is also a new menu in the Brasserie where, if the sun is shining, one can enjoy riverside dining on the south-facing terrace. With such delightful backdrops, no wonder so many couples get married here.

Recommended in the area

Chedworth Roman Villa; Cirencester; Cotswold Wildlife Park

George Hotel

★★★ 81% ◎◎ HOTEL

Address: St Georges Rd, CHELTENHAM, GL50 3DZ
Tel: 01242 235751 **Fax:** 01242 224359
E-mail: hotel@stayatthegeorge.co.uk
Website: www.stayatthegeorge.co.uk
Map ref: 2, SO92 **Directions:** M5 junct 11 follow
town centre signs. At 2nd lights left into Gloucester
Rd, past rail station over mini-rdbt. At lights right into
St Georges Rd. Hotel 0.75m on left
Rooms: 31 (1 GF) **D** £120-£185 (incl. bkfst)
Facilities: STV Complimentary membership to local
health club Live music at wknds ♫ Wi-fi
Parking: 30 **Notes:** ⊗

The only independent hotel in the centre of
Cheltenham, its location is perfect for the upmarket
shopping areas of Montpellier and the Promenade.
Built in the 1840s, it has an abundance of original
features, none of them compromised by later
additions. The individually designed bedrooms
have all been finished to a high standard and are
equipped with bathrobes, DVD player (with films
free from the hotel's library), Wi-fi and mineral water.
LCD TV screen sizes rise in relation to the type of
room booked, thus a Junior Suite comes with a
32-inch, a Classic with a 22-inch. Lively Monty's
Brasserie (Monty's Braz to aficionados), adjacent
to the hotel, specialises in modern cuisine and
cocktails and has retained its two AA Rosettes

for high quality and consistently good food for
four years running. It opens seven days a week
for morning coffee, lunch and dinner, and always
features a range of fish and shellfish, and dishes
such as beef Wellington, duo of Cotswold lamb,
corn-fed chicken and butternut squash ravioli. The
hotel's Grade II* listing precludes the installation
of a lift, but assistance is provided for those with
luggage. For the same reason, the bedrooms aren't
air-conditioned, although the Brasserie, Cocktail Bar
and private dining rooms are.

Recommended in the area

Pitville Pump Room; Holst Birthplace Museum;
Chedworth Roman Villa

Cotswolds88 Hotel

★★★★ 81% ◎◎ SMALL HOTEL
Address: Kemps Ln, PAINSWICK, GL6 6YB
Tel: 01452 813688
Fax: 01452 814059
E-mail: reservations@cotswolds88hotel.com
Website: www.cotswolds88hotel.com
Map ref: 2, SO80
Directions: From Stroud towards Cheltenham on
A46, in Painswick centre right at St Marys Church
into Victoria St. Take left into St Marys St, right into
Tibbiwell St, then right into Kemps Lane
Rooms: 17 (8 annexe) (2 fmly) **Facilities:** FTV
Treatment room Wi-fi **Parking:** 17

Built on an ancient Roman site, this late-Palladian
mansion is a fine example of its style, although
various later architects have left their mark,
including Arts and Crafts impresario, Detmar Blow.
The interior is – to use the hotel's own word – funky,
blending off-the-wall vintage pieces and splashes
of colour with touches of psychedelia. Some of
the individually styled, en suite bedrooms are
decorated with limited-edition wallpaper inspired
by Leigh Bowery, one-time model of Lucian Freud;
most have good views of the surrounding hills.
Abstract images of the hotel and grounds by
internationally renowned photo-artist David Hiscock
feature throughout the building in various forms.
The 88Room restaurant, on the ground floor, offers
from its contemporary menu slow-braised shoulder
of lamb and roasted rump, mashed potato and
Provençal sauce and potato-wrapped fillet of halibut
with creamed leeks, sautéed trompette mushrooms
and red wine jus; and risotto with sliced black truffle
and poached egg yolk. The terrace is also a good
place to eat. The intimate bar serves signature
cocktails, while residents may relax with tea and
homemade scones in the private lounge and library,
or on the balcony. Would-be kitchen supremos can
book a master class with head chef, Lee Scott.

Recommended in the area
Painswick Rococo Garden; Cheltenham Racecourse;
City of Bath

Burleigh Court Hotel

★★★ 79% ◉◉ HOTEL

Address: Burleigh, Minchinhampton, STROUD,
GL5 2PF
Tel: 01453 883804 **Fax:** 01453 886870
E-mail: burleighcourt@aol.com
Website: www.burleighcourthotel.co.uk
Map ref: 2, SO80 **Directions:** From Stroud A419
towards Cirencester. Right after 2.5m signed Burleigh
& Minchinhampton. Left after 500yds signed Burleigh
Court. Hotel 300yds on right
Rooms: 18 (7 annexe) (2 fmly) (3 GF) **S** £90-£110;
D £140-£200 (incl. bkfst)
Facilities: ↘ ⚘ Wi-fi Child facilities **Parking:** 40

Way below this early-19th-century, three-storey,
Cotswold stone manor house runs the River
Frome on its way through Golden Valley. During
nearly two centuries of existence, the house has
been considerably remodelled, including some
additions in the 1920s by Clough Williams-Ellis,
creator of Portmeirion in North Wales. From
some of its individually decorated and furnished
bedrooms there are views across its beautifully
maintained gardens, while others look across the
valley. The coach house bedrooms are located
close to the Victorian plunge pool. These rooms,
like those around the courtyard garden, are ideal
for families. With its open log fires and soft sofas,
the oak-panelled lounge bar is the perfect place
for a cocktail or a liqueur. On the menu in the
two-AA Rosette dining room expect confit belly of
Gloucester Old Spot pork; black pepper-roasted
Cornish monkfish tail; and wild mushroom and
chestnut risotto, all making best use of home-
grown herbs, salad leaves, vegetables, and other
fresh produce from local suppliers. There's an
extensive bar menu too and in the reception lounge
overlooking the front lawn and gardens you can
enjoy morning coffee and afternoon cream tea.

Recommended in the area

Painswick Rococo Garden; Prinknash Abbey Pottery;
Ruskin Mill

Lords of the Manor

★★★★ ◉◉◉ COUNTRY HOUSE HOTEL

Address: UPPER SLAUGHTER, GL54 2JD
Tel: 01451 820243
Fax: 01451 820696
E-mail: reservations@lordsofthemanor.com
Website: www.lordsofthemanor.com
Map ref: 3, SP12
Directions: 2m W of A429. Exit A40 onto A429,
take 'The Slaughters' turn. Through Lower Slaughter
for 1m to Upper Slaughter. Hotel on right
Rooms: 26 (4 fmly) (9 GF)
Facilities: FTV Fishing ⤸ Wi-fi
Parking: 40

In a timeless corner of the Cotswolds, this 17th-century, honey-coloured stone, former rectory is set in eight acres of landscaped gardens and rolling parkland. Privately owned, it is a second home to the Munir family, who have invested substantially in it since they acquired it in 1997. Elegant public rooms overlook immaculate lawns, and bedrooms have great character and charm, with all the amenities expected of a hotel of this stature. The restaurant serves consistently impressive, three-AA Rosette cuisine, typified by local estate hare Wellington with quince purée, caramelised parsnip and hare jus; and pan-fried fillet of red mullet with mussel tortellini, braised fennel, tomato confit and bouillabaisse sauce. The rambling cellars hold a wide selection of fine wines from the New and Old Worlds, among them an extensive Italian collection, including some from boutique wineries in Sicily. Wine-tasting sessions, which guests are invited to take part in, are held every Friday and Saturday before dinner. You won't find a gym, jogging track or Jacuzzi here, but you can walk through the walled gardens and sit under the shade of a pear tree, or find a restful bench by the lake. If it's muddy, you're welcome to borrow wellies.

Recommended in the area

Bourton Model Village; Cotswold Farm Park;
Broadway

Greater Manchester

New and renovated buildings line the canal basin, Manchester

Egerton House

★★★ 81% ◎ HOTEL

Address: Blackburn Rd, Egerton, BOLTON, BL7 9SB
Tel: 01204 307171
Fax: 01204 593030
E-mail: reservation@egertonhouse-hotel.co.uk
Website: www.egertonhouse-hotel.co.uk
Map ref: 6, SD70
Directions: M61, A666 (Bolton road), pass Asda on right. Hotel 2m on just passed war memorial on right
Rooms: 29 (7 fmly) **S** £73-£76; **D** £83-£96 (incl. bkfst)
Facilities: FTV Wi-fi
Parking: 135
Notes: ⊗

This beautiful privately-owned country-house hotel enjoys a secluded location in three acres of developed gardens just three miles away from Bolton. A family home for over 200 years, Egerton House has a warm and welcoming feel and plenty of character, making it a delightful retreat with the beauty of the Lancashire Hills right on the doorstep. Indeed, once you've settled into the cosy lounge with its open fire and lovely views of the grounds, it would be easy to forget the outside world exists. All 29 en suite rooms are non-smoking and come with flat-screen TV with Freeview, tea- and coffee-making facilities, iron and ironing board and trouser press. Complimentary Wi-fi access is available throughout the hotel. Dinner and Sunday lunch are served in

The Dining Room, an AA Rosette-awarded smart and contemporary space where the focus of the set menu is high-quality regional produce put to use in classic English and French dishes such as slow roast pork belly with butter mash, shallot and green beans or fillet of turbot, with cocotte potatoes, salsify, smoked bacon, shallot, wild mushrooms and garlic butter. Whether you're staying for business or pleasure, you can expect first-class, friendly service from a dedicated team. The hotel is an ideal venue for meetings, private gatherings and weddings.

Recommended in the area

Bolton Museum, Art Gallery & Aquarium; Smithills Hall; Trafford Centre

The Saddleworth Hotel

★★★★ 83% ◎◎◎ COUNTRY HOUSE HOTEL

Address: Huddersfield Road, DELPH, Oldham,
Manchester, OL3 5LX
Tel: 01457 871888
Fax: 01457 871889
E-mail: enquiries@thesaddleworthhotel.co.uk
Website: www.thesaddleworthhotel.co.uk
Map ref: 6, SD00 **Directions:** M62 junct 21, A640
to Huddersfield. At Junction Inn take A6052 to Delph;
at White Lion left onto unclassified road, in 0.5m left
on A62 towards Huddersfield. Hotel 0.5m on right
Rooms: 13 (5 annexe) (3 fmly) (1 GF)
Facilities: STV ↘ Wi-fi **Parking:** 142 **Notes:** ⊗

Once a coaching station on one of the busiest
routes across the Pennine Hills, the Saddleworth
Hotel sits in nine acres of beautiful gardens and
woodland in the picturesque Castleshaw Valley.
The house was built in the 17th century and has
been lovingly restored and sympathetically updated
by the live-in owners. There are many interesting
period features, including the panelling and fireplace
in the Ballroom, which were taken from historic
Weasenham Hall in East Anglia, and the wrought
iron French doors leading to the garden which
date back to 1795 and were recovered from a
Newmarket stud, but originally came from a château
in Bordeaux. Even the lighting has been carefully
chosen – the ceiling sparkles with Swarovski ceiling
lights and the crystal chandeliers, once at home on
an ocean liner, add to the ambience. The bedrooms
have their own individual character and are
elegantly furnished and equipped with all the latest
technology, while the luxury continues in the en
suite marble bathrooms. The Saddleworth Hotel is a
popular venue for parties, weddings, fine dining and
afternoon tea. The restaurant serves a combination
of traditional English and continental cuisine,
complemented by a choice of over 100 fine wines.

Recommended in the area

Standedge Tunnel and narrow boats; walking the
Pennine Way; llama trekking

The Lowry Hotel

★★★★★ 83% ◉◉ HOTEL

Address: 50 Dearmans Place, Chapel Wharf, Salford,
MANCHESTER, M3 5LH
Tel: 0161 827 4000 **Fax:** 0161 827 4001
E-mail: enquiries.lowry@roccofortehotels.com
Website: www.roccofortehotels.com
Map ref: 6, SJ89 **Directions:** M6 junct 19, A556/
M56/A5103 for 4.5m. At rdbt take A57(M) to lights,
right onto Water St. Left to New Quay St/Trinity Way.
At 1st lights right into Chapel St for hotel
Rooms: 165 (7 fmly) **S** from £152; **D** from £122
Facilities: Spa STV FTV Gym Swimming facilities
available nearby ♫ Wi-fi **Parking:** 100

Designing a new hotel for this site by the River
Irwell must have been an exciting architectural
challenge. The result does not disappoint. With
a dramatic curved-glass front, it stands next to
Santiago Calatrava's landmark Trinity Bridge, which
links the separate city of Salford with the centre
of Manchester. Spacious, air-conditioned rooms
and luxury suites are presented in neutral tones,
dark woods and with plush furnishings. Marble
bathrooms and walk-in wardrobes head a roll-call
of room facilities that also includes two phone
lines, voice messaging, high-speed internet access,
interactive satellite TV, iPod docking station, CD
player (on request), mini-bar and safe. The menu in
the River Bar and Restaurant has two AA Rosettes
for Modern British dishes like pan-roasted turbot
with violet artichokes, cippolini onions, brioche
and basil-spinach pistou; and Lancashire fillet and
braised cheek of beef, courgettes, wild asparagus
and smoked potato. A separate dining room with
river views seats up to twenty. The Spa offers a
selection of health treatments, a gym, sauna and
relaxation rooms. The on-site car park with valet
parking carries a charge.

Recommended in the area

The Lowry; Chinatown; Museum of Science &
Industry; National Football Museum

Hampshire

In summer, bracken and heather carpet the heathland of the New Forest National Park

Esseborne Manor

★★★ 80% ◉◉ HOTEL

Address: Hurstbourne Tarrant, ANDOVER, SP11 0ER
Tel: 01264 736444
Fax: 01264 736725
E-mail: info@esseborne-manor.co.uk
Website: www.esseborne-manor.co.uk
Map ref: 3, SU34
Directions: Halfway between Andover & Newbury
on A343, 1m N of Hurstbourne Tarrant
Rooms: 19 (8 annexe) (2 fmly) (6 GF) **S** £80-£110;
D £100-£180 (incl. bkfst)
Facilities: STV FTV ⊴ ⊎ Wi-fi
Parking: 50

A long drive leads to this privately-owned Victorian country-house hotel, set in three acres of gardens high on the hill above the lovely Bourne Valley. The surrounding high downland makes this a perfect spot for country walks, with lots of delightful village pubs for refreshment along the way. All the bedrooms, overlooking the gardens and farmlands beyond, are individually decorated, and some have Jacuzzis and four-poster beds. Feature rooms include Lymington, with a luxurious Victorian bath overlooking the croquet lawn; Ferndown, with a canopy bed and a private patio; and the Honeymoon Suite, with a separate lounge and rococo-style king-size bed. The Dining Room, with its fabric-lined walls, provides a warm and elegant setting for the chef's fine English cuisine, using local produce and herbs from the hotel's own gardens. A choice of fixed-price menus is offered, including a Menu du Vin that includes a specially selected glass of wine with each course. There's also an extensive wine list should you prefer to select your own. The dinner menu might include such main courses as slow-roast pheasant and fillet of cod with crushed new potato and tomato fondue. Complimentary golf at Hampshire Golf Club and daily membership of Nuffield Health Club in Newbury is available to guests.

Recommended in the area
Highclere Castle; Winchester; Broadlands

Oakley Hall Hotel

★★★★ 83% ◉ COUNTRY HOUSE HOTEL
Address: Rectory Rd, BASINGSTOKE, RG23 7EL
Tel: 01256 783350   **Fax:** 01256 783351
E-mail: enquiries@oakleyhall-park.com
Website: www.oakleyhall-park.com
Map ref: 3, SU65 **Directions:** M3 junct 7, follow
Basingstoke signs. In 500yds before lights turn left
onto A30 towards Oakley, immediately right onto
unclass road towards Oakley. In 3m left at T-junct into
Rectory Rd. Left onto B3400. Hotel signed 1st on left
Rooms: 18 (18 annexe) (8 fmly) (18 GF) **S** £119-£295;
D £119-£295 (incl. bkfst) **Facilities:** FTV Clay pigeon
shooting Wi-fi **Parking:** 100 **Notes:** ⊗

An impressive drive leads to this country house
hotel, built in 1795 and once owned by the
Bramstons, close friends of Jane Austen, whose
father was rector at nearby Steventon. It has been
beautifully, indeed expensively, restored and offers
luxury rooms and a swish contemporary restaurant
with classy mirrors, leather seats, well-dressed
tables and a striking striped carpet. The views
across the rolling north Hampshire countryside
are delightful – no wonder it's a popular wedding
venue. In the AA Rosette Winchester restaurant
the broadly modern European cuisine typically
includes spiced monkfish tail with pak choi, basmati
rice and coriander beurre blanc; pan-fried fillet of
organic Laverstoke pork (from the 2,500-acre farm
down the road run by 1979 Formula One champion,
Jody Scheckter) in pancetta with grain mustard
mash, black pudding and roast root vegetables;
and rösti with mushroom and spinach mille-feuille,
artichoke, pumpkin purée and balsamic and tomato
dressing. Afternoon tea is served either on the
Garden Terrace or in the Library. The bedrooms,
many located around the courtyard, are spacious
and well equipped; others are tucked away in an
18th-century, gingerbread-style cottage beneath the
trees on the rear lawns. Within the main house are
nine elegant meeting rooms.

Recommended in the area
Milestones; Basing House; The Vyne (NT)

Cloud Hotel

★ ★ SMALL HOTEL

Address: Meerut Rd, BROCKENHURST, SO42 7TD
Tel: 01590 622165 & 622354
Fax: 01590 622818
E-mail: enquiries@cloudhotel.co.uk
Website: www.cloudhotel.co.uk
Map ref: 3, SU30
Directions: M27 junct 1 signed New Forest, A337
through Lyndhurst to Brockenhurst. On entering
Brockenhurst 1st right. Hotel 300mtrs
Rooms: 18 (1 fmly) (2 GF)
Facilities: FTV Wi-fi **Parking:** 20
Notes: ⊗ ⅰ under 12yrs

The famous New Forest ponies can often be seen near the entrance to this award-winning hotel, owned for 36 years by acclaimed businesswoman, international speaker and charity fundraiser Avril Owton. She was once one of the famous Tiller Girls dance troupe, which now gives its name to the bar. Avril's stage days are also recalled by heaps of high-kicking memorabilia on display around the hotel. The rooms, all en suite, are decorated in an up-to-date style and the majority, including the one with a four-poster, have either uninterrupted views of the forest or of the garden. The forest is again to hand through the windows of Encore Restaurant, now sporting a new, less chintzy look, where largely traditional English food includes roast lamb with

stuffing and honey mint sauce; chargrilled sirloin steak with red onion and port sauce; poached supreme of salmon with mushroom fish sauce; and roast vegetable lasagne. After lunch or dinner take coffee in the conservatory and admire the well-maintained gardens, where, in summer, you may have something to eat. The hotel is open to non-residents for lunch, dinner and cream teas; in fact, traditional tea parties are proving popular for all sorts of celebrations.

Recommended in the area

Exbury Gardens; Beaulieu Motor Museum; New Forest Safaris

The Pig

★★★ ◉◉ COUNTRY HOUSE HOTEL
Address: Beaulieu Rd, BROCKENHURST,
SO42 7QL
Tel: 01590 622354
Fax: 01590 622856
Website: www.thepighotel.co.uk
Map ref: 3, SU30
Directions: At Brockenhurst onto B3055 Beaulieu
Road. 1m on left up private road
Rooms: 26 (3 annexe) (1 GF) **D** £125-£220
(excl. bkfst)
Facilities: ⌣ Wi-fi Foraging CONF
Parking: 23

A radical change of name marks the transformation of a country house hotel into more of a restaurant with rooms. In the heart of the New Forest National Park, its owners admit to a shabby chic, evolving interior, rather than a designed one. This makes it feel warm, relaxed, interesting and homely, all muted colours, lots of restored and reconditioned pieces, and a laid-back bar to chill out in. The stables have been converted into duplex suites and rooms with their own courtyards, and rejoice in farmyard names like The Pig Hut, The Pig Shed and The Hen House. Chef James Golding has two 'lieutenants' – Garry, his forager, and Mike, his kitchen gardener, whose recommendations largely determine the '25-mile menu', the sourcing radius for 80 per cent of the kitchen's fresh ingredients. Dishes are served in an authentically reproduced Victorian greenhouse dining room, complete with bare wooden tables and mismatched bone-handled cutlery. Among James's specialities are grilled Solent brill on the bone; and New Forest venison and damson pie. A wander around the grounds reveals hammocks between trees and the odd bench placed in a tranquil corner. The Lime Wood hotel at Lyndhurst is The Pig's 'big sister'.

Recommended in the area

The New Forest; Bucklers Hard Historical Village; Exbury Gardens

Lime Wood

★★★★★ ⊛⊛⊛ COUNTRY HOUSE HOTEL
Address: Beaulieu Rd, LYNDHURST, SO43 7FZ
Tel: 023 8028 7177
Fax: 023 8028 7199
E-mail: info@limewood.co.uk
Website: www.limewood.co.uk
Map ref: 3, SU30
Directions: Exit A35 onto B3056 towards Beaulieu, hotel 1m on right
Rooms: 29 (13 annexe) (9 fmly) (3 GF) **S** £245-£775; **D** £245-£775
Facilities: Spa STV FTV ⊗ Fishing Gym Wi-fi Foraging CONF **Parking:** 60

This immaculately renovated, Regency country house hotel and spa in the heart of the New Forest National Park was originally a hunting lodge. Its five-year transformation involved a rich collaboration of creative talent, extensive use of local materials like ash and stone, and the application of subtle colours, so that the interiors harmonise with their surroundings. Rooms and suites, divided between the main house and the garden lodges, are large, with wooden floors, king-size beds, and a mix of antiques and hand-picked art. Other features include a well-stocked pantry, satellite TV, DVD player and iPod docking station. Many of the bathrooms are spacious enough to have room for a free-standing bath. There's a choice between two restaurants: the glamorous, three-AA Rosette Dining Room – think ravioli with creamy polenta, violet artichokes and truffles – and The Scullery, which is more of a smoked salmon with organic beets and soured cream type of place, which offers all-day dining in a country-house kitchen setting. Chef Luke Holder's passion for local, organic produce surfaces on the menus in a multitude of other ways too, from wild mushrooms and New Forest venison, to home-reared beef and lamb. The Pig at Brockenhurst is Lime Wood's 'little sister'.

Recommended in the area

The New Forest Museum; Bolderwood Deer Sanctuary; Furzey Gardens

Westover Hall Hotel

★★★ 88% ◉◉ COUNTRY HOUSE HOTEL
Address: Park Ln, MILFORD ON SEA, SO41 0PT
Tel: 01590 643044
Fax: 01590 644490
E-mail: info@westoverhallhotel.com
Website: www.westoverhallhotel.com
Map ref: 3, SZ29
Directions: M3 & M27 W onto A337 to Lymington,
follow signs to Milford on Sea onto B3058, hotel
outside village centre towards cliff
Rooms: 15 (3 annexe) (2 fmly) (2 GF) **S** £99-£210;
D £120-£270 (incl. bkfst)
Facilities: Wi-fi **Parking:** 50

Just a short walk from the beach, this privately
owned boutique hotel enjoys uninterrupted views
across Christchurch Bay to The Needles and the
Isle of Wight. Arts and Crafts in style, it features
a minstrels' gallery, magnificent stained-glass
windows, extensive oak panelling and a galleried
entrance hall. In the lounge is a remarkable tiled
fireplace by the late-Victorian ceramicist, William de
Morgan, while the library bar features contemporary
and ethnic furniture. Bedrooms vary in size and
aspect, but all are decorated with flair and style, and
from those facing south you can see Hurst Castle
in the east and Hengistbury Head in the west. The
same panorama awaits diners in the informal Vista
Bistro (sample dish: seared scallops, samphire
and peas) and One Park Lane, the two-AA Rosette
restaurant, where the five-course, fine-dining
menu might list tournedos with oxtail, horseradish
purée and wild mushroom; ballottine of guinea
fowl with wild boar, bread sauce and fennel; and
monkfish with red lentil and tarragon, as well as
accompanying wine suggestions. To really push
the boat out, try the nine-course tasting menu. The
terrace is the ideal location for an alfresco lunch, or
why not take a picnic to the hotel's own beach hut?

Recommended in the area

Beaulieu Palace & Motor Museum; Hurst Castle;
Hengistbury Head

Chewton Glen Hotel & Spa

★★★★★ ◎◎◎ COUNTRY HOUSE HOTEL
Address: Christchurch Rd, NEW MILTON, BH25 6QS
Tel: 01425 275341 **Fax:** 01425 272310
E-mail: reservations@chewtonglen.com
Website: www.chewtonglen.com
Map ref: 3, SZ29 **Directions:** A35 from Lyndhurst
for 10m, left at staggered junct. Follow tourist sign for
hotel through Walkford, take 2nd left
Rooms: 58 (11 GF) Rooms and Suites £269–£2000
Facilities: Spa FTV ⊙ ⚲ ♪ 9 ⚑ Putt green ⚑ Gym
Hydrotherapy spa Dance studio Cycling & jogging
trail Clay shooting Archery ♫ Wi-fi Child facilities
Parking: 200 **Notes:** ⊗

The sea is just 10 minutes' walk from this superb
18th-century country-house hotel. Bedrooms
are individually styled with luxurious fabrics and
furnishings. All bedrooms enjoy the benefits of
air conditioning, satellite TV, radio, DVD and CD
players, and direct-dial telephone. There are also
a number of suites, some duplex, and all with
secluded private gardens. Guests can enjoy the
health and beauty treatments, both traditional
and modern, of the elegant high-tech spa, where
everything from a massage to a facial or body polish
is available. The restaurant offers a wide variety
of cuisines, using as much fresh local produce as
possible and vegetarian and low-calorie dishes can
be provided. The nearby New Forest offers wild
mushrooms, vegetables and game; seafood may
come from Christchurch and Lymington nearby.
The wine list is drawn from a cellar of over 700 bins.
Short residential packages are available including:
Gourmet Dining Breaks, Spa Breaks and Celebration
Breaks. Children of all ages are welcome at the
hotel. The height of luxury will apply literally to the
new Tree House suites available from late summer
2012. These elegantly crafted suites are set high
among the forest trees and offer tranquility and
privacy along with stunning forest views.

Recommended in the area

New Forest National Park; National Motor Museum,
Beaulieu; Buckler's Hard historic village

The White Horse Hotel & Brasserie

★★★ 85% ◉ HOTEL

Address: 19 Market Place, ROMSEY, SO51 8ZJ
Tel: 01794 512431
Fax: 01794 517485
E-mail: reservations@silkshotels.com
Website: www.silkshotels.com
Map ref: 3, SU32
Directions: In town centre
Rooms: 31 (4 fmly) **S** £95-£115; **D** £115-£135
Facilities: FTV Wi-fi
Parking: 6

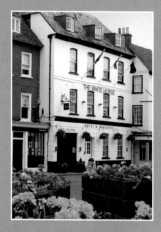

The old market town of Romsey is famous for its abbey, which is within striking distance of this 14th-century boutique hotel; for being Lord Palmerston's birthplace – his statue stands across the road; and for Broadlands, the Palladian-style home of Earl Mountbatten, barely half a mile away. Hotel bedrooms are individually styled to a high standard, with fabrics by Lewis & Wood and Sanderson, crisp white bed linen, hot drinks tray, bath robes, fluffy towels, curtains with blackout linings, and even traditional-type coat-hangers in the wardrobes. Many of the smaller bathrooms have been made into lavish walk-in shower rooms, with high-pressure showers, tiled walls and big mirrors. The two-floor Loft Suites have a bedroom on the upper level, connected by a solid oak staircase to the sitting area with sofa bed below. The Brasserie is open all day for grills and the likes of roasted supreme of corn-fed chicken; pan-fried wild sea bass fillet; and pine-nut and spinach gnocchi with goat's cheese. Freshly baked breads are a house speciality. The coral- and shell-decorated bar is home to an extensive whisky (and whiskey) collection, some extremely rare, draught Hampshire ales, sandwiches and light meals.

Recommended in the area

Mottisfont Abbey and Garden; Winchester Cathedral; Broadlands

River Test, Romsey

Herefordshire

North Hill in the Malvern Hills, Great Malvern

Feathers Hotel

★★★ 81% ◉ HOTEL

Address: High St, LEDBURY, HR8 1DS
Tel: 01531 635266 & 0800 074 9377
Fax: 01531 638955
E-mail: enquiries@feathersledbury.co.uk
Website: www.feathersledbury.co.uk
Map ref: 2, SO73
Directions: S from Worcester on A449, E from Hereford on A438, N from Gloucester on A417. Hotel in town centre
Rooms: 22 (3 annexe) (2 fmly) **S** £95–£127.50; **D** £140–£245 (incl. bkfst) **Facilities:** STV ◉ Gym Steam room Wi-fi **Parking:** 30

Originally The Plume of Feathers, this hotel dates back to at least 1564, and is one of many Tudor survivals in this historic market town. In the late 18th century, cladding was applied to cover up its then unfashionable black and white exterior, but early in the 20th century, when good taste made a comeback, it was removed. 'Wonky' (the hotel's description) exposed beams are visible in the bedrooms, and in the Coaching Rooms early-17th-century wall paintings can be seen. Every room has a flat-screen TV, internet access and hot drinks tray. Fuggles Brasserie is log fire-warmed and decorated with hops, and here you can expect Herefordshire steak; Cotswold venison; Monmouthshire duck breast; and grilled skate wing. The sumptuously furnished and decorated Quills Restaurant is used as the breakfast room, and then in the evening becomes a private fine-dining room. The newly renovated Top Bar offers a seasonal 'Quickies' lunch menu, serves afternoon tea and is also well known for its cocktails. The old stables have been turned into a leisure spa and conference rooms, and two self-catering apartments, Lanark House and Eve's Cottage, were added in 2011. On a warm day, enjoy a drink and a light lunch under a parasol in the peaceful walled garden.

Recommended in the area

Eastnor Castle; Westons Ciders Visitor Centre; River Wye river cruise

Hertfordshire

Bridgewater Monument, Ashridge Park

The Grove

★★★★★ 87% ◉◉◉ HOTEL

Address: Chandler's Cross, RICKMANSWORTH,
WD3 4TG
Tel: 01923 807807
Fax: 01923 221008
E-mail: info@thegrove.co.uk
Website: www.thegrove.co.uk
Map ref: 3, TQ09 **Directions:** M25 junct 19, A411
towards Watford. Hotel on right
Rooms: 217 (69 fmly) (35 GF) **S** £285-£975;
D £310-£1000 (incl. bkfst) **Facilities:** Spa STV FTV ⊛
⚞ supervised ⚲ 18 ⚲ Putt green ⚲ Gym Giant chess
Orchid house Wi-fi **Parking:** 400 **Notes:** ⊗

The history of The Grove, a magnificent 18th-century stately home set within 300 acres of park and woodland, and easily reached from London, is rich and interesting. In its heyday, having been the seat of the Earls of Clarendon, it was a venue for lavish country house parties, attended by royalty. Today, the hotel calls its mix of traditional elegance with contemporary design, 'groovy grand'. The guest rooms range from the merely luxurious in the West Wing, to the positively palatial in the individually designed Mansion suites, many with fireplaces and four-poster beds. There is a choice of three dining venues, each with an outdoor terrace. Head for three-Rosette Colette's for fine dining in elegant surroundings, The Glasshouse for a gourmet buffet, or The Stables for simply presented, contemporary twists on British classics. The award-winning Sequoia spa is a tranquil sanctuary while the Walled Garden is a world-within-a-world with tennis courts, an outdoor swimming pool and an urban beach for activity lovers. Also here, the Potting Shed is the perfect place to relax, with its antiques and comfy armchairs. Children are well catered for too – the outdoor space gives kids the room to run free. The hotel's 18-hole golf course is playable all year and has been host to the World Championships.

Recommended in the area

ZSL Whipsnade Zoo; St Albans Cathedral; Warner Bros Studio Tour – The Making of Harry Potter

St Michael's Manor

★★★★ 77% ◉◉ HOTEL

Address: Fishpool St, ST ALBANS, AL3 4RY
Tel: 01727 864444
Fax: 01727 848909
E-mail: reservations@stmichaelsmanor.com
Website: www.stmichaelsmanor.com
Map ref: 3, TL10
Directions: From St Albans Abbey follow Fishpool Street towards St Michael's village. Hotel 0.5m on left
Rooms: 30 (8 annexe) (3 fmly) (4 GF) (6 smoking)
S £130-£350; **D** £160-£350 (incl. bkfst)
Facilities: STV FTV ☙ Licenced fishing in season Guided tours Wi-fi **Parking:** 60 **Notes:** ⊗

This opulently decorated and furnished manor house hotel stands in five acres of gardens close to the famous cathedral and abbey church of St Alban in the centre of the old Roman city of Verulamium. The hotel was built in 1585 by John Gape, whose family continued to live here for almost 400 years, and whose initials you can see on the ceiling of the oak-panelled lounge. The house was converted into a hotel in the early 1960s by today's owners and managers, the Newling Ward family. The individually styled bedrooms, named after trees in the garden, all have satellite TV, DVD player, Wi-fi, iron, hot drinks tray, games and other little luxuries. Many overlook the one-acre lake and gardens. There are similar views from the orangery-style Lake Restaurant, where two specially commissioned pictures of the cathedral and of the hotel itself are given pride of place. The Modern British style of the carte leads to dishes such as roast wood pigeon; fillet of halibut; and asparagus and wild mushroom tart. The weekly changing Lake Menu is more brasserie in style, with a choice of two or three courses, including coffee. The lounge bar menu includes perennial favourites, such as fish and chips, burgers, and cream teas.

Recommended in the area

St Albans Cathedral and Abbey; Verulamium Park; Verulamium Museum

Kent

Canterbury Cathedral, Canterbury

Eastwell Manor

★★★★ ◎ HOTEL

Address: Eastwell Park, Boughton Lees, ASHFORD, TN25 4HR
Tel: 01233 213000
Fax: 01233 635530
E-mail: enquiries@eastwellmanor.co.uk
Website: www.eastwellmanor.co.uk
Map ref: 4, TR04 **Directions:** M20 junct 9, follow A251 signs. Hotel on left as entering Boughton Aluph
Rooms: 62 (39 annexe) (2 fmly) (15 GF) **S** £110-£190; **D** £140-£445 (incl. bkfst) **Facilities:** Spa STV ⓢ ↘ ↙ 9 ⛳ Putt green ⤴ Gym Boules ♫ Wi-fi
Parking: 200

Eastwell Manor, dating back to the Norman Conquest, lies in 62 acres of grounds, including a formal Italian garden, lawns and parkland. In the 16th century Richard Plantagenet lived here, and Queen Victoria and King Edward VII were frequent visitors. Its age is apparent in the lounges, restaurant and bar, with their original fireplaces, carved panelling and fine antiques. Twenty-three individually designed bedrooms are named after previous owners. The luxury mews cottages in the grounds have been converted from Victorian stables; each has a kitchen, sitting room and dining facilities, and are available on a self-catering basis. Complimentary Wi-fi is available throughout. The informal, all-day brasserie in The Pavilion looks out across the countryside, while the more formal but intimate dining destination is the Manor Restaurant. Here, diners are entertained by the resident pianist while choosing from a French and Modern British-inspired menu. The Pavilion Spa houses a 20-metre pool in a Roman baths-style setting, hydrotherapy pool, sauna, Jacuzzi, steam room and techno-gym. The beauty and therapy area, Dreams, pampers both men and women. There is also a 20-metre outdoor heated pool, all-weather tennis court and the 'Eastwell 9' Golf Course (2,132 yards, par 32).

Recommended in the area

Canterbury Cathedral; Sissinghurst Castle; Leeds Castle; Godinton House

Little Silver Country Hotel

★★★ 79% HOTEL

Address: Ashford Rd, St Michael's, TENTERDEN,
TN30 6SP
Tel: 01233 850321 & 0845 166 2516
Fax: 01233 850647
E-mail: enquiries@little-silver.co.uk
Website: www.little-silver.co.uk
Map ref: 4, TQ83
Directions: M20 junct 8, A274 signed Tenterden
Rooms: 16 (2 fmly) (6 GF) **S** £62-£125; **D** £97-£199
(incl. bkfst)
Facilities: STV FTV Wi-fi
Parking: 70 **Notes:** ⊛

This family-friendly hotel in landscaped gardens has been carefully renovated in contemporary style, while retaining its original Tudor-style timbering. In the individually furnished bedrooms you'll find a power shower or bath, flat-screen TV with countless channels, radio, Wi-fi, and hospitality tray with biscuits. Some of the rooms offer a four-poster and spa bath, while the Platinum suite, giving excellent views over the landscaped gardens, not only has its own private staircase, but also a spa bath, separate dressing room, lounge and unusual round bed. Two rooms have been specially built to allow easy access for guests with wheelchairs. The hotel belongs to the 'Produced in Kent' organisation, which promotes food and drink sourced within the county. Oaks Restaurant is set in the Orangery, where the menu lists essentially traditional and seasonal dishes, such as starters of Gressingham duck terrine; and tender asparagus spears; and main courses of slow-braised beef and mushroom pie; pan-seared pork tenderloin; fish of the day; and fusilli with roasted red pepper sauce. An extensive wine list includes a selection from the New World, as well as some from local vineyards. Staff receive a lot of praise on dedicated websites for their helpfulness. The hotel is licensed for civil marriages.

Recommended in the area

Sissinghurst Castle Garden; Leeds Castle; Rye; Canterbury; Bodiam Castle; Smallhythe Place

The Brew House Hotel

★★★★ 77% ◎ HOTEL

Address: 1 Warwick Park, TUNBRIDGE WELLS,
(ROYAL) TN2 5TA
Tel: 01892 520587
Fax: 01892 534979
E-mail: reception@brewhousehotel.com
Website: www.brewhousehotel.com
Map ref: 4, TQ53
Directions: A267, 1st left onto Warwick Park, hotel
immediately on left
Rooms: 15 (5 annexe) (2 fmly) **D** £95-£199
(incl. bkfst) **Facilities:** STV FTV Gym ♫ Wi-fi
Parking: 8 **Notes:** ⊗

Close to the famous Pantiles, this impressive boutique hotel opened its doors in 2007, following a spell as a South East Tourist Board office, and then as the headquarters of table football company, Subbuteo. Originally, it was indeed a brewery, which explains why stone-faced Bacchus, the Roman god of wine, stares out from the building's façade. Air-conditioned bedrooms are divided into three categories: standard, superior and de luxe, all of them individually designed in contemporary style, with queen-size double beds fitted with Egyptian cotton linen. In some of the en suite bathrooms you can flick a switch and the 'smart glass' wall turns from transparent to opaque. Additional room features are an LCD flat-screen TV, hot drinks tray, mini-bar and free Wi-fi. In the restaurant the strikingly modern furniture is echoed by the Modern European food prepared from carefully selected local ingredients by head chef Andrew Giles and his team. Favourites include slow-roasted shoulder of Lamberhurst lamb; Barbury duck breast; fillet of wild sea bass; whole Whitstable slip sole; and beetroot and goat's cheese salad. For a complimentary two-course meal, sign up for the gym. The old school house, behind the main building, is the hotel's main function room.

Recommended in the area

Hever Castle; Penshurst Place; Leeds Castle

Lancashire

The River Hodder, Forest of Bowland, Lancashire

Northcote

★ ★ ★ ★ ◉ ◉ ◉ ◉ SMALL HOTEL

Address: Northcote Rd, LANGHO, BB6 8BE

Tel: 01254 240555

Fax: 01254 246568

E-mail: reception@northcote.com

Website: www.northcote.com

Map ref: 6, SD73

Directions: M6 junct 31, 9m to Northcote. Follow
Clitheroe (A59) signs. Hotel on left before rdbt

Rooms: 14 (2 fmly) (4 GF) **S** £210-£225; **D** £245-£270
(incl. bkfst)

Facilities: STV FTV ⓑ Wi-fi

Parking: 50 **Notes:** ⊗

Built in the 1880s, Northcote still has the ambience
of a Victorian family home and the focus is on
eating well, as, no doubt, it was when it belonged
to a textile baron. Its former ownership explains
its proximity to Lancashire's industrial heartland
to the south, but stretching northwards across
the River Ribble is Longridge Fell and the Forest of
Bowland. The excellent road network also makes it
easy to reach the Yorkshire Dales. Proprietors Nigel
Haworth and Craig Bancroft describe their hotel as
a restaurant with rooms, and the food is certainly a
very good reason to come here. Nigel is a staunch
supporter of the county's many artisan food
producers and, with their ingredients and organic
fruit, vegetables and herbs from the hotel's own
gardens, creates memorable culinary delights. The
excellent dining experience here is complemented
by the extensive range of wines to choose from
– some 400 bins. The bedrooms have individual,
contemporary decor that is stunning in its originality
and the quality of the fabrics and wall coverings.
Each room has a high-tech sound system with iPod
connector, TV with 200 satellite channels, DVD and
CD player and complimentary Wi-fi. Cosy bathrobes
are provided, along with Molton Brown hair and
skincare products.

Recommended in the area

Clitheroe; Ribble Valley; Gawthorpe Hall (NT)

Bedford Hotel

★★★ 80% HOTEL

Address: 307-313 Clifton Drive South,
LYTHAM ST ANNES, FY8 1HN
Tel: 01253 724636
Fax: 01253 729244
E-mail: reservations@bedford-hotel.com
Website: www.bedford-hotel.com
Map ref: 6, SD32 **Directions:** From M55 follow
signs for airport to last lights. Left through 2 sets of
lights. Hotel 300yds on left
Rooms: 45 (6 GF) **S** £60-£65; **D** £90-£160 (incl. bkfst)
Facilities: FTV Gym Hydrotherapy spa bath Wi-fi
Parking: 25 **Notes:** ⊗

A popular, family-run hotel close to town centre shops, boutiques and restaurants, and the sandy beach. Also within easy walking distance is the world-famous Royal Lytham and St Annes Golf Club, host to the 2012 British Open Championship. Spacious public areas include a choice of lounges, a coffee shop, the Circe Suite lounge bar, an impressive ballroom, fitness facilities, and a hydrotherapy spa pool in which you can watch TV while you soak. Furnished in coordinated fabrics, the Standard, Superior and Club bedrooms come in all shapes and sizes, each with en suite bathroom, digital Freeview TV, direct-dial phone, radio, Wi-fi, hot drinks tray, toiletries, bathrobes, iron and ironing board. A laundry valet service is also available.

Widely known for its range of freshly prepared local and international dishes, the award-winning Cartland Restaurant offers both a set menu and à la carte, from which you could choose a typical three-course dinner of steamed Morecambe Bay mussels in white wine with a hint of chilli, garlic and ginger; followed by slow-roasted chump of Pendle lamb with château potatoes, redcurrant and mint sauce; then crumbly Lancashire apple tart with gingerbread ice cream. Just three miles away are the bright lights of Blackpool. Hotel car parking is free.

Recommended in the area

Beach, pier and promenade; Royal Lytham and St Annes Golf Club; Blackpool

Leicestershire

The gold-toned stone battlements of Belvoir Castle overlook the Vale of Belvoir

Sketchley Grange

★★★★ 81% ◎◎ HOTEL

Address: Sketchley Lane, Burbage, HINCKLEY,
LE10 3HU
Tel: 01455 251133
Fax: 01455 631384
E-mail: info@sketchleygrange.co.uk
Website: www.sketchleygrange.co.uk
Map ref: 3, SP49 **Directions:** SE of town, off A5/
M69 junct 1, take B4109 to Hinckley. Left at 2nd rdbt.
1st right onto Sketchley Lane
Rooms: 94 (9 fmly) (6 GF) **S** £65-£130; **D** £65-£130
Facilities: Spa STV FTV ③ Gym Steam room Sauna
Wi-fi **Parking:** 270

Motorway connections are not far away, not that
you'd know from the unexpectedly tranquil location
of this Mock Tudor hotel, surrounded by beautiful
willow gardens and open country. Rooms range
from luxurious Master Suites, spacious enough to
comfortably accommodate an emperor-size bed,
to the Classic Collection of traditionally decorated
en suite doubles, twins, triples and family rooms.
Easily accessible ground-floor rooms with a wheel-in
shower are set aside for less able guests. The honour
of holding two AA Rosettes goes to The Dining
Room, the elegant fine-dining restaurant serving, for
example, sautéed fillet of Ayrshire beef; and poached
wild turbot. The more contemporary Restaurant
52°, overlooking the beautiful gardens, has a more
cosmopolitan menu, represented by Thai red chicken
curry; and wild mushroom and leek tagliatelle. Here
on Sundays a table magician provides entertainment.
For a cappuccino or a quick bite between meetings,
head for the Terrace Bar & Lounge. All overnight
guests enjoy complimentary use of Romans
Health and Leisure Club, which houses a 17-metre
swimming pool, sauna and steam room, gym,
outdoor hot tub, beauty therapy suites, hair salon and
crèche. The largest of the meeting and event rooms
can accommodate up to 300 delegates.

Recommended in the area

Warwick Castle; Twycross Zoo; Bosworth Battlefield
Heritage Centre and Country Park

Kilworth House

★ ★ ★ ★ ◎ HOTEL

Address: Lutterworth Rd, NORTH KILWORTH,
LE17 6JE
Tel: 01858 880058
Fax: 01858 880349
E-mail: info@kilworthhouse.co.uk
Website: www.kilworthhouse.co.uk
Map ref: 3, SP68
Directions: A4304 towards Market Harborough,
after Walcote, hotel 1.5m on right
Rooms: 44 (2 fmly) (13 GF) **D** £180-£340
Facilities: FTV Fishing ❥ Gym Beauty therapy
rooms Wi-fi **Parking:** 140 **Notes:** ⊛

This grand, Grade II listed country house sits amid
38 acres of landscaped parkland. It's an enchanting
place – a blend of Victorian opulence and
contemporary luxury with a warm and welcoming
atmosphere. There are 11 bedrooms on the first
floor of the house, including two with four-poster
beds, all furnished with a mixture of antiques and
rich fabrics, but with the latest technology. Across
the knot garden courtyard are a further 33 rooms, all
individually designed in an elegant, country-house
style. The one-Rosette Wordsworth Restaurant,
with its double oak and stained-glass doors, domed
ceiling, glittering chandeliers, open fireplaces and
views over the knot garden, is a gloriously ornate
setting for some fine Modern British cuisine. For
a less formal alternative, or perhaps, for morning
coffee or afternoon tea, take a seat in the beautifully
restored Victorian Orangery, which has a special
ambience both day and night. With its well-equipped
and modern conference facilities, private dining
rooms, attentive staff, beauty therapy suite, fitness
room, and vast grounds where Muntjac deer dart
across woodland trails and the lake is well-stocked
with fish, it's no wonder Kilworth House draws in
business and leisure guests in equal measure.

Recommended in the area

Kilworth Springs Golf Club; Stanford Hall;
Rutland Water; Foxton Locks

London

St James's Park, London

Four Seasons Hotel London at Canary Wharf

★★★★★ ⊚ HOTEL

Address: Westferry Circus, Canary Wharf, LONDON, E14 8RS

Tel: 020 7510 1999 **Fax:** 020 7510 1998

E-mail: reservations.caw@fourseasons.com

Website: www.fourseasons.com/canarywharf

Map ref: 4, TQ38 **Directions:** From A13 follow Westferry Circus signs. Hotel off 3rd exit Westferry Circus rdbt **Rooms:** 142 **S** £160-£365; **D** £160-£365

Facilities: Spa STV FTV ⊙ supervised ♨ Gym Fitness centre Wi-fi **Parking:** 26

Ships once came to these London Docks with cargoes from all over the world; in the case of West India Dock it was spices from the East. Today, this is the waterfront location for a very 21st-century hotel in what has become London's dynamic financial district. Furnished in American black walnut, the spacious guest rooms and suites offer panoramic views of the River Thames and the city beyond. Fully equipped for business needs, their standard amenities include an all-news cable network, two-line speakerphones and high-speed internet access. The marble bathrooms, which the hotel claims are among the largest in London, incorporate a deep-soaking tub and separate glass-enclosed shower. Quadrato Restaurant offers contemporary Italian dishes, including their signature *Sfizzi e Stuzzichi* (Italian-style tapas) and a wide range of pasta dishes. The restaurant overlooks a large private garden and a heated, 20-metre infinity pool, visible through floor-to-ceiling glass walls. Quadrato Bar in the hotel lobby also offers Italian specialities and light meals, cocktails, afternoon teas and other herbal infusions. The fitness centre is fully equipped and guests have complimentary access to the state-of-the-art Virgin Active Health Club. A high-speed catamaran service links a jetty in front of the hotel with Embankment Pier at Charing Cross.

Recommended in the area

Maritime Greenwich; Tower Bridge; The O2

The Landmark London

★★★★★ ◎◎ HOTEL

Address: 222 Marylebone Rd, LONDON, NW1 6JQ
Tel: 020 7631 8000
Fax: 020 7631 8080
E-mail: reservations@thelandmark.co.uk
Website: www.landmarklondon.co.uk
Map ref: 4, TQ38
Directions: Adjacent to Marylebone Station. Hotel on Marylebone Rd
Rooms: 300 (71 fmly) (52 smoking)
Facilities: Spa STV FTV ⓢ Gym Beauty treatments & massages ♫ Wi-fi
Parking: 80 **Notes:** ⊛

The Landmark London ranks among the finest of the capital's grande dame hotels. Built in 1899, it personifies classic Victorian opulence, and is perfectly located in one of London's most upmarket districts, close to all of the capital's main attractions. The guest rooms are some of the largest in London, averaging 55 square metres, and all 300 have an executive desk, private bar, high-speed internet access as well as a marble bathroom. The Landmark London's spectacular Winter Garden restaurant is situated beneath the soaring eight-storey glass atrium and offers seasonal Modern British cuisine, and is also popular for brunch, lunch and delicious afternoon tea. For a more informal setting, the twotwentytwo restaurant and bar fits the bill, offering a relaxing place to meet, eat and drink. Meanwhile for late-night drinks, champagne and cocktails, the Mirror Bar is the place to head for. The exclusive Landmark Spa and Health Club offers a complete wellbeing experience; it features a 15-metre chlorine-free swimming pool, a heat therapy sanarium, a steam room, whirlpool, a state-of-the-art gym and four lavish treatment rooms. For pure indulgence, try one of the ESPA or VOYA spa treatments.

Recommended in the area

Marylebone High Street; Regent's Park; London Zoo; Wembley Stadium

Meliá White House

★★★★ 80% ◎◎ HOTEL

Address: Albany St, Regents Park, LONDON, NW1 3UP

Tel: 020 7391 3000

Fax: 020 7388 0091

E-mail: melia.white.house@solmelia.com

Website: www.melia-whitehouse.com

Map ref: 4, TQ38

Directions: Opposite Gt Portland St underground station & next to Regent's Park/Warren Street underground station

Rooms: 581 (7 fmly) (61 smoking)

Facilities: STV FTV Gym ♫ Wi-fi **Notes:** ⊗

Managed by the Spanish Solmelia company, this impressive art deco property is located just to the south of Regent's Park, and only a few blocks north of Oxford Street. Spacious public areas offer a high degree of comfort and include an elegant cocktail bar. The en suite bedrooms come in a variety of sizes and are comfortable, stylish and well equipped with air conditioning, hairdryer, magnifying mirror, tea and coffee tray, safe, trouser press, satellite TV, radio, direct-dial phone, and high-speed Wi-fi connection via laptop or TV. Room service is available 24 hours a day. Diners looking for somewhere fashionable to eat will approve of L'Albufera, an elegant, award-winning Spanish restaurant; for greater informality, The Place

Brasserie offers buffet breakfast, lunch and dinner, with an emphasis on Mediterranean cuisine. Relax in comfortable Longfords Bar, while listening to live music (from Wednesdays to Saturdays). Among the hotel's other amenities are an air-conditioned gym with the latest cardiovascular equipment, and a modern therapy room full of treatments that 'alleviate and rejuvenate'. For those looking to stay longer in the capital, there are various apartments to choose from. The hotel also has a business centre and eight conference or banqueting rooms.

Recommended in the area

Madame Tussaud's; Regent's Park; Oxford Street; Camden Town

London Bridge Hotel

★★★★ 79% HOTEL

Address: 8-18 London Bridge St, LONDON, SE1 9SG
Tel: 020 7855 2200
Fax: 020 7855 2233
E-mail: sales@londonbridgehotel.com
Website: www.londonbridgehotel.com
Map ref: 4, TQ38
Directions: Access through London Bridge station
(bus/taxi yard), into London Bridge St (one-way).
Hotel on left, 50yds from station
Rooms: 138 (12 fmly) (5 smoking) **S** £143-£384;
D £143-£384
Facilities: STV FTV Gym Wi-fi **Notes:** ⊗

In the heart of vibrant Southwark, an area rich in
architecture, museums, theatres and shopping
opportunities, this is a tremendously chic, privately
owned hotel with a stately entrance and a stunning
interior that blends classical features with an ultra-
modern interior. A calming blend of cream and
earth tones combines with textures contrasting
between smooth leather, polished wood, suede and
coarse weave fabrics. There's a touch of colour in
the Londinium restaurant, named in recognition of
the Roman artefacts unearthed during the building
development, and where red suede upholstery is
set against polished walnut floors. Still chic, and
with a contemporary but relaxed atmosphere is
the newly opened Quarter Bar and Lounge. The
bedrooms are supremely relaxing and comfortable;
fibre-optic reading lights, flat-screen TVs and
complimentary Wi-fi are among the in-room
facilities. De luxe rooms have a king-size bed, plus
a sofa bed and walk-in closet, while the executive
rooms and suites are designed with business guests
in mind. The City, London's financial heart, is, after
all, just a short walk away, across London Bridge.

Recommended in the area

Tate Modern; Shakespeare's Globe Theatre;
Borough Market

Cavendish London

★★★★ 80% ⊛ HOTEL

Address: 81 Jermyn St, LONDON, SW1Y 6JF
Tel: 020 7930 2111
Fax: 020 7839 2125
E-mail: info@thecavendishlondon.com
Website: www.thecavendishlondon.com
Map ref: 4, TQ38
Directions: From Piccadilly, (pass The Ritz),
1st right into Duke St before Fortnum & Mason
Rooms: 230 (12 fmly)
Facilities: STV Wi-fi
Parking: 50
Notes: ⊛

Situated on the prestigious Jermyn Street, in the heart of Piccadilly, the smart Cavendish Hotel offers guests the ultimate in luxury. Although the location makes it ideal for sampling the thrill of both London's theatres and its renowned shopping opportunities, it also provides a chance to escape the hustle and bustle of the city. It was run in Edwardian times by Rosa Lewis, the 'Duchess of Duke Street', famous for her hospitality and cooking, and the tradition continues to this day. Inside, however, the hotel now features cutting-edge design, carried through from the public areas to the bedrooms, which have some of the best views in London. All guest rooms – including spacious executive rooms and suites – boast elegant furnishings and subtle lighting, complemented by Villeroy and Boch bathrooms. Each room comes fully equipped with the latest technology, including flat-screen LCD TV with over 600 channels, an iPod docking station and high-speed broadband. The AA Rosette-awarded Petrichor at The Cavendish Restaurant serves an indulgent breakfast, as well as informal lunches and dinners. The emphasis on British cuisine using sustainably sourced ingredients has gained Petrichor a Gold Accreditation from the Sustainable Restaurant Association.

Recommended in the area

Fortnum & Mason; Buckingham Palace; Piccadilly Circus

Dukes London

★★★★★ 85% HOTEL

Address: 35 St James's Place, LONDON, SW1A 1NY
Tel: 020 7491 4840 **Fax:** 020 7493 1264
E-mail: bookings@dukeshotel.com
Website: www.dukeshotel.com
Map ref: 4, TQ38
Directions: From Pall Mall turn into St James's
then 2nd left into St James's Place. Hotel in
courtyard on left
Rooms: 90 (4 GF)
Facilities: STV FTV Gym Steam room Health club
Personal training Wi-fi
Notes: ⊛

This boutique hotel has been welcoming its guests for over a century. Just a short open-carriage ride away are the royal residences of St James's Palace and Clarence House, the official residence of The Prince of Wales and The Duchess of Cornwall. The luxurious rooms and suites, including the Penthouse Suite that overlooks Green Park, provide hand-made chocolates, organic toiletries, newspapers, magazines and much more besides. Women travelling alone may opt for a Duchess room, with a female member of staff on hand for all room service and housekeeping requirements, and a quiet corner table in the restaurant if required. Even the complimentary slippers are smaller in size. Award-winning chef Nigel Mendham's seasonal menus

in the elegant Thirty Six restaurant offer classic British dishes, while the wine list includes a special reserve selection of predominantly Old World reds. The Drawing Room and Conservatory overlook a peaceful courtyard garden and serve morning coffee, a light lunch and afternoon tea. From 8pm, the garden opens for post-dinner drinks and cigars. In Dukes Bar, the regular metropolitan after-work crowd come in for the cocktails and dry martinis. The Health Club features an Italian marble steam room, modern gym and beauty treatment room.

Recommended in the area

St James's Park; National Gallery; Burlington Arcade

The Halkin Hotel

★★★★★ ◉◉◉ TOWN HOUSE HOTEL

Address: Halkin St, Belgravia, LONDON, SW1X 7DJ
Tel: 020 7333 1000
Fax: 020 7333 1100
E-mail: res@halkin.como.bz
Website: www.halkin.como.bz
Map ref: 4, TQ38
Directions: Between Belgrave Sq & Grosvenor Place. Via Chapel St into Headfort Place, left into Halkin St
Rooms: 41
Facilities: STV FTV Complimentary use of gym & spa at sister hotel Wi-fi **Notes:** ⊗

Behind the Georgian-style façade is one of London's smartest hotels. Discreetly situated in a quiet street, The Halkin is surrounded by elegant buildings, smart shops, and is just a short stroll from Hyde Park Corner, Knightsbridge and Buckingham Palace. Inside, the style is contemporary Italian, much of the impact being derived from the use of luxury textiles in cool shades of taupe and cream. The bedrooms and suites are equipped to the highest standard with smart, all-marble bathrooms – among the largest in London – and many extras, including three dual-line phones with voicemail and modem connection, high-speed internet, fax, interactive cable TV with CD and DVD services, air conditioning and personal bar. Each floor has been designed thematically – earth, wind, fire, water and the universe. Public areas include a lounge, the airy Halkin Bar, for light meals, delicious morning coffees or afternoon tea, drinks and cocktails. And then there's nahm, David Thompson's award-winning Thai restaurant, where service from Armani-clad staff is attentive and friendly. Breakfast is also served in this room; choices include classic English breakfast fare. Guests may use the gym or enjoy the COMO Shambhala Health Club at The Halkin's sister hotel, The Metropolitan.

Recommended in the area

Buckingham Palace; Harrods & Harvey Nichols, Knightsbridge; Hyde Park

Jumeirah Carlton Tower

★★★★★ ◎◎ HOTEL

Address: Cadogan Place, LONDON, SW1X 9PY
Tel: 020 7235 1234
Fax: 020 7235 9129
E-mail: jctinfo@jumeirah.com
Website: www.jumeirahcarltontower.com
Map ref: 4, TQ38 **Directions:** A4 towards
Knightsbridge, right onto Sloane St. Hotel on left
before Cadogan Place
Rooms: 216 (59 fmly) (70 smoking)
Facilities: Spa STV FTV ◎ supervised ♨ Gym Golf
simulator (50 courses) ♫ Wi-fi
Parking: 170 **Notes:** ⊗

A long-standing Knightsbridge landmark, this luxury hotel is within walking distance of Harrods, Harvey Nichols and the exclusive designer boutiques of Sloane Street. Most of the guest rooms overlook the private gardens of Cadogan Place and London's skyline beyond. All have wireless and high-speed internet access, flat plasma-screen TV, direct-dial phones in (one in the bathroom), voicemail, writing desk, Bose music system, and top-of-the-range toiletries. In the Rib Room restaurant, refurbished by international interior designer Martin Brudnizki, the menu showcases head chef Ian Rudge's traditional British cuisine, while sommelier Louise Gordon oversees the cellar containing over 500 wines and Champagne choices. Chinoiserie, by day a quiet setting for breakfast and afternoon tea, is by night the place for a drink while a resident harpist plays. Afternoon tea is served to the accompaniment of historic sound-bites from famous literary figures. High up on the ninth floor, the Club Room in the Peak Health Club & Spa offers light healthy meals and snacks, fruit cocktails and smoothies. GILT Cocktail Lounge, strikingly finished in cream, gold and black, serves a range of Champagne and Bellinis. Club facilities include a fully equipped gym, state-of-the-art golf simulator, aerobics studio, sauna, steam room and 20-metre indoor pool.

Recommended in the area
Hyde Park; Harrods; Harvey Nichols

The Capital

★★★★★ TOWN HOUSE HOTEL

Address: Basil St, Knightsbridge, LONDON, SW3 1AT
Tel: 020 7589 5171
Fax: 020 7225 0011
E-mail: reservations@capitalhotel.co.uk
Website: www.capitalhotel.co.uk
Map ref: 4, TQ38
Directions: 20yds from Harrods & Knightsbridge
underground station
Rooms: 49 **S** fr £175–£240; **D** fr £245–£495
Facilities: STV Wi-fi
Parking: 12
Notes: ⊗

Just yards from Harrods, Harvey Nichols and Sloane Street, and within easy reach of the West End, this hotel offers luxury accommodation and personal service in the heart of one of London's most prestigious neighbourhoods. Opened in 1971 by David Levin, it is to this day privately owned and run by the Levin family. Muted tones characterise the chic decor, which combines contemporary and antique furniture. The Capital's 49 bedrooms and suites come in a variety of styles and each has a luxurious marble bathroom. All the suites and double rooms have super-king-size beds with handmade mattresses and Egyptian cotton bedding. The Capital Restaurant has long held a reputation for being one of the finest in the country, and that

looks set to continue with the appointment of award-winning French chef Jérôme Ponchelle (the AA Rosette award was not confirmed at the time of going to press). Afternoon tea is served in The Capital's elegant sitting room, and cocktails are a speciality in the intimate and stylish bar. Cesar, head barman, is renowned for his ability to engage with guests over the delights of whisky and food pairing. An added benefit to this hotel is its private parking within central London.

Recommended in the area

Harrods; Buckingham Palace; Hyde Park

The Levin

★★★★ TOWN HOUSE HOTEL

Address: 28 Basil St, Knightsbridge, LONDON,
SW3 1AS
Tel: 020 7589 6286
Fax: 020 7823 7826
E-mail: reservations@thelevin.co.uk
Website: www.thelevinhotel.co.uk
Map ref: 4, TQ38
Directions: 20yds from Harrods & Knightsbridge
underground station
Rooms: 12 (1 GF) **D** £240-£500
(incl. Continental bkfst)
Facilities: STV FTV Wi-fi **Parking:** 8 **Notes:** ⊗

It would be hard to beat The Levin's location, tucked away in quiet Basil Street yet literally a stone's throw from Harrods. This sophisticated boutique hotel offers all the comforts of home to discerning travellers who crave a central London hotel with personality and charm. That it has in spades, thanks to owner and operator David Levin and his team of highly experienced, professional and friendly staff. The Levin's 12 contemporary bedrooms are designed to please customers with an eye for detail and love of beautiful things. Each bedroom is complemented by a marble bathroom and, for the ultimate in glamour, rooms even come with their own in-room champagne and cocktail bar. In the public areas the hotel's design takes its lead from the 1930s – think pistachio-coloured love seats, Tibetan silk rugs and baby-blue chandeliers. Breakfast, lunch, afternoon tea and dinner are served in the warm and buzzy Le Metro Bistro which, like the hotel itself, is one of Knightsbridge's best-kept secrets. Long treasured by the locals, it serves an all-day menu of British classics with a selection of small plates and larger favourites, complemented by an eclectic and impressive selection of wines by the glass.

Recommended in the area

Harrods; Hyde Park; South Kensington museums

K+K Hotel George

★★★ 85% HOTEL

Address: 1-15 Templeton Place, Earl's Court,
LONDON, SW5 9NB
Tel: 020 7598 8700 & 020 7598 8707
Fax: 020 7370 2285
E-mail: hotelgeorge@kkhotels.co.uk
Website: www.kkhotels.com/george
Map ref: 4, TQ38 **Directions:** Earls Court Rd
(A3220), right at Trebovir Rd, right at Templeton Place
Rooms: 154 (38 fmly) (8 GF) (14 smoking) **S** fr £130;
D fr £150
Facilities: STV FTV Gym Wellness area with
exercise machines Sauna Wi-fi **Parking:** 22

K+K Hotel George is a first class, contemporary boutique-style hotel behind a historic facade in a quiet residential street in Earl's Court, Kensington – just 200 metres from the underground station (Earl's Court). All 154 air-conditioned guest rooms have en suite bathrooms or walk-in showers and free high speed internet access is available via LAN and Wi-fi. A fabulous buffet breakfast is included in the room rate. Other facilities include two meeting rooms, an internet lounge and a cosy hotel bar which is open till late. There is also secure reserved parking for 22 cars. For R&R, guests can enjoy the private and tranquil award-winning garden or use the fitness and sauna areas. K+K Hotel George is the ideal base for visits to the Science, Natural History and Victoria & Albert museums, as well as the Royal Albert Hall. Shopping heaven is found nearby at Harrods, Harvey Nichols and Westfield London, as well as in the fabulous boutiques on Sloane Street and the famous King's Road. The hotel is just two-minutes' walk to Earls Court exhibition centre and a 12-minute walk or one tube stop to Olympia exhibition centre. Football fans can cheer the local teams of Chelsea FC, Fulham FC and Queens Park Rangers. There are numerous restaurants and bars in the neighbourhood.

Recommended in the area

V&A Museum; Holland Park; Kensington Palace

Wyndham Grand London Chelsea Harbour

★★★★★ 83% ◉ HOTEL

Address: Chelsea Harbour, LONDON, SW10 0XG
Tel: 020 7823 3000 **Fax:** 020 7351 6525
E-mail: wyndhamlondon@wyndham.com
Website: www.wyndham.com
Map ref: 4, TQ38 **Directions:** A4 to Earls Court Rd
S towards river. Right into Kings Rd, left into Lots Rd.
Rooms: 158 (36 fmly) (46 smoking) **S** fr £182;
D fr £182 (incl. bkfst)
Facilities: Spa STV FTV ◑ Gym Sauna Steam room
♫ Wi-fi **Parking:** 2000

Not so long ago this area on the north bank of
the River Thames was an industrial wasteland,
by passed by everyone except those who had
to work here. How different it is now, with luxury
apartments, a marina and this all-suite hotel, with its
air-conditioned rooms, many with private balconies,
and spacious, luxury bathrooms. The rooms are
all elegantly furnished, with two satellite TVs, VCR,
three direct-dial phones, fax, modem and voicemail,
mini-bar, bathrobes, branded umbrella and safe.
Four penthouse suites are set up for private
dining, entertaining and meetings. The harbourside restaurant, Chelsea Riverside Brasserie, offers
contemporary dining from light snacks to three-
course meals. A typical lunch menu offers Shetland
mussels; traditional fish and chips; steak and fries;
as well as pasta dishes and sandwiches. The grill
section of the dinner menu includes specially
aged Aberdeenshire beef, and its signature dish of
line-caught Cornish sea bass. Visit the Lounge for
afternoon tea, sandwiches, homemade scones,
pastries and a choice of loose (the hotel is quite
specific on this) teas. The spa incorporates a gym
pool with integrated body and shoulder jets, walk-in
sauna, steam room and six treatment rooms.

Recommended in the area
The King's Road; Knightsbridge; Saatchi Gallery

Best Western Premier Mostyn Hotel

★★★★ 77% ◉◉◉ HOTEL

Address: 4 Bryanston St, LONDON, W1H 7BY
Tel: 020 7935 2361
Fax: 020 7487 2759
E-mail: info@mostynhotel.co.uk
Website: www.bw-mostynhotel.co.uk
Map ref: 4, TQ38
Directions: Nearest underground stations: Marble Arch & Bond St
Rooms: 121 (15 fmly) (9 GF) **S** £200-£250; **D** £230-£270
Facilities: Spa STV FTV ♨ Gym ♫ Wi-fi
Notes: ⊗

London is big enough for there to be many districts where a hotel can be called 'well located'. This one certainly qualifies, since it is only a few minutes' walk from Oxford Street, Marble Arch and Hyde Park. Originally built in the 18th century for Lady Black, a lady-in-waiting to the court of George II, much of the original architecture has been retained, in particular the magnificent ornate ceilings in the conference rooms and the three-AA Rosette restaurant. Air-conditioned bedrooms and en suite bathrooms, complete with rain shower, come in varying sizes, and are all furnished with bright and trendy soft furnishings, and equipped with direct-dial phone, trouser press, hot drinks tray, flat-screen satellite TV, hairdryer, electronic safe, media hub and free internet access. Extra benefits for Club Room guests include luxury robes and slippers, complimentary drink and breakfast, late check-out and complimentary car parking. Three lavish suites, arranged over two floors, incorporate galleried bedrooms and lounges. The public areas include a cocktail bar/lounge; the Fire & Spice all-day dining concept; the Texture Restaurant, offering impressive, modern cooking, and the Trimiri Spa. There is free Wi-fi throughout the hotel. Wheelchair access is under construction at the time of writing.

Recommended in the area

Hyde Park; Marble Arch; Wallace Collection

Brown's Hotel

★★★★★ ◎◎ HOTEL

Address: Albemarle St, Mayfair, LONDON, W1S 4BP
Tel: 020 7493 6020
Fax: 020 7493 9381
E-mail: reservations.browns@roccofortehotels.com
Website: www.roccofortehotels.com
Map ref: 4, TQ38
Directions: A short walk from Green Park,
Bond St & Piccadilly
Rooms: 117 (12 smoking) **S** £245-£525 (incl bkfst)
D £325-£605 (incl. bkfst)
Facilities: Spa STV Gym ♫ Wi-fi
Notes: ⊗

Very much the elder statesman among London hotels (built in 1837, it was the capital's first), its dignified atmosphere has appealed to many distinguished guests over the decades. Beautifully designed rooms and suites by Lord Forte's daughter, Olga Polizzi, are all generously provided with quality extras, including a mini library, among which might be Rudyard Kipling's *Jungle Book*, written while he was a guest here. The restaurant, HIX at The Albemarle (Mark Hix is the hotel's Director of Food) has beautiful wood panelling, a vaulted ceiling and works on the walls by Bridget Riley, Tracey Emin and other leading British artists. Open for breakfast, lunch, pre-theatre and dinner, its two-AA Rosette menus offer great British classics, such as boiled ham hock with pease pudding and Tewkesbury mustard sauce; light fish and shellfish dishes, such as Newlyn monkfish curry; and traditional lunchtime roasts from the carving trolley. There are over 400 wines to choose from. The English Tea Room serves lighter meals and legendary afternoon teas. Live jazz is performed Monday to Saturday from 9pm to midnight in the bar named after, and displaying works by, top British photographer Terence Donovan. A luxurious spa and state-of-the-art gymnasium offer ways of recharging the batteries.

Recommended in the area
Bond Street shopping; the West End; Green Park

The Langham, London

★★★★★ 86% ◉◉ HOTEL

Address: Portland Place, LONDON, W1B 1JA
Tel: 020 7636 1000
Fax: 020 7323 2340
E-mail: lon.info@langhamhotels.com
Website: www.langhamlondon.com
Map ref: 4, TQ38
Directions: N of Regent St, left opposite All Soul's Church
Rooms: 378 (8 fmly) (15 smoking) **S** £199-£9000; **D** £199-£9000
Facilities: Spa STV ⊗ supervised Gym Health club Sauna Steam room ♫ Wi-fi **Notes:** ⊗

The Langham, London has been enchanting guests since it opened as Europe's first 'Grand Hotel' in 1865. From the grandeur of its elegant entrance to the timeless style of its public rooms and bedrooms, this certainly ranks among London's top luxury hotels. All 380 exquisitely appointed guest rooms evoke a warm, residential feel. Choose from the modern and elegant Grand rooms or the traditionally styled Classic rooms. For breakfast, lunch and dinner, Roux at The Landau offers classically constructed French dishes together with some classic British dishes. The chic and glamorous bar, Artesian, serves imaginative cocktails and houses a selection of more than 70 rums. Afternoon tea is served in the dazzling Palm Court, which was awarded London's Top Afternoon Tea 2010 by the Tea Guild. Choose from either the Wonderland traditional afternoon tea or the signature Bijoux Tea. The luxury Chuan Spa offers rejuvinating treatments based on the philosophies of Traditional Chinese Medicine. The hotel also features a state-of-the-art gym, 16-metre pool, men's and women's saunas, steam rooms and solarium.

Recommended in the area

Regent Street; Regent's Park; Marylebone Village

London Marriott Hotel Marble Arch

★★★★ 84% HOTEL

Address: 134 George St, LONDON, W1H 5DN
Tel: 020 7723 1277
Fax: 020 7402 0666
E-mail:
mhrs.lonma.sales.mkt.cood@marriotthotels.com
Website: www.londonmarriottmarblearch.co.uk
Map ref: 4, TQ38 **Directions:** From Marble Arch
turn into Edgware Rd, then 4th right into George St.
Left into Dorset St for entrance
Rooms: 240 (100 fmly) (20 smoking) From £135
(room only); from £150 (incl. bkfst) **Facilities:** STV
FTV ⓢ supervised Gym Wi-fi **Parking:** 83 **Notes:** ⊗

Now nearly 40 years old, this hotel has recently been given a tasteful facelift. It stands a few blocks away from the famous white Carrara monument of Marble Arch, which many people are surprised to learn originally stood in front of Buckingham Palace. In 1851 it was moved to its present location, somewhat marooned on a huge traffic island opposite Speakers' Corner in Hyde Park. Spacious, snazzily decorated accommodation includes family rooms capable of accommodating up to four people, with in-room facilities including a 32-inch flat-screen TV, dedicated work area, wireless high-speed internet access (charges apply to non-Marriott Rewards members) and laptop-size safe. The hotel prides itself on its special bedding package, which features thicker than normal mattresses, down mattress toppers and Egyptian cotton sheets. Executive room guests benefit from upgraded amenities and access to the Executive Lounge, serving complimentary Continental breakfast and refreshments throughout the day. The newly opened Brasserie Centrale offers freshly prepared international dishes at breakfast and dinner, while Chats Café Bar serves beverages and hot and cold snacks at any time of day. The big stores and smart shops of Oxford Street, Bond Street and Regent Street are all within easy reach.

Recommended in the area

Hyde Park; Marble Arch; Kensington Gardens

The Westbury Hotel

★★★★★ 81% ◉◉ HOTEL

Address: Bond St, LONDON, W1S 2YF
Tel: 020 7629 7755
Fax: 020 7495 1163
E-mail: reservations@westburymayfair.com
Website: www.westburymayfair.com
Map ref: 4, TQ38
Directions: From Oxford Circus S down Regent St, right onto Conduit St, hotel at junct of Conduit St and Bond St
Rooms: 246 (80 fmly) **D** £190.80-£3000
Facilities: STV FTV Gym Fitness centre Steam room Sauna Wi-fi **Notes:** ⊗

Stay here and you can shop till you drop, for this is Mayfair, London's exclusive fashion and boutique district. Not only does Bond Street run straight through its centre, but the retail therapy honeypots of Regent and Oxford streets, Piccadilly and Park Lane border it on four sides. A recent multimillion pound refurbishment of the hotel has resulted in individually designed bedrooms with contemporary furnishings, soft neutral colours and modern prints. A splendid job was done too on the en suite bathrooms and they now sport superior Italian marble imported from quarries in Lucca and Bergamo. There's a wide choice of food: The fine-dining restaurant (formerly Artisan) has re-opened under the name Alyn Williams at The Westbury, the man himself having worked for many years with Gordon Ramsay and Marcus Wareing; then there's Tsukiji Sushi Restaurant where head chef Show Choong presents New Japanese cuisine in sleek, red wood surroundings; and, finally, The Gallery, a new all-day restaurant, open for breakfast, lunch and dinner, where the food would be familiar to guests who have dined in the South of France and Northern Italy. In charge here is Brian Fantoni, formerly of Claridge's and The Savoy. The opulent Polo Bar serves an impressive choice of cocktails and light dishes.

Recommended in the area
Royal Academy of Arts; Faraday Museum; Piccadilly

Lancaster London

★★★★ 83% ◎◎ HOTEL

Address: Lancaster Ter, LONDON, W2 2TY
Tel: 020 7262 6737
Fax: 020 7724 3191
E-mail: book@lancasterlondon.com
Website: www.lancasterlondon.com
Map ref: 4, TQ38 **Directions:** Hotel is adjacent to
Lancaster Gate underground station
Rooms: 416 (11 fmly)
Facilities: STV Wi-fi Air con
Parking: 65
Notes: ⊗ Xmas/New Year CONF Civ Wed Leisure
breaks available

Lancaster London offers world-class guest service coupled with a strong corporate social responsibility ethos. The hotel has recently been recognised for its continued commitment to the vision of "walking softly on the planet" by being awarded the AA Eco Hotel of the Year award for 2011/12. The hotel's facilities include an elegant lounge bar, two award-winning restaurants and some of London's largest, most flexible banqueting and event facilities. Perfect for both business and leisure visits, the 416 guest rooms offer every luxury, with beautiful oak furniture, deep-pile carpets and exquisite marble bathrooms. Modern facilities include flat-screen TVs, high-speed Wi-fi access and multilingual voicemail. The hotel is situated next to Hyde Park, the largest of the Royal Parks, offering some of the best views, not only of the park but also the London skyline. You will find the Lancaster London a destination hard to beat. Marble Arch and Oxford Street's shops are a five-minute stroll from the hotel, with Knightsbridge and Harrods just 10 minutes away by taxi. The City of London's financial district is 15 minutes direct by London underground. Heathrow Airport is a mere 20-minute ride on the Heathrow Express from nearby Paddington station. Lancaster London puts you at the very centre of this vibrant metropolis.

Recommended in the area
Kensington Gardens and Hyde Park; Marble Arch; Royal Albert Hall

Royal Garden Hotel

★★★★★ ◉◉◉ HOTEL

Address: 2-24 Kensington High St, LONDON, W8 4PT
Tel: 020 7937 8000
Fax: 020 7361 1991
E-mail: sales@royalgardenhotel.co.uk
Website: www.royalgardenhotel.co.uk
Map ref: 4, TQ38
Directions: Adjacent to Kensington Palace
Rooms: 394
Facilities: Spa STV Gym Health & fitness centre Wi-fi
Notes: ⊗

In the heart of Kensington, the Royal Garden Hotel is the perfect place to stay whether on business or exploring London. There are 394 beautifully appointed bedrooms to choose from, including 37 suites, plus two restaurants, three bars, a 24-hour business centre and 24-hour room service. The hotel also has a choice of 10 conference and banqueting rooms that can accommodate up to 550 delegates. The Soma centre is the holistic health centre and spa, offering a gym, sauna and steam room, plus a wide range of beauty treatments and classes in yoga, Pilates and kick-boxing. Head to the award-winning Min Jiang restaurant on the 10th floor for an authentic Chinese experience in an elegant setting looking out over Kensington Gardens, Hyde Park and the London skyline beyond. Enjoy superb dim sum and be sure not to miss the famous Beijing duck roasted in a special wood-burning oven. Alternatively, the Park Terrace restaurant, lounge and bar on the ground floor is open for breakfast, lunch, afternoon tea, dinner and all-day snacks. Here, the setting is relaxed and informal, the focus is on fresh British produce, and there are large windows through which to enjoy the vista of Kensington Gardens and Palace.

Recommended in the area

Harrods; Hyde Park; Serpentine Gallery; Kensington Gardens; Natural History Museum; V&A Museum

Visitors cross the Millennium Bridge to reach St Paul's Cathedral, London

Greater London

Herds of red deer and fallow deer can be seen grazing in Richmond Park

Manor Hotel & Restaurant

★★★ 79% HOTEL

Address: Berwick Pond Rd, RAINHAM, RM13 9EL
Tel: 01708 555586
Fax: 01708 630055
E-mail: info@themanoressex.co.uk
Website: www.themanoressex.co.uk
Map ref: 4, TQ58
Directions: M25 junct 30/31, A13, 1st exit signed Wennington, right, at main lights right onto Upminster Rd North, left into Berwick Pond Rd
Rooms: 15 (1 fmly) **S** £100-£115; **D** £130-£155 (incl. bkfst) **Facilities:** STV Wi-fi
Parking: 60 **Notes:** ⊗

Set well back from the road, the former Berwick Manor is located just about where you start to leave Greater London behind, and rural Essex starts to get a look in. While the M25 motorway and towns like Romford and Rainham are not far away, the hotel makes a perfect base from which to explore the pretty villages of this often overlooked county. Having been expertly restored, the hotel offers well-appointed, contemporary overnight accommodation in double or twin rooms, an elegantly proportioned executive suite and a sumptuous penthouse. Each room has an en suite shower room, luxurious cotton bed linen, direct-dial phone, satellite TV, Wi-fi and radio. A hot drinks tray and ironing facilities are also provided. Lunch and dinner are served in the attractive restaurant, where menus typically offer medallions of beef with horseradish mash; pan-fried halibut; and chunky vegetable, lentil and goat's cheese filo parcel. The Terrace menu is amazingly good value, with homemade lamb meatballs; bangers and mash; and battered fish and chips all priced at a fiver. A very manageable wine list ranges around the world from Argentina to Spain. The hotel is one of only a few in the county licensed to hold outdoor wedding ceremonies.

Recommended in the area

RSPB Rainham Marshes Nature Reserve; Coal House Fort, East Tilbury; Thurrock Shopping Centre

Bingham

★★★ 81% ◎◎◎ TOWN HOUSE HOTEL

Address: 61-63 Petersham Rd, RICHMOND UPON
THAMES, TW10 6UT
Tel: 020 8940 0902
Fax: 020 8948 8737
E-mail: info@thebingham.co.uk
Website: www.thebingham.co.uk
Map ref: 3, TQ38
Directions: On A307
Rooms: 15 (2 fmly) **S** £170; **D** £190-£285
Facilities: FTV In room treatments Wi-fi
Parking: 8
Notes: ⊗

A chic Georgian townhouse, restaurant and bar right on the River Thames, close to the town centre and, for those who like unusual museums, even closer to that belonging to Royal British Legion's poppy factory. In 1821, Lady Anne Bingham, daughter of the 2nd Lord Lucan, added the wonderfully ornate room now known as the Bingham Bar, and poets Katherine Harris Bradley and Edith Emma Cooper, who wrote together as Michael Field, lived here later that century. Refurbished to the max, the lavish interior features statement chandeliers and mirrored walls, and it is plain to see that similar care has been taken in designing the air-conditioned guest rooms, all featuring Art Deco furniture (two with four-posters), digital TVs with DVD players, complimentary Wi-fi and digital radios with iPod docks. River and Super River Rooms not only enjoy the obvious views, but whirlpool baths too. The AA has awarded three Rosettes to the softly lit restaurant, where modern British dishes include squab pigeon; slow-cooked suckling pig; and roast halibut, all extremely imaginatively accompanied. The cocktail bar is a glamorous place for afternoon tea, or something stronger, which you can take out to the terrace overlooking the river.

Recommended in the area

Kew Gardens; Hampton Court; Wimbledon Lawn Tennis

Merseyside

Crosby Beach, Merseyside. One of the 100 cast iron figures of Antony Gormley's sculpture *Another Place*

The RiverHill Hotel

★★★ 80% HOTEL

Address: Talbot Rd, Prenton, BIRKENHEAD, CH43 2HJ
Tel: 0151 653 3773
Fax: 0151 653 7162
E-mail: reception@theriverhill.co.uk
Website: www.theriverhill.co.uk
Map ref: 6, SJ38
Directions: M53 junct 3, A552. Left onto B5151 at lights, hotel 0.5m on right
Rooms: 15 (1 fmly)
Facilities: STV FTV Free use of local leisure facilities Wi-fi **Parking:** 32 **Notes:** ⊗

The privately-owned RiverHill Hotel stands in its own beautiful grounds in the quiet residential area of Oxton, which is conveniently placed for public transport links to Liverpool and has easy access to the Irish ferry terminal, Cammell Lairds, Chester and the motorway networks. The individually decorated en suite bedrooms offer everything you need for a comfortable and enjoyable stay – a flat-screen TV, direct dial telephone, in-room safe, trouser press, hairdryer and complimentary fresh fruit, water, snacks and hot drinks facilities. There are two bridal suites, each with a four-poster bed and the option of choosing a champagne breakfast perhaps by way of marking a celebration. The elegant Bay Tree Restaurant offers a menu of dishes based on locally sourced ingredients, such as grilled fillet of beef wrapped in bacon, topped with stilton cheese and served with a burgundy sauce. Meals are complemented by a range of quality wines. The Wirall is an ideal place for spending leisure time, with no less than 14 golf courses including the Royal Liverpool and Wallasey, plus many art galleries, museums and historical landmarks. A warm welcome awaits from the owners and their staff, who are happy to help with any guest requirements.

Recommended in the area

Speke Hall (NT); Bidston Observatory; Ness Botanic Gardens

Vincent Hotel

★★★★ 81% @@ TOWN HOUSE HOTEL

Address: 98 Lord St, SOUTHPORT, PR8 1JR
Tel: 01704 883800
Fax: 01704 883830
E-mail: manager@thevincenthotel.com
Website: www.thevincenthotel.com
Map ref: 6, SD31
Directions: M58 junct 3, follow signs to Ormskirk
& Southport
Rooms: 60 **S** £83-£199; **D** £83-£695
Facilities: Spa STV FTV Gym Wi-fi
Parking: 50
Notes: ⊗

Opened in 2008, this cool addition to Southport's famous Lord Street (likened by some to a Parisian boulevard), offers six floors of trendily designed, air-conditioned guest studios and residences (they're not officially called bedrooms here). In addition, suites range from the Junior to the V-Penthouse, with its own steam room, balcony and outdoor Jacuzzi. All rooms have ultra comfortable king-size or twin beds with Frette cotton sheets, goose-down pillows, and up-to-the-minute technology, including free high-speed internet, wall-mounted high-definition LCD TV, workstation, pay-per-view movies and two direct-dial phones. Certain rooms can even be interconnected to create more living space. V-Café is open throughout the day from 7am till late, serving Continental breakfast, morning coffee, afternoon tea, home-made soups, steaks and grills, fish and shellfish, pastas, and a full range of handmade sushi and sashimi. In four short years it has already been awarded two AA Rosettes. After 6pm, the lights are dimmed, candles are lit and soft music plays. Hotel guests may also drink in the members-only McGee's cocktail bar, named after Tony McGee, a top photographer friend of the hotel's proprietor. Other facilities include the V-Spa, V-Gym and V-Galleria Suites, used for weddings and corporate events.

Recommended in the area

Southport Pier; Southport Botanic Garens; Liverpool

Thornton Hall Hotel and Spa

★★★★ 81% ⊛⊛⊛ HOTEL

Address: Neston Rd, THORNTON HOUGH, Wirral, CH63 1JF

Tel: 0151 336 3938 & 353 3717 **Fax:** 0151 336 7864

E-mail: reservations@thorntonhallhotel.com

Website: www.thorntonhallhotel.com

Map ref: 6, SJ38 **Directions:** M53 junct 4, B5151/ Neston onto B5136 to Thornton Hough (signed)

Rooms: 63 (6 fmly) (28 GF) **Facilities:** Spa STV FTV ⊙ ⊌ Gym Beauty spa & clinic Hairdressing salon free Wi-fi throughout **Parking:** 250 **Notes:** ⊗

Dating from the mid-1800s, this family-owned country house hotel on the Wirral peninsula has been carefully extended and restored. Public areas include an impressive leisure spa, a choice of restaurants and a spacious bar. Suites and bedrooms vary in style and include feature rooms in the main house and more contemporary rooms in the garden wing. While leaving its original oak carvings intact, a six-figure refurbishment of Lawns Restaurant has created a premier fine-dining experience, which, under the watchful eye of new executive chef David Gillmore, now holds a third AA Rosette for its international cooking. A typical evening meal selected from the carte could comprise borscht, or Aberdaron crab as a starter; followed by Cheshire lamb rump or grilled monkfish; and dessert of fig and blackberry parfait, or chilled chocolate fondant. Tasting, fixed price and vegetarian menus are also available. Times Restaurant within the Health Club is a more contemporary place to eat and drink, outdoors if you prefer. Regarded as one of the best in the North West, the holistic spa has a 20-metre pool, outdoor hot tubs, sauna, steam room and well-equipped fitness suite, while The Lodge offers a wide range of clinical and skincare treatments.

Recommended in the area

Liverpool; Croxteth Hall & Country Park; Sefton Park; Chester; Ness Gardens; Chester Zoo

Grove House

★★★ 80% HOTEL

Address: Grove Rd, WALLASEY, CH45 3HF
Tel: 0151 639 3947 & 630 4558
Fax: 0151 639 0028
E-mail: reception@thegrovehouse.co.uk
Website: www.thegrovehouse.co.uk
Map ref: 6, SJ29
Directions: M53 junct 1, A554 (Wallasey New Brighton), right after church into Harrison Drive, left after Windsors Garage into Grove Rd
Rooms: 14 (7 fmly) **S** £69; **D** £90-£135 (incl. bkfst)
Facilities: FTV Wi-fi
Parking: 28 **Notes:** ⊗

Located on the Wirral peninsula, Grove House Hotel has miles of coastal walks, a variety of water-based activities and first-class golf courses right on its doorstep. It's also a convenient base for exploring the city of Liverpool, with its World Heritage listed waterfront and excellent museums and entertainment venues. The hotel boasts a pretty garden and is peacefully situated in a residential area of the town, yet it's only a short distance from the seafront promenade and the underground station for Liverpool, and just a mile away from the M53. The bedrooms are beautifully furnished and equipped with facilities for making hot drinks, a trouser press and direct-dial telephone, and each has a luxurious bathroom. One of the rooms is large enough to accommodate a family, and there is also a bridal suite with four-poster bed, which can be booked to include a champagne breakfast. The bar-lounge is a great place to relax at the end of the day before enjoying a meal in the oak-panelled restaurant, which overlooks the garden. Here, service is impeccable and the excellent choice of dishes on both the carte and set menus is complemented by a wide-ranging wine list. All in all, this is a friendly place offering high standards and good value.

Recommended in the area

Heritage Centre of Port Sunlight; Williamson Art Gallery & Museum; Ellesmere Port Boat Museum

Norfolk

Barton Broad, Norfolk Broads National Park

The Blakeney Hotel

★★★★ 76% ◉ HOTEL

Address: The Quay, BLAKENEY, Holt, NR25 7NE
Tel: 01263 740797
Fax: 01263 740795
E-mail: reception@blakeneyhotel.co.uk
Website: www.blakeneyhotel.co.uk
Map ref: 8, TG04 **Directions:** From A148
between Fakenham & Holt, take B1156 to
Langham & Blakeney
Rooms: 63 (16 annexe) (20 fmly) (17 GF) **S** £89-£145;
D £178-£314 (incl. bkfst & dinner)
Facilities: FTV ⊗ Gym Billiards Snooker Table tennis
Sauna Steam room Spa bath Wi-fi **Parking:** 60

A traditional, privately owned hotel on the quayside, with awesome views across the estuary and salt marshes to Blakeney Point, an Area of Outstanding Natural Beauty. Bedrooms and private bathrooms are smartly decorated and equipped with all the usual extras. Those rooms looking northwards over the water are great for observing wildlife. Some rooms have balconies or south-facing garden views, while others have patios leading on to those gardens. Dogs are permitted in a few ground floor rooms. The restaurant, bar and terrace also look out over the water, providing a great backdrop to a hearty English breakfast, lunch or dinner from the seasonally based à la carte or daily set menu. The restaurant's cooking style, for which it has held an AA Rosette for five years, includes dishes such as Blakeney fish soup with Gruyère and saffron rouille crouton; oven-baked fillet of pork with confit potatoes, glazed vegetables and apple compote; grilled fillet of plaice with crushed new potatoes, spring onions and fine beans; and baked flat mushroom with roast vegetables, glazed with Binham Blue, a creamy cheese made near Wells-next-the-Sea. The leisure area incorporates a sauna, steam room, spa bath, mini-gym and an indoor heated swimming pool overlooking the sun terrace.

Recommended in the area

Seal trips to Blakeney Point; National Trust properties; North Norfolk Railway

Hoste Arms Hotel

★★★ 88% ◎◎ HOTEL

Address: The Green, BURNHAM MARKET, King's
Lynn, PE31 8HD
Tel: 01328 738777
Fax: 01328 730103
E-mail: reception@hostearms.co.uk
Website: www.hostearms.co.uk
Map ref: 8, TF84 **Directions:** Signed on B1155, 5m
W of Wells-next-the-Sea
Rooms: 34 (7 GF) **S** £122-£241; **D** £149-£241
(incl. bkfst)
Facilities: Spa STV Beauty treatment rooms Wi-fi
Parking: 45

The Hoste Arms, originally a 17th-century coaching inn with pantiled roof, is a truly delightful country house hotel located in one of Norfolk's prettiest villages, just a few miles from the beautiful Norfolk coast. Have a drink in front of the log fire in the cosy front bar, lunch in the light-filled conservatory, or dine in the fine, wood-panelled restaurant. Go for a walk, maybe, in the pretty walled garden behind the Moroccan-themed terrace at the rear of the property. Stay in one of the spacious, extremely comfortable and thoughtfully equipped bedrooms, each tastefully styled by hotel owner, Jeanne Whittome. The two-AA Rosette dining room is supplied with excellent, locally sourced food by a kitchen laying claim to the 'biggest Aga in the world',

a culinary tour de force designed by the hotel's founder, the late Paul Whittome, his former head chef, and Aga itself. With such good oysters from these coastal waters, start with six Brancasters; then follow with loin of Holkham venison; or roasted breast and confit leg of Goosnargh duck. A new beauty spa and Japanese Garden opened in March 2011 offering an assortment of massages and treatments in a modern and luxurious setting.

Recommended in the area

Holkham Hall; Brancaster Beach; Sandringham

Caley Hall

★★★ 85% ◉ HOTEL

Address: Old Hunstanton Rd, HUNSTANTON,
PE36 6HH
Tel: 01485 533486
Fax: 01485 533348
E-mail: mail@caleyhallhotel.co.uk
Website: www.caleyhallhotel.co.uk
Map ref: 8, TF64
Directions: 1 mile from Hunstanton, on A149
Rooms: 39 (20 fmly) (30 GF) **S** £50-£200;
D £80-£200 (incl. bkfst)
Facilities: STV Wi-fi Child facilities
Parking: 50

Located where the north Norfolk coast curves southwest into The Wash, this is a good base for long walks along wide beaches and exploring unspoilt countryside dotted with sleepy villages. Caley Hall is a lovely 17th-century brick-and-flint house which, from the front, presents a fairly modest farmhouse appearance, but former barns, stables and extensions tucked away at the back have been beautifully converted to provide additional accommodation. Most of the rooms, all with en suite bathrooms, are at ground level, grouped around several sheltered patio areas, and have satellite TV, DVD and CD players, a fridge and tea- and coffee-making facilities. There's individual heating in each room, so guests can adjust the temperature. The deluxe rooms are more spacious, one has a four-poster bed, and there's a suite with a whirlpool bath, plus some rooms for mobility-impaired guests. The restaurant is housed in the old stables, but the decor is chic rather than rustic, with high-back leather chairs and modern light-wood tables. Breakfast, lunch and dinner are served, with an evening menu that might include grilled sea bass, braised local beef, a traditional roast and vegetarian options. There's also a bright, spacious bar, open all day, with lots of cosy, soft leather sofas.

Recommended in the area

Sandringham; Titchwell RSPB Reserve; Holkham Hall

St Giles House

★★★★ 81% ◉◉ HOTEL

Address: 41-45 St Giles Street, NORWICH, NR2 1JR
Tel: 01603 275180
Fax: 0845 299 1905
E-mail: reception@stgileshousehotel.com
Website: www.stgileshousehotel.com
Map ref: 4, TG20
Directions: A11 into central Norwich. Left at rdbt (Chapelfield Shopping Centre). 3rd exit at next rdbt. Left onto St Giles St. Hotel on left
Rooms: 24 (incl. bkfst)
Facilities: Spa FTV Wi-fi
Parking: 30 **Notes:** ⊗

In the centre of historic Norwich, a baroque-style, Grade II listed building and an adjacent Georgian building have been stunningly restored and transformed into this luxurious boutique hotel. Exceptionally chic throughout, several features are outstanding, including the spectacular glass dome and crystal chandelier in the main lounge of the Walnut Suite, one of the hotel's three function and conference suites. Many original features have been retained throughout the building, including fabulous wood panelling, ornamental plasterwork and marble floors. All of the bedrooms and suites are spacious, luxurious and have been individually designed. They are equipped with flat-screen TVs and DVD players, mini-bars and tea and coffee-making equipment and free Wi-fi access. The stylish, open-plan, wood-panelled lounge bar and restaurant offers contemporary dining in a relaxing atmosphere, and the menus focus on local ingredients, with a commitment to providing top quality as well as good value. In good weather, guests can enjoy cocktails or alfresco dining on the delightful Parisian-style terrace. The hotel also has two smaller, individual and stylish dining rooms that are ideal for pivate parties and functions.

Recommended in the area

Norwich Cathedral; Norwich Castle; Theatre Royal

Titchwell Manor

★★★ 86% ◎◎ HOTEL

Address: TITCHWELL, PE31 8BB
Tel: 01485 210221
Fax: 01485 210104
E-mail: margaret@titchwellmanor.com
Website: www.titchwellmanor.com
Map ref: 8, TF74
Directions: On A149 (coast road) between
Brancaster & Thornham
Rooms: 26 (18 annexe) (4 fmly) (16 GF) **S** £45-£125;
D £90-£250 (incl. bkfst)
Facilities: FTV Wi-fi
Parking: 50

Golfers come for the two championship courses nearby; nature lovers come for the rich birdlife of the marshes; foodies come for the cuisine of head chef Eric Snaith, and others come just for the relaxing atmosphere and stylish accommodation. Situated near Brancaster and Burnham Market, this elegant property commands stunning views towards the coast and RSPB reserve; it is a common sight to see Marsh Harriers circling overhead. The guest rooms are in a converted barn, in a cottage, around a herb-filled courtyard and in the main building – a brick-and-flint Victorian former farmhouse. All boast chic, contemporary furnishings and some have sea views. There are family rooms and even dog-friendly rooms complete with bowls and biscuits. The fine dining Conservatory Restaurant offers a selection of innovative, beautifully presented, daily-changing dishes either from a set menu or a tasting menu, while the newly created Eating Rooms, that leads onto a sea-view terrace, is the perfect place for more informal eating or for just relaxing with a drink. The gardens are a real delight and a favourite spot with guests is the summerhouse where total peace and tranquillity can be enjoyed.

Recommended in the area

RSPB Titchwell Marsh Reserve; Peddars Way and Norfolk Coast Path; Norfolk Lavender

Northamptonshire

Canons Ashby House, Daventry, near Northampton

Rushton Hall Hotel and Spa

★★★★ 83% ◉◉ COUNTRY HOUSE HOTEL

Address: KETTERING, NN14 1RR

Tel: 01536 713001

Fax: 01536 713010

E-mail: enquiries@rushtonhall.com

Website: www.rushtonhall.com

Map ref: 3, SP87

Directions: A14 junct 7, A43 to Corby then A6003 to Rushton, turn after bridge

Rooms: 46 (5 fmly) (3 GF) **S** £150-£350; **D** £150-£350 (incl. bkfst) **Facilities:** Spa FTV ⓘ ♨ ◡ Gym Billiard table Sauna Steam room Wi-fi

Parking: 140

Rushton Hall is a magnificent Grade I listed Elizabethan country house, surrounded by beautiful, tranquil countryside where a wide range of activities and country pursuits are available. The east Midlands road network makes it easy to get to, so it is a popular conference and wedding venue. The grandeur of the building is balanced by an ambience of comfort, where guests can relax by one of the big open fireplaces and enjoy the attentive hospitality. Bedrooms are richly decorated in individual style, from elegant superior rooms to wood-panelled rooms with magnificent four-poster beds. All have internet access and flat-screen TVs, and some of the en suite bathrooms have a large bath and separate shower. The restaurant occupies the grand oak-panelled dining room and as much attention is paid to the sourcing of freshest ingredients as to the creation of the menus – mains might include a delicious seared fillet of halibut with brandade croquette, cockles and capers. Lunch and afternoon tea are served in the Great Hall or in the courtyard when the weather is good. Guests have the use of a fitness suite, outdoor tennis court, billiard table, swimming pool, indoor and outdoor spa, steam room, sauna and sun shower. Beauty treatments are also available.

Recommended in the area

Triangular Lodge; Boughton House; Rockingham Speedway; Rockingham Castle; Rutland Water

Northumberland

Dunstanburgh Castle, Craster, on the beautiful Northumberland coast

Langley Castle

★★★★ 82% ◉◉ HOTEL

Address: Langley, HEXHAM, NE47 5LU
Tel: 01434 688888
Fax: 01434 684019
E-mail: manager@langleycastle.com
Website: www.langleycastle.com
Map ref: 11, NY96
Directions: From A69 S on A686 for 2m.
Hotel is on right
Rooms: 27 (18 annexe) (8 fmly) (9 GF)
Facilities: STV Wi-fi
Parking: 70
Notes: ⊗

A genuine 14th-century castle, restored and transformed into a magnificent and comfortable hotel, set in its own 12-acre woodland estate. The guest bedchambers have private facilities, and some boast window seats set into 7ft-thick walls, four-poster beds, and even a sauna and spa bath. CastleView and CastleView Lodge, converted Grade I listed buildings within the grounds, offer additional guest rooms. All the bedrooms have draped canopies over the beds, satellite TV and stunning views up to the main castle. The splendid drawing room, with blazing log fire, traceries and stained glass, together with the oak-panelled cocktail bar, complement the intimate atmosphere of the Josephine Restaurant. The food served here is of the highest order, making the most of fresh, local produce, with fish and game a speciality on the table d'hôte menu. For early diners the Early Knight menu offers sophisticated choices between lunchtime and 6pm. The exclusive nature of the castle makes Langley the perfect destination to be pampered in unique surroundings, and it's ideally located for discovering the delights of Hadrian's Wall, Bamburgh Castle, Holy Island and the Scottish Borders. The Castle is only 30 minutes from Newcastle city centre and 40 minutes from Newcastle Airport.

Recommended in the area

Hadrian's Wall; Bamburgh Castle; Hexham Abbey

Nottinghamshire

Newstead Abbey and Upper Lake, near Nottingham

The Grange Hotel

★★★ 83% ⍟ HOTEL

Address: 73 London Rd, NEWARK, NG24 1RZ
Tel: 01636 703399
Fax: 01636 702328
E-mail: info@grangenewark.co.uk
Website: www.grangenewark.co.uk
Map ref: 7, SK75
Directions: From A1 follow signs to Balderton, hotel opposite Polish War Graves
Rooms: 19 (9 annexe) (1 fmly) **S** £83-£120;
D £97-£160 (incl. bkfst)
Facilities: FTV Wi-fi
Parking: 17 **Notes:** ⊗

A family-run, Victorian-era hotel in a conservation area, just a short walk from the town centre. Skilfully renovated, Newark Civic Trust gave the hotel an award for the way that many of the original features had been retained. Public rooms include a bar called Potters, with framed illustrations of old crockery, and a residents' lounge. Beyond Potters is a stone-flagged patio shaded by tall yews and the immaculate landscaped garden, indeed winner in 2011 of the 'East Midlands in Bloom' gold medal for best hotel garden. The bedrooms, some with four-posters, all feature excellent bathrooms with bath and shower, co-ordinated soft furnishings, desk space with phone and computer access point, TV, radio alarm, beverage-making and ironing facilities,

hairdryer, trouser press and, last but not least, a rubber duck for the very young. High-ceilinged Cutlers restaurant, named after the antique cutlery on display, offers a frequently changing carte menu, with main courses such as braised blade of beef; baked herb-crusted sea bass; and broccoli, cheese and potato bake. That it attracts non-residents as well as hotel guests says much about the restaurant's local reputation. Weddings and business functions are expertly catered for.

Recommended in the area

Newark Castle & Gardens; Newark International Antiques Fair; Newark Air Museum

Hart's Hotel

★★★★ 82% ◉◉ HOTEL

Address: Standard Hill, Park Row, NOTTINGHAM,
NG1 6FN
Tel: 0115 988 1900
Fax: 0115 947 7600
E-mail: reception@hartsnottingham.co.uk
Website: www.hartsnottingham.co.uk
Map ref: 7, SK53
Directions: At junct of Park Row & Ropewalk
Rooms: 32 (1 fmly) (7 GF) **D** £125-£265
Facilities: STV FTV Small unsupervised exercise
room Wi-fi
Parking: 16

A privately owned boutique hotel built to an award-winning design on the former ramparts of Nottingham's medieval castle, and close to the bustling city centre. Light, contemporary rooms feature top quality beds with sumptuous goose-down pillows and duvets, and Egyptian cotton bed linen. Mini-bars are stocked with wines, beers and fresh milk for your cafetière coffee, while other standard features include CD, radio, flat-screen digital TV with Blu-ray and DVD player, satellite channels, internet access, DDI lines and voicemail. Some rooms have French doors leading out into the pretty garden – a perfect spot for a relaxing gin and tonic before dinner in Hart's Restaurant. Dine on modern British cooking in one of the intimate booths and choose from owner Tim Hart's wine list, which has a generous selection from smaller producers. An alternative to the restaurant is the more casual Park Bar, with original artwork on display, high-backed sofas, red leather armchairs, and courtyard seating. Hart's Upstairs is a popular venue for private parties, weddings and business meetings. From the hotel's garden there are extensive views across the city and beyond. A nightly charge is made for the secure, barrier-controlled car park.

Recommended in the area

City of Caves; Nottingham Royal Centre; Nottingham Playhouse

Newstead Abbey formal gardens

Oxfordshire

Radcliffe Camera, Oxford

The Feathers Hotel

★★★★ 79% ◎◎ TOWN HOUSE HOTEL

Address: Market St, WOODSTOCK, OX20 1SX
Tel: 01993 812291
Fax: 01993 813158
E-mail: enquiries@feathers.co.uk
Website: www.feathers.co.uk
Map ref: 3, SP41
Directions: From A44 (Oxford to Woodstock),
1st left after lights. Hotel on left
Rooms: 21 (5 annexe) (4 fmly) (2 GF) **S** £104-£189;
D £104-£349 (incl. bkfst)
Facilities: FTV Wi-fi

It was in the Sixties that a former landlord's love of stuffed birds led the 17th-century Dorchester Inn to change its name to The Feathers. With its ivy-covered façade, oak beams and open fireplaces, time appears to have stood still here, a feeling endorsed by an antique clock permanently stuck at ten to eight. Unfortunately, time waits for no man, not even in this intimate, town centre hotel, but you can try and slow it down, perhaps in the cosy drawing room, the Courtyard Bar, the atmospheric restaurant, or in one of the individually styled, highly appointed bedrooms. These come in all shapes and sizes, with lush fabrics, funky lighting, free-standing stone basin and, imaginatively, a decanter full of jelly beans. The two-AA Rosette restaurant serves Modern English dishes such as Tamworth pork trotter with sticky braised belly and cheek, butternut squash and caramelised apple; halibut with chicken wing; and celeriac and sage risotto with roast chestnuts. Or go for the Gin Experience menu, whereby the taste and texture of each dish depends on one of several special gins selected by Chef. There's a tasting menu too, while coffee, lunch, cream tea and supper are served in the more informal, all-day bar.

Recommended in the area

Blenheim Palace; City of Oxford; Bicester Shopping Village

Rutland

Normanton Church, Rutland Weir

Hambleton Hall

★★★★ ◎◎◎◎ COUNTRY HOUSE HOTEL
Address: Hambleton, OAKHAM, LE15 8TH
Tel: 01572 756991
Fax: 01572 724721
E-mail: hotel@hambletonhall.com
Website: www.hambletonhall.com
Map ref: 3, SK80
Directions: 3m E off A606
Rooms: 17 (2 annexe) **S** £195-£215; **D** £245-£625
(incl. bkfst)
Facilities: STV FTV ⟍ ⅊ ⅊ Private access to
lake Wi-fi
Parking: 40

This family-run hotel is a magnificent Victorian house, standing in its own beautiful gardens and enjoying fine views over Rutland Water, the largest man-made lake in western Europe. The bedrooms are highly individual in character, furnished with fine fabrics and sumptuous furniture; ranging from the largest master rooms, which have king-size beds and far-reaching, wonderful views of the lake, to smaller standard rooms that overlook the beautifully manicured lawns and handsome cedar trees. The most luxurious accommodation is in the Croquet Pavilion, a two-bedroom folly, just 50 yards from the main building with a private terrace affording views of Rutland Water. The cuisine here is outstanding. On frequently changing menus the kitchen bases the dishes on fresh, seasonal and locally sourced produce. The hotel won the AA Wine Award for England and was also the Overall Winner for 2011; each month there is a wine dinner. In the public areas there are open fireplaces in the cosy bar and an elegant drawing room. The hotel is popular for prestigious private functions of all kinds, including wedding receptions. For corporate guests there is full business support, including secretarial and translation services.

Recommended in the area

Burghley House; Rutland Water; Grimsthorpe Castle; Kelmarsh Hall Gardens

Shropshire

Ludlow Castle and St Laurence's Church, Ludlow

The Feathers Hotel

★★★ 80% ● HOTEL

Address: The Bull Ring, LUDLOW, SY8 1AA
Tel: 01584 875261
Fax: 01584 876030
E-mail: feathers.ludlow@btconnect.com
Website: www.feathersatludlow.co.uk
Map ref: 6, SO57
Directions: From A49 follow town centre signs to centre. Hotel on left
Rooms: 40 (3 fmly) **S** £79-£89; **D** £99-£115 (incl. bkfst)
Facilities: STV FTV Wi-fi
Parking: 33

The New York Times described this old inn's famous Jacobean frontage as "the most handsome in the world", a fine enough tribute but not one that does justice to the amazing geometry of its black-and-white timberwork. Centrally placed in town, the hotel is within easy reach of many historic buildings, and excellent craft and antiques shops. The hotel has a café terrace and a cosy public lounge to rest in after sightseeing. Guest rooms, all recently refurbished, comprise some with a four-poster, many doubles, several twins, and single and family rooms. Additionally, there are a few individually designed luxury rooms equipped with plush fabrics, spa bath and power shower. All rooms are en suite with both bath and shower, and include flat-screen colour television, hospitality tray and direct-dial phone. Many of the rooms in the oldest part of the building feature original exposed beams. In the restaurant, head chef Stuart Forman's traditional and contemporary menu is firmly rooted in fresh, local produce, with examples such as roast fillet of Gloucester Old Spot pork, baked apple with stuffing, wilted kale and Stowford Press sauce; and roast tail of monkfish wrapped in Parma ham with paprika-sautéed potatoes and lemon and caper dressing. The hotel is popular during Ludlow's major festivals.

Recommended in the area

Ludlow Castle; St Laurence's Church; Whitcliff and Mortimer Forest

Rowton Castle Hotel

★★★ 88% ◎ HOTEL

Address: Halfway House, SHREWSBURY, SY5 9EP
Tel: 01743 884044
Fax: 01743 884949
E-mail: post@rowtoncastle.com
Website: www.rowtoncastle.com
Map ref: 6, SJ41
Directions: From A5 near Shrewsbury take A458 to Welshpool. Hotel 4m on right
Rooms: 19 (3 fmly)
Facilities: ✑ Wi-fi
Parking: 100
Notes: ❸

A castle has stood in the grounds at Rowton for nearly 800 years. The building has seen many changes and alterations over the centuries but has remained primarily a family home. It has now been transformed into a luxury country hotel, retaining the spendour of yesteryear whilst providing the facilities anticipated by the most discerning of guests. Rowton Castle is a beautiful 17th-century, Grade II listed building, set in 17 acres of tranquil grounds, six miles west of the historic town of Shrewsbury. The castle boasts 19 individually designed bedrooms, seven with period four-poster beds. Each beautifully appointed room has a fully equipped bathroom, TV, direct-dial telephone, Wi-fi and excellent beverage-making facilities. Personal service and attention to detail are hallmarks of Rowton Castle's excellent reputation and this is ably demonstrated in the hotel's award-winning Cedar Restaurant. Oak panelling with 17th-century carving, velvet armchairs and intimate lighting are a perfect backdrop to this fine-dining experience. An extensive fixed-price menu offers a mouthwatering selection for all tastes, complemented by an interesting choice of wines from around the world. Rowton Castle is a fairytale venue for weddings and has excellent conference facilities.

Recommended in the area

The Long Mynd; Welshpool and Llanfair Light Railway; Offa's Dyke Path

Somerset

Pulteney Bridge, Bath

Bailbrook House Hotel

★★★ 75% HOTEL

Address: Eveleigh Av, London Road West, BATH,
BA1 7JD
Tel: 01225 855100
Fax: 01225 855200
E-mail: bailbrook@hilwoodresorts.com
Website: www.bailbrookhouse.co.uk
Map ref: 2, ST76 **Directions:** M4 junct 18/A46, at
bottom of long hill take slip road to city centre. At
rdbt take 1st exit, London Rd. Hotel 200mtrs on left
Rooms: 78 (78 annexe) (2 fmly) (26 GF)
Facilities: FTV ⅃ Gym Sauna Wi-fi
Parking: 120 **Notes:** ⊗

For the most modern hotel facilities in a seriously historic setting, this Grade II*-listed, early 19th-century mansion might be hard to beat. Built of honey-coloured Bath stone for a wealthy lawyer, it stands in 20 acres of gardens on the outskirts of England's only World Heritage City. During the 1970s it was converted into a training college for air traffic controllers, and then became a residential conference centre. Conference facilities are still offered today, alongside a restaurant, bar, main function suite and spacious, beautifully appointed en suite bedrooms. The rooms are in Bailbrook Court, a contemporary building next to the main house, and all have a work area, two phone lines, free internet connection, remote-control TV, hot drinks tray, iron and ironing board. The day might start with a full English or continental breakfast, then lunch in the bar or on the terrace, and finally dinner in the restaurant, Gabriels, whose menu lists tian of crab; grilled fillet mignon; braised salmon; and mushroom Stroganoff. Leisure facilities include an all-weather tennis court, fitness suite, sauna, spa bath and games room. Advice to satnav users: the hotel's actual postcode leads to a small country lane, whereas BA1 7DA hits the spot.

Recommended in the area

The Pump Room; Roman Baths; Bath Abbey

Dukes

★★★ 82% ◉◉ SMALL HOTEL
Address: Great Pulteney St, BATH, BA2 4DN
Tel: 01225 787960
Fax: 01225 787961
E-mail: info@dukesbath.co.uk
Website: www.dukesbath.co.uk
Map ref: 2, ST76
Directions: A46 to Bath, at rdbt right on A4. 4th set
of lights turn left (A36), then right into Great Pulteney
St. Hotel on left
Rooms: 17 (5 fmly) (2 GF) **S** £99-£132;
D £139-£251.40 (incl. bkfst)
Facilities: FTV Wi-fi

An expertly restored, bow-fronted, Grade I listed Georgian townhouse where the rooms are decorated with period furniture, fine fabrics, prints and portraits. Surviving original plasterwork includes delicate features such as Adams-style urns and floral swags. In winter a blazing log fire in the lounge gives a warm welcome, while in summer the peaceful courtyard terrace, with a sparkling fountain, is perfect for a relaxing meal or drink. The en suite bedrooms and six suites (two with four-posters) have been restored to their original spacious dimensions. Many have enormous sash windows and splendid views over Great Pulteney Street, the Bath skyline or the surrounding countryside. Each differs in size and design, some Georgian themed, others more contemporary. All have bath and/or power shower, large fluffy towels and bathrobes, digital TV, Wi-fi access and hairdryer. The Cavendish Restaurant and Bar offers modern British seasonal cooking, using carefully sourced, locally grown and reared organic and free-range produce. A fixed-price lunch menu offers two or three courses and the dinner menu is à la carte. There are two smaller, more intimate, dining rooms which can be reserved for private receptions.

Recommended in the area

Thermae Bath Spa; Roman Baths; Royal Crescent and Circus

Queensberry

★★★ ◎◎◎ HOTEL

Address: Russel St, BATH, BA1 2QF
Tel: 01225 447928
Fax: 01225 446065
E-mail: reservations@thequeensberry.co.uk
Website: www.thequeensberry.co.uk
Map ref: 2, ST76
Directions: 100mtrs from the Assembly Rooms
Rooms: 29 (2 fmly) (2 GF) **S** £130-£190; **D** £130-£460
Facilities: FTV Wi-fi
Parking: 9
Notes: ⊗

Four Georgian town houses form this charming hotel, located in a quiet residential street close to the city centre. The hotel is run with a passion by Laurence and Helen Beere who, together with their staff, maintain a refreshingly old-fashioned attitude to guest service, making a stay here a memorable one. The spacious bedrooms are individually designed, combining up-to-date comfort and sophistication with the buildings' original features. Expect marble bathrooms, flat-screen TVs and White Company toiletries. There is a choice of sumptuously furnished drawing rooms, an inviting bar and secluded terraced gardens. The stylish Olive Tree restaurant offers innovative menus of modern British dishes with Mediterranean influences; in the main, local and trusted suppliers are relied upon to provide the seasonal ingredients that create the award-winning cuisine, with dishes such as fillet of Stokes Marsh beef with prosciutto, veal kidney, cocotte potatoes and artichoke. The popular 'quintessentially British' Old Q Bar is a great place to relax and enjoy a drink and choose a snack or light meal from the bar menu. All the attractions of historic Bath are just a few minutes' walk away, and if arriving by car, the hotel offers a valet service.

Recommended in the area

Thermae Bath Spa; Beckford's Tower; Claverton Pumping Station

Suffolk

The Tide Mill, Woodbridge

Wentworth

★★★ 88% ◎◎ HOTEL

Address: Wentworth Rd, ALDEBURGH, IP15 5BD
Tel: 01728 452312
Fax: 01728 454343
E-mail: stay@wentworth-aldeburgh.co.uk
Website: www.wentworth-aldeburgh.com
Map ref: 4, TM45
Directions: Off A12 onto A1094, 6m to Aldeburgh,
with church on left, left at bottom of hill
Rooms: 35 (7 annexe) (2 fmly) (5 GF) **S** £83-£129;
D £141-£290 (incl. bkfst & dinner)
Facilities: FTV Wi-fi
Parking: 30

This triple-gabled hotel has been managed by the
Pritt family since 1920, and the continuous thread
is responsible for the fact that the Wentworth is
everything a seaside hotel should be. The attractive
and well-maintained public rooms include three
lounges furnished with comfortable chairs and
sofas, which are sunny spots in summer and cosy
places to relax by an open fire in winter. Outside
are two sea-facing gardens in which to soak up
the sun with a morning coffee, light lunch or cream
tea. Many of the regularly refurbished en suite
bedrooms have good views of the North Sea, for
which the hotel thoughtfully provides binoculars.
Seven rooms in Darfield House, just opposite the
main building, are particularly spacious and well
appointed. For those who find stairs difficult (there's
no lift) there are five ground-floor rooms. Room
sizes and outlook do vary, and these differences
are reflected in the tariff. You can start the day
here with a locally smoked kipper, as part of your
'full-house' cooked breakfast. At lunchtime, the
terrace bar menu offers a wide choice, from a fresh
crab sandwich to traditional cod and chips, and the
elegant candlelit restaurant has a daily changing
dinner menu based on fresh local produce.

Recommended in the area

Minsmere (RSPB) Reserve; Snape Maltings
(Aldeburgh Festival); Suffolk Heritage Coast

Bildeston Crown

★ ★ ★ ◎◎◎ HOTEL

Address: 104 High St, BILDESTON, IP7 7EB
Tel: 01449 740510
E-mail: hayley@thebildestoncrown.co.uk
Website: www.thebildestoncrown.co.uk
Map ref: 4, TL94
Directions: A12 junct 31, turn right onto B1070
& follow signs to Hadleigh. At T-junct turn left
onto A1141, then immediately right onto B1115.
Hotel 0.5m
Rooms: 13 **Facilities:** STV FTV Wi-fi
Parking: 30

In a village deep in picturesque countryside, stands this 15th-century, heavily timbered coaching inn. Original features, including log fires, oak beams and period furniture ensure that you'll remain conscious of its ancestry. Much thought has gone into the bedrooms, each of which includes flat-screen TV, an extensive library of music available via a built-in wall control panel, concealed speakers in the en suite bathroom and shower area, and internet access. The luxurious Black Fuschia room, with dramatic black decor and a super-king-size bed, is apparently 'not for the faint-hearted'. At the centre of the Crown lies the comfortable restaurant, where paintings line the rich, red walls, beams cross the ceiling and locally sourced seasonal cuisine ranges from the classic to interpretations of the traditional. A typical dinner might be pan-seared fillet of mackerel with leek tart, followed by breast of Suffolk chicken with confit leg and poached lobster, and set-milk cream with balsamic figs to finish. Red Poll beef from the hotel owner's own herd is always a possibility, and there's also an eight-course tasting menu. On a fine day, eat or drink in the central courtyard, or try one of the two bars where the full restaurant menu is also available.

Recommended in the area

Lavenham; Colne Valley Railway; Constable Country

Hintlesham Hall

★ ★ ★ ★ ◎◎ HOTEL

Address: George St, HINTLESHAM, IP8 3NS
Tel: 01473 652334
Fax: 01473 652463
E-mail: reservations@hintleshamhall.com
Website: www.hintleshamhall.com
Map ref: 4, TM04
Directions: 4m W of Ipswich on A1071 to Hadleigh & Sudbury
Rooms: 33 (10 GF) **S** £119-£149; **D** £129-£199 (incl. bkfst) **Facilities:** FTV ⊃ ⅃ 18 ⌇ Putt green ⌣ Gym Health & Beauty services Clay pigeon shooting ♫ Wi-fi **Parking:** 60

Hospitality and service are absolute priorities at this imposing 16th-century, Grade I listed country house hotel in 175 acres of landscaped gardens and grounds. The building is distinguished by its Georgian additions, most notably the façade, as well as by earlier Stuart interior embellishments. Works of art and antiques abound throughout, particularly in the spacious public rooms and restaurants. Individually decorated bedrooms and suites come in varying shapes, sizes and styles, but consistently applied are their high degree of comfort, tasteful furnishings and thoughtful extras. Wander around the grounds before heading for the grand Salon, largest of the three dining rooms, and Head Chef Alan Ford's well-balanced carte, from which examples include grilled fillet of haddock served in a mussel and clam chowder, and tournedos of beef with braised oxtail and horseradish. Many of the dishes encompass fresh herbs from the famous garden, designed by the late Robert Carrier, who bought the then derelict Hall in 1972. The award-winning 350-bin wine list includes a generous selection of half bottles. Health and beauty and specialist treatments, and a gym with instructors, complement the seasonal pool. A championship PGA golf course is adjacent to the Hall.

Recommended in the area

Constable Country; Aldeburgh; Newmarket Racecourse

Milsoms Kesgrave Hall

★★★★ 76% ◉ HOTEL

Address: Hall Rd, Kesgrave, IPSWICH, IP5 2PU
Tel: 01473 333741
Fax: 01473 617614
E-mail: reception@kesgravehall.com
Website: www.milsomshotels.com
Map ref: 4, TM14
Directions: A12 N of Ipswich, left at Ipswich/
Woodbridge rdbt onto B1214. Right after 0.5m into
Hall Rd. Hotel 200yds on left
Rooms: 23 (8 annexe) (4 fmly) (8 GF) **S** £115-£200;
D £125-£275
Facilities: STV FTV ♨ Wi-fi **Parking:** 100

A joint venture between Milsom Hotels and Hills Group, this superb 18th-century, Grade II-listed Georgian mansion stands in nearly 40 acres of parkland. Just turning into the driveway gives you a fair clue about what to expect. Decorated and furnished in a contemporary style, its large open-plan public areas include a smart bar with original Gothic mirrors, a lounge with plush sofas, and a restaurant from which you can watch the chefs in the 'Engine Room'. Bedrooms are tastefully appointed and thoughtfully equipped, with huge walk-in shower (or bathtub in the room itself), crisp white linen, fluffy towels, mini-bar, satellite TV, MP3 player, Wi-fi and hot drinks tray. With an AA Rosette to their credit, Head Chef Stuart Oliver and

his team are full-on champions of Suffolk produce, with Dedham Vale steaks; pan-fried Sutton Hoo chicken breast; sausages and salami from Lane Farm, Brundish; and Kesgrave Hall shellfish and fish pie. A daily specials board declares further support for what's local and seasonal. Children can choose from their own menu. Although you cannot book, the all-day menu means you can eat when you choose; on Sundays, the lunch menu is available until 4.30 pm, then the full evening carte from 5 pm.

Recommended in the area

Suffolk Heritage Coast; Aldeburgh & Snape; Sutton Hoo (NT)

The Olde Bull Inn

★★★ 83% ⊛ HOTEL

Address: The Street, Barton Mills, MILDENHALL,
IP28 6AA
Tel: 01638 711001
Fax: 01638 712003
E-mail: bookings@bullinn-bartonmills.com
Website: www.bullinn-bartonmills.com
Map ref: 4, TL77 **Directions:** Off A11 between
Newmarket & Mildenhall, signed Barton Mills.
Hotel by Five Ways rdbt
Rooms: 14 (2 annexe) (2 fmly) (2 GF) **S** £70-£99;
D £85-£125 (incl. bkfst) **Facilities:** STV FTV Wi-fi
Parking: 60 **Notes:** ⊛

This 16th-century coaching inn in the lovely village of Barton Mills was rescued from dereliction and reopened as a hotel more than ten years ago. In more recent times the current owners have transformed the bedrooms into charming boutique accommodation with a mixture of period details, designer fabrics and wallpapers and contemporary furniture. Every bedroom is individually designed and has an en suite bathroom along with flat-screen TV with Freeview, direct-dial telephone, beverage tray and hairdryer. Food is one of the biggest draws at The Olde Bull Inn, with everything made in-house using the best, freshest ingredients from local suppliers. The charming Oak Room Restaurant has an AA Rosette and serves modern British food, including the signature 'fillet steak tower' – best local beef covered in a creamy pepper sauce, layered with onions and resting on a parsnip and potato rösti. The daily specials board always offers something seasonal to supplement the main menu, such as Brancaster mussels or Thornham oysters. Less formal meals and snacks – along with a range of local real ales – are served in the cosy bar with its log fire, and in the summer you can dine alfresco in the courtyard.

Recommended in the area

Shopping & punting in Cambridge; Center Parcs spa at Elveden Forest; Go Ape! at Thetford Forest

Tuddenham Mill

★★★★ 81% ◉◉ HOTEL

Address: High St, Tuddenham St Mary, NEWMARKET,
IP28 6SQ
Tel: 01638 713552
E-mail: info@tuddenhammill.co.uk
Website: www.tuddenhammill.co.uk
Map ref: 4, TL66
Rooms: 15 **S** £185-£395 (incl. bkfst)
Parking: 60

The Domesday Book records a mill at Tuddenham in 1086, although the present structure was not erected until 1775. The 53-foot chimney was added in 1855, when a steam engine was installed. A century later the mill was derelict, but happily the cast-iron water wheel survived and can now be seen in the bar. The mill was recently meticulously renovated by a dedicated team of architects, engineers and craftsmen working closely with planners and conservation officers to ensure its success. Today's contemporary-style bedrooms are separately housed next to the main building, each one with co-ordinated fabrics and soft furnishings, furniture designed and sourced in Italy, walk-in shower, Bose sound system and Loewe flat-screen TV. Some have a huge double-ended stone bath that's apparently big enough for three! You can still see the old beams in the walls and up in the high pitched roofs. Seasonally inspired, contemporary food is on offer and those looking for a real treat should sample the lunchtime or evening taster menu. Eat in, outside by the pond, or upstairs at one of the much sought-after window tables which have a view of the mill stream, now cleared of centuries of silt and debris to create a natural haven for otters, herons and fish.

Recommended in the area

The National Stud; National Horse Racing Museum; Moulton Packhorse Bridge

Westleton Crown

★★★ 79% ◉◉ HOTEL

Address: The Street, WESTLETON, IP17 3AD
Tel: 01728 648777
Fax: 01728 648239
E-mail: info@westletoncrown.co.uk
Website: www.westletoncrown.co.uk
Map ref: 4, TM46
Directions: A12 N, turn right for Westleton just after
Yoxford. Hotel opposite on entering Westleton
Rooms: 34 (22 annexe) (5 fmly) (13 GF) **S** £80-£100;
D £90-£215 (incl. bkfst)
Facilities: FTV Wi-fi
Parking: 34

Whether you want to get away from it all on a short
break or simply need somewhere for a longer stay
on the Suffolk coast, the Westleton Crown has it
all. Dating back to the 12th century, this traditional
coaching inn retains the character and rustic
charm of its heritage, but with all the comforts the
21st-century traveller could hope for. The bar has
the feel of a genuine local, with a warm welcome
and plenty of Suffolk ales to enjoy. Meals may be
taken in the bar, elegant dining room or stylish
Garden Room, as well as in the charming terraced
gardens during warmer weather. Food is taken
extremely seriously at the Westleton Crown, with
everything – from tasty bread to soups, patés
and ice cream – made in-house from the finest,
freshest ingredients. Menus are imaginative and
varied and complemented by an extensive wine
list. The bedrooms are individually designed and
exceptionally comfortable. Those in the main inn are
more traditional in style, while more contemporary
rooms can be found in the converted stables and
cottages. Whichever you choose, expect flat-screen
TVs, tea and coffee-making facilities, beautiful
bathrooms and luxuriously large beds with fully
sprung mattresses, goose down duvets and crisp
white Egyptian cotton linen.

Recommended in the area

Minsmere (RSPB) Reserve; Dunwich; Snape Maltings

The lighthouse and beach huts at Southwold, Suffolk

Surrey

18th-century Leith Hill Tower, Leith Hill, near Dorking

the runnymede-on-thames

★★★★ 80% HOTEL

Address: Windsor Rd, EGHAM, TW20 0AG
Tel: 01784 220600
Fax: 01784 436340
E-mail: info@therunnymede.co.uk
Website: www.therunnymede.co.uk
Map ref: 3, SU07 **Directions:** M25 junct 13, onto
A308 towards Windsor
Rooms: 181 (19 fmly) **S** £127-£263; **D** £164-£302
(incl. bkfst) **Facilities:** Spa STV ⊙ supervised ↘
supervised ⚓ ⚑ Gym Dance studio Children's play
area River boat hire Group treatment suite Wi-fi
Child facilities **Parking:** 300 **Notes:** ⊗

From its peaceful location beside the River Thames, this large modern hotel offers an excellent range of leisure and corporate facilities. Guest rooms, with either river or courtyard views, are stylishly furnished and offer many delights, from cosy duvets to fast broadband access. In the Leftbank Restaurant, produce is carefully sourced and the result is 'an eclectic fusion' of Mediterranean and British food; an extensive wine list includes some imaginative bins. The Lock, beside the Bell Lock Weir, is the hotel's newest eatery where guests can dine alfresco when the weather permits. With a bistro-style atmosphere it provides a menu of 'simple and bold' dishes such as potato leek and gruyere tart, Casterbridge rib eye steak, big chips and bearnaise sauce and The Lock Kitchen burger served with big chips. With its riverside terrace and gardens, the lounge is the place for afternoon tea or even a cocktail or two. Guests here can choose to do a little or as much as they like for this is an excellent place to relax. Perhaps swim in the 18-metre pool, relax in the whirlpool bath, enjoy a sauna or the eucalyptus steam room, or work up a sweat in the dance studio, gym or on the tennis courts. Just nearby are Royal Windsor and Heathrow, and central London is only 40 minutes down the road.

Recommended in the area

Windsor Castle; Legoland; Magna Carta Memorial

East Sussex

Cooden Beach Hotel

★★★ 80% HOTEL

Address: Cooden Beach, BEXHILL, TN39 4TT
Tel: 01424 842281
Fax: 01424 846142
E-mail: rooms@thecoodenbeachhotel.co.uk
Website: www.thecoodenbeachhotel.co.uk
Map ref: 4, TQ70
Directions: A259 towards Cooden. Signed at rdbt
in Little Common Village. Hotel at end of road
Rooms: 41 (8 annexe) (10 fmly) (4 GF)
Facilities: FTV ⊕ Gym Sauna Steam room Spa bath
♫ Wi-fi
Parking: 60

From many of the bedrooms in this privately owned, beach-facing hotel, there are splendid uninterrupted views of the English Channel. Standing in two acres of immaculate gardens, with private access to the shore, its mock-Tudor architecture betrays its late-1920s construction. Most of the charmingly decorated bedrooms have a king-size bed with supportive Tempur mattress, and all of them have newly installed en suite facilities, as well as satellite TV, hairdryer, direct-dial phone and hot drinks tray. The Oceana Restaurant looks straight out to sea and offers traditional English food, such as its signature dish, 'posh' fish and chips, made with tempura batter, and served with chunky chips and mushy peas. That's not all, of course: other options include roast lamb shank; pan-fried tuna steak; and Mediterranean tart with Dolcelatte cheese. Sunday lunch is in the Cooden Carvery, while the Cooden Tavern serves morning coffee and afternoon tea, and bar food and daily specials until 9 pm. From the Club Terrace you can watch the yachts and, out on the horizon, big ships heading for distant ports. The recently refurbished Leisure Club features a heated pool, gym, sauna, steam room and spa bath, while the hotel's golf packages are available for the Cooden Beach course next door.

Recommended in the area

Bodiam Castle (NT); Rye; Drusillas Zoo Park

Devonshire Park

★★★ 79% HOTEL

Address: 27-29 Carlisle Rd, EASTBOURNE, BN21 4JR
Tel: 01323 728144
Fax: 01323 419734
E-mail: info@devonshire-park-hotel.co.uk
Website: www.devonshire-park-hotel.co.uk
Map ref: 4, TV69
Directions: Follow signs to seafront, exit at Wish Tower. Hotel opposite Congress Theatre
Rooms: 35 (8 GF) **S** £50-£75; **D** fr £65 (incl. bkfst)
Facilities: STV Wi-fi
Parking: 25
Notes: ⊗ ⚲ under 12yrs

This family run, country-house style hotel is extremely well placed; opposite is Devonshire Park, where the Eastbourne International tennis tournament serves as a warm-up to Wimbledon. Close by are the Towner Gallery, Congress Theatre, Winter Garden, town centre and seafront. Attractively furnished rooms in this elegant property, which was built in the resort's Victorian heyday, are spacious, and many have a king-size bed and both a bath and separate walk-in shower. Extras include luxury toiletries, Wi-fi, satellite TV and iPod dock. Views to the rear take in the South Downs, and three of the larger suites have a private patio. In the intimate four-room restaurant, the daily changing menu reflects fresh ingredients sourced from local suppliers earlier that morning. Dishes might include pan-fried Romney Marsh lamb noisettes with rosemary and redcurrant jus; grilled trout with courgette rösti and lime and pink peppercorn dressing; and pumpkin ravioli in rich tomato and cream sauce. A carefully considered wine list offers a wide choice. Pre-theatre dinner can be easily arranged. Guests can enjoy coffee and light lunch in the bar upstairs, relax in one of the lounges or, in the summer, at a table on the front lawn.

Recommended in the area

Devonshire Park International Tennis Centre; Eastbourne promenade; South Downs National Park

Newick Park Hotel & Country Estate

★★★ ◉◉ HOTEL

Address: NEWICK, BN8 4SB
Tel: 01825 723633 **Fax:** 01825 723969
E-mail: bookings@newickpark.co.uk
Website: www.newickpark.co.uk
Map ref: 4, TQ42
Directions: Exit A272 at Newick Green, 1m, pass
church & pub. Turn left, hotel 0.25m on right
Rooms: 16 (3 annexe) (5 fmly) (1 GF) **S** £125-£245;
D £165-£285 (incl. bkfst)
Facilities: FTV ⚲ Fishing ⚓ Clay pigeon shooting
Helicopter rides Quad biking Tank driving Laser quest
Wi-fi **Parking:** 52

Grade II* listed and surrounded by its own private
park of 255 acres, this lovely Georgian house offers
complete peace and privacy. There's a definite
family-home atmosphere in the comfortable
study, sitting room and lounge bar, with huge log
fires, interesting antiques and attentive staff. The
spacious, individually designed bedrooms are
tastefully furnished, comprehensively equipped and
look out over the park and South Downs; some have
a king-size bed, others a four-poster. The restaurant
team, led by Chris Moore, always searches out the
best local produce, the first port of call being the
estate and organically run kitchen garden. That the
food is excellent is acknowledged by the two AA
Rosettes held since 1996 for, typically, fillet of sea

trout with crab; roast shoulder of pork with salsa
verde; and red pepper risotto. Wi-fi internet access
is provided free of charge and there are two light
and airy function rooms for meetings. Guests can
have fun riding a quad bike, driving a tank or clay-
pigeon shooting, all with full instruction. Weddings
and other special occasions are often celebrated
here. Glyndebourne Festival Opera is only fifteen
minutes away and there are many castles, historic
houses and gardens within easy reach.

Recommended in the area

Glyndebourne Opera; Sheffield Park Gardens;
Brighton's Lanes

Mermaid Inn

★★★ 81% ◎ HOTEL

Address: Mermaid St, RYE, TN31 7EY
Tel: 01797 223065 & 223788
Fax: 01797 225069
E-mail: info@mermaidinn.com
Website: www.mermaidinn.com
Map ref: 4, TQ92
Directions: A259, follow signs to town centre, then into Mermaid St
Rooms: 31 (5 fmly) **S** £90-£110; **D** £180-£260 (incl. bkfst) **Facilities:** Wi-fi
Parking: 25
Notes: ⊗

As you step from the cobbles of Mermaid Street into this ancient timbered and foliage-covered building, you walk straight into nearly 600 years of history. The inn you see today was built in 1420 from ships' timbers and baulks of Sussex oak. Hidden in the Lounge Bar fireplace is a priest's hole, used when it was a crime to be caught harbouring a Roman Catholic. The bedrooms feature fine panelling, latticed windows and fireplaces carved from Caen stone used as ships' ballast and rescued from the harbour. The Elizabethan Chamber and Dr Syn's Bedchamber both have magnificent carved beds, and concealed behind the bookcase in Dr Syn's is a secret stairway. The second-storey rooms are particularly intriguing, with curved timbers supporting the ceilings, and dormer windows affording a view over the town's red-tiled roofs. All rooms are en suite, with LCD TV, hospitality tray, 24-hour room service and free Wi-fi, while in some you may have company in the form (if that's the right word) of one of several ghosts. The linenfold-panelled restaurant, holder of an AA Rosette, is where the British and French cooking includes free-range Beckley chicken breast; braised Canterbury pork belly; pan-fried Rye Bay sea bass; and fricassée of woodland mushrooms.

Recommended in the area

Camber Castle; Camber Sands beach; Lamb House (NT)

West Sussex

Fulking Escarpment on the South Downs Way

Felbridge Hotel & Spa

★★★★ 86% ◉◉ HOTEL

Address: London Rd, EAST GRINSTEAD, RH19 2BH
Tel: 01342 337700
Fax: 01342 337715
E-mail: sales@felbridgehotel.co.uk
Website: www.felbridgehotel.co.uk
Map ref: 4, TQ33
Directions: From W: M23 junct 10, follow signs to A22. From N: M25 junct 6. Hotel on A22 at Felbridge
Rooms: 120 (16 fmly) (53 GF) (9 smoking)
S £89-£160; **D** £89-£160 **Facilities:** Spa STV FTV ⓡ supervised ⊰ Gym Sauna Steam room Hairdresser Wi-fi **Parking:** 300 **Notes:** ⊗

Comprehensively modernised in 2007, this luxurious hotel is within easy reach of the M25 and London Gatwick airport, as well as the Sussex coast. Fashionably designed, air-conditioned bedrooms have a power shower, Egyptian cotton towels, ultra-comfortable bed, flat-screen TV and iBAHN high-speed internet access; robes, slippers and luxurious products are provided in the suites. For chilling out, head for the contemporary design and comfortable seating of QUBE Bar; for an informal meal, try the Bay Tree Brasserie; while for fine-dining it has to be Anise, the peaceful, two-AA Rosette restaurant where a locally sourced, three-course dinner might comprise a starter of cumin-seasoned scallops with bacon, apple and black pudding; a main course of either confit duck leg with parsnip, Savoy cabbage and anise jus; or wild sea bass fillet with curried cauliflower, lime and coconut foam; and, for dessert, dark chocolate fondant with hazelnut mousse, caramelised hazelnuts and chocolate liqueur. Staff are on hand to talk diners through the extensive wine list. Other hotel facilities include the Chakra Spa and Fitness Centre, offering guests and health club members use of its fully equipped gymnasium, tennis courts, heated swimming pool, sauna, steam room as well as the 10-person spa pool.

Recommended in the area

Chartwell; Bluebell Railway; Wakehurst Place

The Goodwood Hotel

★★★★ 79% ◎◎ HOTEL
Address: GOODWOOD, Chichester, PO18 0QB
Tel: 01243 775537
Fax: 01243 520120
E-mail: reservations@goodwood.com
Website: www.goodwood.com
Map ref: 3, SU80
Directions: Off A285, 3m NE of Chichester
Rooms: 91 (48 GF) **S** £105-£300 (incl. bkfst)
Facilities: Spa STV FTV ◎ ≟ 18 ⚑ Putt green Gym
Golf driving range Sauna Steam room Fitness studio
Wi-fi
Parking: 350

In the centre of the 12,000-acre Goodwood Estate, home of the Dukes of Richmond for more than three centuries, is this attractive, privately owned hotel. It offers lots of ways to enjoy yourself, both indoors and outdoors, a range of meeting rooms, and conference and banqueting facilities. Bedrooms are all of a consistently high standard; the newly restored suites are furnished with modern furniture and antiques. Each of the individually styled Character rooms in the 18th-century part of the building combines modern details with historic links to the Estate; the Garden rooms open on to their own terrace; the freshly refurbished Signature rooms have dark-wood furniture and eclectic collections of books; and last, but not least, are the Classic rooms, many with interconnecting doors. There's a good range of eating options: in the Richmond Arms, where much of what you eat comes from the estate farm; in the Richmond Arms Bar in the 17th-century coaching inn, with an original open fireplace; and in the buzzing, brasserie-style Goodwood Bar and Grill. Overnight guests can also choose to dine in The Kennels, a private members' clubhouse. Open to the public all year round is the Aero Club Café, situated right in the heart of Goodwood airfield.

Recommended in the area

Fishbourne Roman Palace; Chichester; West Wittering

Spread Eagle Hotel and Spa

★★★ 80% ◉◉ HOTEL

Address: South St, MIDHURST, GU29 9NH
Tel: 01730 816911 **Fax:** 01730 815668
E-mail: spreadeagle@hshotels.co.uk
Website:
www.hshotels.co.uk/spread/spreadeagle-main.htm
Map ref: 3, SU82
Directions: M25 junct 10, A3 to Milford, take A286
to Midhurst. Hotel adjacent to market square
Rooms: 38 (4 annexe) (8 GF) **S** £95-£340;
D £125-£340 (incl. bkfst) **Facilities:** Spa STV FTV ◉
Gym Health & beauty treatment rooms Steam room
Sauna Fitness trainer Wi-fi **Parking:** 75

Since part of this historic hotel, with grounds
running down to Midhurst's South Pond, dates back
to 1430, its sloping floors and inglenook fireplaces
should come as no surprise. Neither, since it stands
right on the street and has a courtyard, should the
fact that it was once a coaching inn. Signs of great
age are everywhere, such as in the oak-beamed
lounge with leaded-light windows and huge open
fire. The Queen's Suite, on the floor above, is where
that allegedly inveterate inn visitor, Elizabeth I,
slept in 1591; it also houses what is possibly the
last surviving wig closet in an English hotel. In the
White Room there's a secret passage reputedly
used by smugglers to evade the King's revenue
men. But even if the walls are panelled in oak, and
even though they are furnished with antiques,
the individually designed bedrooms provide
everything for the modern traveller. The hallway
leads to the candlelit restaurant, which, with its
inglenook fireplace and stained-glass windows, is
the showcase for the accomplished Modern Classic
cuisine that has earned Nathan Marshal two AA
Rosettes. During the summer lunch is also served
in the Conservatory and Terrace. The spa has an
impressive, Scandinavian-style vaulted glass ceiling
and plenty of wet areas.

Recommended in the area

Goodwood Estate; Petworth House; Cowdray Park;
West Dean Gardens

Weald and Downland Open Air Museum, near Chichester

Warwickshire

The River Avon flows past majestic Warwick Castle, Warwick

Menzies Welcombe Hotel Spa & Golf Course

★★★★ 83% ◎◎ HOTEL

Address: Warwick Rd, STRATFORD-UPON-AVON, CV37 0NR

Tel: 01789 295252 **Fax:** 01789 414666

E-mail: welcombe@menzieshotels.co.uk

Website: www.menzieshotels.co.uk

Map ref: 3, SP25 **Directions:** M40 junct 15, A46 towards Stratford-upon-Avon, at rdbt follow signs for A439. Hotel 3m on right **Rooms:** 78 (12 fmly) (11 GF) (6 smoking) **Facilities:** Spa STV ⊕ ₤ 18 ♨ Putt green Gym Wi-fi **Parking:** 200 **Notes:** ⊗

Built in the Jacobean style in 1866, this imposing hotel stands in a 157-acre estate, part of which is devoted to an immaculately maintained Italian garden and water features. It was built as a calendar house, in which the main architectural elements represent the divisions of a year, thus there are seven entrances, 12 fireplaces, 52 chimneys and 365 windows. Among the attractions are the 18-hole championship golf course, luxury spa with indoor swimming pool, external vitality pool, treatment and thermal experience rooms, gymnasium and aerobics studio. And then there are the luxurious bedrooms, ranging from contemporary air-conditioned garden rooms, to four-poster rooms and, in the Coach House, self-contained one-, two-

and three-roomed apartments. The splendid oak-panelled lounge leads into Trevelyan, the two-AA Rosette restaurant that overlooks the landscaped gardens and rolling countryside beyond. Here the carte offers English and European dishes, such as skate wing and brown shrimps with grilled fennel; roast stuffed saddle of rabbit; and cannon of lamb with pancetta and thyme potato cake. Relax in front of the grand open fireplace in the lounge, or out on the terrace. Eleven private function suites may be used for weddings, private and business functions.

Recommended in the area

Royal Shakespeare Theatre; Holy Trinity Church; Anne Hathaway's Cottage

West Midlands

Futuristic Selfridges department store building, near the Bull Ring Shopping Centre, Birmingham

Fairlawns Hotel & Spa

★★★ 85% ◎◎ HOTEL

Address: 178 Little Aston Rd, WALSALL, WS9 0NU
Tel: 01922 455122
Fax: 01922 743148
E-mail: reception@fairlawns.co.uk
Website: www.fairlawns.co.uk
Map ref: 6, SP09 **Directions:** Off A452 towards
Aldridge at x-roads with A454. Hotel 600yds on right
Rooms: 58 (8 fmly) (1 GF) (3 smoking)
S £82.50-£167.50; **D** £110-£180 (incl. bkfst)
Facilities: Spa STV FTV ⊗ supervised ♨ ♨ Gym
Dance studio Beauty salon Bathing suite Floatation
suite Sauna Aromatherapy room Wi-fi **Parking:** 150

Owned and run by the Pette family since 1984, this hotel lies in open countryside yet is close to Walsall, Sutton Coldfield and Lichfield and has good motorway access. Standing in nine acres of landscaped grounds, it also boasts an adult health club and spa, and guests have complimentary use of all the facilities, including a 20-metre indoor pool, two gyms, aerobic dance studio and an impressive hydrotherapy suite. Beauty treatments and special spa days can also be arranged. Outside there are tennis courts and a trim trail for fitness enthusiasts as well as pretty gardens to relax in and enjoy. The comfortable bedrooms, some modern, some more traditional, include family rooms and suites. All have modern facilities such as free high-speed Wi-fi access, digital flat-screen TV with Sky Sports channels, hairdryer, ironing facilities and good-quality toiletries (note that some smoking rooms are available). Quieter rooms and suites are located in a separate wing, away from normal hotel activities. The award-winning Fairlawns Restaurant offers lunch and dinner in comfortable, elegant surroundings, with attentive service and imaginative food, especially seafood, and it is little wonder that this is a popular local dining venue.

Recommended in the area

Walsall Art Gallery; Lichfield Cathedral; Cannock Chase, Area of Outstanding Natural Beauty

Isle of Wight

The Needles, Isle of Wight

The Royal Hotel

★★★★ 79% ◉◉ HOTEL

Address: Belgrave Rd, VENTNOR, PO38 1JJ
Tel: 01983 852186
Fax: 01983 855395
E-mail: enquiries@royalhoteliow.co.uk
Website: www.royalhoteliow.co.uk
Map ref: 3, SZ57
Directions: A3055 into Ventnor follow one-way system, after lights left into Belgrave Rd. The hotel is on the right
Rooms: 53 (9 fmly) **S** £105-£140; **D** £175-£275 (incl. bkfst)
Facilities: ⚓ Wi-fi **Parking:** 50 **Notes:** ⊗

This elegant hotel has been a destination for the discerning traveller for more than 150 years. Grand yet intimate, this beautiful early Victorian hotel (built in 1832) has 54 bedrooms and is set in stunning sub-tropical gardens. The tone is English country house with a contemporary twist, using silks, velvets and elegant toile de jouy fabrics. Many of The Royal's principal bedrooms have delightful views over the garden or Ventnor Bay, and all are individually styled and equipped with flat-screen TVs and direct-dial telephones. A visit to the elegant two-Rosette restaurant, with its high ceilings and crystal chandeliers, is an absolute must. Passion, time and culinary invention go into putting together a constantly changing seasonal menu, which makes the most of excellent local produce. And when the weather is good, you can enjoy al fresco dining on the Riviera Terrace complete with stunning sea views. To sum up, this hotel offers award-winning dining, warm, attentive service and a fabulous location – quite simply the perfect destination for a family holiday or stylish getaway.

Recommended in the area:

Coastal walks; Ventnor Botanic Garden; Appuldurcombe House

George Hotel

★★★ ◎◎ HOTEL

Address: Quay St, YARMOUTH, Isle of Wight,
PO41 0PE
Tel: 01983 760331
Fax: 01983 760425
E-mail: res@thegeorge.co.uk
Website: www.thegeorge.co.uk
Map ref: 3, SZ39
Directions: Between castle & pier
Rooms: 19 (1 GF) **S** £137.50; **D** £190-£287
(incl. bkfst)
Facilities: STV Sailing from Yarmouth Mountain
biking Wi-fi **Notes:** ⊗ ⋇ under 10yrs

This delightful 17th-century townhouse hotel enjoys a wonderful location at the water's edge, adjacent to the castle and pier in this bustling harbour town. Steeped in history and heritage, the hotel was once home to the island's Governor, Sir Roberth Holmes who often entertained the then King Charles II. The wow factor greets guests as they cross the large and light entrance and onto the uneven floors of mellow stone flags before reaching the impressive, sweeping staircase. Comfort is key here – the cosy lounge is traditional with tapestry cushions and velvet curtains. Dining takes place in the Brasserie, a bright room with wonderful views over the Solent. Menus are seasonal, contemporary style with a European influence, and fish features regularly. The bedrooms are individually decorated with pretty fabrics and have many thoughtful extras – many of the rooms have views out over the Solent or the busy harbour and two have timber balconies which look out to sea. The George also offers an exciting programme of events throughout the year.

Recommended in the area:
Osborne House; Carisbrooke Castle; Ventnor Botanic Gardens

Wiltshire

The Westbury White Horse, Salisbury Plain

Lucknam Park

★★★★★ ◉◉◉ COUNTRY HOUSE HOTEL
Address: COLERNE, SN14 8AZ
Tel: 01225 742777 **Fax:** 01225 743536
E-mail: reservations@lucknampark.co.uk
Website: www.lucknampark.co.uk
Map ref: 2, ST87 **Directions:** M4 junct 17, A350
towards Chippenham, then A420 towards Bristol
for 3m. At Ford left to Colerne, 3m, right at x-rds,
entrance on right **Rooms:** 42 (18 annexe) (16 GF)
S £315-£1065; **D** £315-£1065
Facilities: Spa STV FTV ◉ ⑤ ❸ Gym Cross country
course Mountain bikes Equestrian centre Five-a-side
football Wi-fi **Parking:** 70 **Notes:** ⊗

Lucknam Park Hotel & Spa is a magnificent listed
Palladian mansion which sits proudly at the end of
a glorious mile-long drive lined with beech and lime
trees. The hotel's individually designed bedrooms,
including 13 impressive suites, are truly luxurious.
For a spot of pampering, head to the stunning
spa, with its 20-metre pool, nine state-of-the-art
treatment rooms, five thermal cabins, indoor and
outdoor hydrotherapy pool, saltwater plunge pool
and innovative skin and bodycare experiences.
Within the spa, The Brasserie, with its open kitchen
and wood-fired oven, offers contemporary and
stylish dining, including a healthy option menu.
For fine-dining at its best, the elegant three AA-
Rosette restaurant The Park, serving accomplished
modern British cuisine, is not to be missed. After
all that wining and dining, you might feel like a bit
of exercise, in which case Lucknam Park has it all:
two floodlit tennis courts, a five-a-side football pitch,
bicycles, walking and jogging trails, croquet and
an extensive equestrian centre are all within the
beautiful grounds. AA Hotel of the Year for England
2010–11.

Recommended in the area

Bath; Lacock Village (NT); Wells Cathedral

Whatley Manor

★★★★★ ◉◉◉◉ HOTEL

Address: Easton Grey, MALMESBURY, SN16 0RB
Tel: 01666 822888
Fax: 01666 826120
E-mail: reservations@whatleymanor.com
Website: www.whatleymanor.com
Map ref: 2, ST98 **Directions:** M4 junct 17, follow
signs to Malmesbury, continue over 2 rdbts. Follow
B4040 & signs for Sherston, hotel 2m on left
Rooms: 23 (4 GF) **D** £305-£865 (incl. bkfst)
Facilities: Spa STV Fishing Gym Cinema Hydro pool
(indoor/outdoor) Wi-fi
Parking: 100 **Notes:** ⚲ under 12yrs

Owners Marco and Alix Landolt once stayed at
Whatley Manor while visiting their son, who was
competing in the Badminton Horse Trials. They fell in
love with it. In 2000, when it came on to the market,
they bought it, then painstakingly brought it back
to its former glory. Dating from the 18th-century, it
stands in 12 acres of land that the Landolts have
turned into 26 distinctive gardens, many based on
1920s plans. Spacious bedrooms, most with views
over these gardens, are individually decorated and
feature Bang & Olufsen sound and vision systems,
and works of art. Several eating options are
available: the Kitchen Garden Terrace for alfresco
breakfasts, lunches and dinners; Le Mazot, a Swiss-
style brasserie; and the four-AA Rosette Dining
Room, where much-acclaimed chef, Martin Burge,
serves classical French cuisine with 21st-century
influences. Examples might be roast partridge with
Morteau sausage; Dover sole with langoustine
mousse and glazed shrimps; and truffle risotto.
Wines can be matched by the sommelier from an
extensive list. On a fine day guests might like to take
a hamper for a picnic in the grounds. The Aquarius
Spa houses one of Britain's largest hydrotherapy
pools. The old Loggia Barn is ideal for wedding
ceremonies.

Recommended in the area
Bath; Cheltenham; Westonbirt Aboretum

Worcestershire

Worcester Cathedral, Worcester

The Granary Hotel & Restaurant

★★★ 80% ◎◎ HOTEL

Address: Heath Ln, Shenstone, KIDDERMINSTER, DY10 4BS
Tel: 01562 777535
Fax: 01562 777722
E-mail: info@granary-hotel.co.uk
Website: www.granary-hotel.co.uk
Map ref: 6, SO87
Directions: On A450 between Stourbridge & Worcester, 1m from Kidderminster
Rooms: 18 (1 fmly) (18 GF) **S** £60-£90; **D** £70-£140 (incl. bkfst)
Facilities: FTV Wi-fi **Parking:** 96

It must have been quite a transformation when, out here in the Worcestershire countryside, a decidedly unglamorous former haulage yard and transport cafe was transformed into this chic boutique hotel. Guests stay in contemporary, en suite bedrooms, and, if they choose one of the two executive suites, can sleep in a four-poster bed made from Indonesian teak. Rooms are well-equipped with extras, including free Wi-fi, digital flat-screen TV and hot drinks tray, and look out over the fields towards Abberley Hill. Public areas include a recently completed cocktail bar, residents' lounge and a two-AA Rosette restaurant. Next door is the hotel's market garden, run along philanthropic lines as a training facility for local people with disabilities, and from where many of the kitchen's fruit, vegetables and herbs come. Dinner might begin with a drink in the new restaurant bar, and then, in the restaurant itself, furnished with Lloyd Loom chairs, perhaps a starter of antipasti, or poached lemon sole with crab mousse; then a main course of Worcestershire lamb fillet with baby shepherd's pie, or pan-fried duck breast with oven-dried morello cherries; and finally a homemade dessert. Light lunches are also available, while a lunchtime carvery is open every day except Mondays and Saturdays.

Recommended in the area

Worcester Cathedral; Shatterford Lakes Wildlife Sanctuary and Fishery; Great Malvern Priory

Cotford Hotel & L'Amuse Bouche Restaurant

★★★ 79% ◉◉ HOTEL

Address: 51 Graham Rd, MALVERN, WR14 2HU
Tel: 01684 572427
Fax: 01684 572952
E-mail: reservations@cotfordhotel.co.uk
Website: www.cotfordhotel.co.uk
Map ref: 2, SO74 **Directions:** From Worcester
follow signs to Malvern on A449. Left into Graham Rd
signed town centre, hotel on right
Rooms: 15 (3 fmly) (1 GF) **S** £69.50-£85; **D** £105-£125
(incl. bkfst) **Facilities:** STV ⤴ Wi-fi **Parking:** 15

This Victorian gothic hotel is set in mature
landscaped grounds at the foot of the beautiful
Malvern Hills. It was built in 1851 as a summer
residence for the Bishop of Worcester, and his
private chapel now houses the award-winning
L'amuse Bouche Restaurant. It is here that guests
will find a taste of French-style cuisine in a quaint
English setting. Before or after a meal, relax in
front of an open fire in the piano lounge or bar, or
perhaps enjoy a drink out on the terrace during the
warmer summer months. The hotel's landscaped
gardens are a joy to explore. The hotel and
restaurant were extensively refurbished in 2011,
but the history of this charming property is still
apparent throughout – from the Bishop's room to
the garden room in the coach house, all the rooms
are brimming with character. Positioned only a few
minutes' walk from historic Malvern town centre
yet with the feeling that it is miles from anywhere,
guests will enjoy the best of both worlds at this
hotel. In an Area of Outstanding Natural Beauty,
Malvern is rich in heritage, the arts and an amazing
range of activities.

Recommended in the area

The Malvern Hills (AONB); Great Malvern Priory; Little
Malvern Court

The Cottage in the Wood Hotel

★★★ 86% ◎◎ HOTEL

Address: Holywell Rd, Malvern Wells, MALVERN,
WR14 4LG
Tel: 01684 588860
Fax: 01684 560662
E-mail: reception@cottageinthewood.co.uk
Website: www.cottageinthewood.co.uk
Map ref: 2, SO74
Directions: 3m S of Great Malvern off A449,
500yds N of B4209, on opposite side of road
Rooms: 30 (23 annexe) (9 GF) **S** £79-£121;
D £99-£198 (incl. bkfst)
Facilities: FTV Wi-fi **Parking:** 40

A uniquely situated hotel perched high on the Malvern Hills, with a panoramic view of the Severn Plain which fringes the Cotswolds. The 30-mile views are no less than stupendous, but you'll also find a hotel which has been in the same family ownership for 25 years, and is run by a team of enthusiastic people who really enjoy what they do. The comfortable bedrooms, most with large Vi-Spring beds, are spread between three buildings – the main house, which was originally a Georgian dower house, Beech Cottage, which was once a cider house, and The Pinnacles (here you'll find the largest rooms with the most spectacular views). Outlook is the name aptly given to the hotel's acclaimed restaurant, with its floor-to-ceiling windows offering diners a stunning aspect. It would be easy for the food to be upstaged by a vista like that, but the kitchen steps up to the mark, using quality local, seasonal ingredients to produce some ambitious but winning modern British dishes. The extensive wine list offers plenty to excite, too. After a hearty breakfast or an indulgent lunch, you can stroll directly onto the open tracts of the Malvern Hills and gaze from the lofty tops where Elgar gained inspiration for the Dream of Gerontius and other famous works.

Recommended in the area

The Three Counties Showground; Worcester; Gloucester

East Riding of Yorkshire

Flamborough Head Lighthouse, Flamborough

Lowther Hotel

★★★ 80% HOTEL

Address: Aire St, GOOLE, DN14 5QW
Tel: 01405 767999
Fax: 01405 769321
Website: www.lowtherhotel.co.uk
Map ref: 7, SE72 **Directions:** M62 junct 36, A614, follow town centre signs. At clock tower rdbt right into Aire St. Hotel at end on left
Rooms: 14 (1 fmly) **S** £85; **D** frE99 (incl. bkfst)
Facilities: FTV ♫ Wi-fi
Parking: 14
Notes: ⊛

The Lowther is a grand Georgian Hotel built in 1824 and was recently granted status as a Grade II* Listed Building. The building holds important historical artefacts such as the Minton tiled floor entrance to the hotel and murals in the private function rooms are nearly 200 years old. All of the 14 bedrooms are en suite, as is the Bartholomew suite. All are luxurious and individually designed and feature 12" pocket-sprung beds, large flat-screen TVs, IPod docking station/alarm, tea and coffee making facilities. Dining options start with the stylish Burlington restaurant which uses the freshest and finest of of ingredients and is a popular choice for a four-course Sunday lunch. Meals are accompanied by a variety of wines from the restaurant's extensive wine list. For a lighter bite, head for the New Bridge Lounge where you can enjoy a snack, relaxing drink or afternoon tea settled in one of the cosy leather armchairs. If it's a cocktail or eveing drink you're after then go to the Absolut Vodka Bar where you'll be well looked after. The hotel is a popular wedding venue and is also well placed for business events – there are four good function rooms and a half-acre private courtyard.

Recommended in the area

Goole Museum and Art Gallery; Howden; Yorkshire Waterways Museum

North Yorkshire

Staithes, North York Moors National Park

Rudding Park Hotel, Spa & Golf

★ ★ ★ ★ ◉◉ HOTEL

Address: Rudding Park, Follifoot, HARROGATE,
HG3 1JH
Tel: 01423 871350 **Fax:** 01423 872286
E-mail: reservations@ruddingpark.com
Website: www.ruddingpark.co.uk
Map ref: 7, SE35 **Directions:** From A61 at rdbt
with A658 take York exit, follow signs to Rudding Park
Rooms: 90 (31 GF) **S** from £112; **D** from £133
(incl. bkfst)
Facilities: Spa Gym ♪ 18-hole Hawtree Course
6-hole short course 14-seat private cinema Wi-fi
Parking: 250 **Notes:** ⊛

Award-winning Rudding Park sits in 300 acres of
beautiful parkland, three miles south of the spa
town of Harrogate. The stylish 90 bedroom hotel
also features a spa, gym and 14-seat cinema.
The hotel, which adjoins the Regency house, was
extended in 2010 with larger bedrooms, many
with private terraces or balconies, and seven with
their own en suite steam room, spa bath or sauna.
The Clocktower restaurant has much to admire: a
hand-made pink crystal chandelier, Moroccan wall
lights, hand painted Brazilian wallpaper, waltzer
seating and two AA Rosettes. Head chef Eddie
Gray's seasonal menus include the Yorkshire Menu
featuring ingredients sourced within a 75-mile
radius of Rudding Park – Sykes House Farm pork

belly and black pudding terrine, for instance. The
stylish bar leads to the Conservatory, where a
400-year-old Catalonian olive tree seems to thrive.
The Spa consists of four treatment rooms, including
a hammam and two relaxation areas. The 18-hole,
par 72 golf course, PGA professional tuition and
floodlit driving range constitute what is reckoned to
be the most comprehensive golfing facility in
the North.

Recommended in the area

Harewood House; Castle Howard; Jorvik Viking
Centre

Black Swan Hotel

★★★ 81% ◎◎ HOTEL

Address: Market Place, HELMSLEY, YO62 5BJ
Tel: 01439 770466
Fax: 01439 770174
E-mail: enquiries@blackswan-helmsley.co.uk
Website: www.blackswan-helmsley.co.uk
Map ref: 7, SE68
Directions: A1 junct 49, A168, A170 east, hotel
14m from Thirsk
Rooms: 45 (4 fmly) **S** £92-£157; **D** £132-£197
(incl. bkfst)
Facilities: STV Wi-fi
Parking: 50

An historic coaching inn turned boutique hotel, located in the heart of a pretty village on the edge of the North Yorks Moors. Its left-hand wing, the black-and-white timbered part, is Elizabethan, while the rest is largely Georgian, which together create a very attractive frontage. Antiques appear throughout the interior, while bedrooms are finished in colours that reflect the moss, heather and stone of the moorland, each room is en suite, with thick duvets, soft towels and bathrobes, luxury toiletries, TV, and hot drinks tray. The bar area's recent complete makeover has endowed it with a zinc-topped counter, silk, leather and wool plaid. The Rutland Restaurant's two AA Rosettes recognise the quality of its three menus – a monthly fixed price, a six-course Signature, and a seasonal carte, sourced from within a 30-mile radius of the hotel. Typical dishes include pan-fried halibut; Waterford House beef fillet; and roasted Lepping duck breast. On Wednesday to Sunday evenings, the award-winning Tearoom is transformed into an informal brasserie. Just 200 yards around the corner from the hotel is the Verbena Spa, where guests can, for a charge, use the saunarium, aromatherapy rooms, monsoon shower, ice cave, hot tub and heated outdoor pool.

Recommended in the area

Rievaulx Abbey; Helmsley Castle; Duncombe Park

Dunsley Hall

★★★ 82% ◎ COUNTRY HOUSE HOTEL

Address: Dunsley, WHITBY, YO21 3TL
Tel: 01947 893437
Fax: 01947 893505
E-mail: reception@dunsleyhall.com
Website: www.dunsleyhall.com
Map ref: 7, SE81
Directions: 3m N of Whitby, signed off A171
Rooms: 26 (2 fmly) (10 GF) **S** fr £105; **D** £159-£208
(incl. bkfst)
Facilities: ⅃ Putt green Wi-fi
Parking: 30
Notes: ⊗

A Victorian shipping magnate built this mellow-stone hideaway in four acres of landscaped gardens, full today (and who knows, maybe then too) of beautiful rhododendrons. Dunsley Hall is now a family-run country-house hotel, with oak-panelling, stained-glass windows and other surviving period gems to ensure a pleasing blend of the old with the best facilities a hotel of today can offer. In the main house, accommodation is available in traditionally designed, individually furnished bedrooms, some with four-poster beds; rooms in the ground floor extension are contemporary yet elegant, while a self-catering cottage provides all the amenities for an independent stay. Wherever you choose, you'll have a view of the grounds, countryside or coast. With Whitby so close you can expect seafood – trio of salmon, red snapper and king prawns, for example – to feature prominently on the Oak Room restaurant's menu, while lighter lunchtime and early evening alternatives are provided in the Pyman Bar. In addition to seafood, local produce is the foundation of all menus. Guests may visit the hotel's working farm at nearby Ramsdale, where 50 acres of farmland are available for outdoor pursuits and team-building events, so bring wellingtons and a warm coat.

Recommended in the area

North Yorks Moors Railway; Captain Cook Museum; Castle Howard

The Churchill Hotel

★★★ 81% ◉◉ HOTEL

Address: 65 Bootham, YORK, YO30 7DQ
Tel: 01904 644456
Fax: 01904 663322
E-mail: info@churchillhotel.com
Website: www.churchillhotel.com
Map ref: 7, SE65
Directions: On A19 (Bootham), W from York
Minster, hotel 250yds on right
Rooms: 32 (4 fmly) (5 GF) **S** £89.95-£134.95;
D £144.90 (incl. bkfst)
Facilities: ♬ Wi-fi
Parking: 40

Built around 1827, this superb example of a late-Georgian mansion stands in its own grounds, a short walk from the Minster and York's other major attractions. Within, period features and artefacts relating to Winston Churchill are incorporated into smart contemporary design. The bedrooms vary in size and style, but share the common values of attention to detail, comfort and quality, their strong lines and bold colours complementing well the original features. The executive bedrooms present vibrant design, crisp white linen on deep, comfortable beds, and high-quality, modern en suite bathrooms. Among the varied features of the suites are bespoke four-poster beds, free-standing copper baths, walk-in showers and hand-crafted furniture designed specifically for the hotel. In the Piano Bar & Restaurant, premier local produce features in innovative dishes such as olive-crusted Newstead Farm lamb loin with fennel, vitelotte potato, aubergine and broad beans; Yorkshire Dales beef fillet with smoked pommes purée, ox tongue, girolles, turnips and kale; market fish of the day; and wild mushroom and truffle risotto with Parmesan. One of the city's nearby attractions is the Theatre Royal, and guests can eat before a performance, either in the restaurant or on the terrace overlooking the historic Bootham district.

Recommended in the area

York Minster; The Shambles; York City Walls

The Grange

★★★★ 77% ◉◉ HOTEL

Address: 1 Clifton, YORK, YO30 6AA
Tel: 01904 644744
Fax: 01904 612453
E-mail: info@grangehotel.co.uk
Website: www.grangehotel.co.uk
Map ref: 7, SE65
Directions: On A19 York/Thirsk road, approx
500yds from city centre
Rooms: 36 (6 GF) **S** £125-£227; **D** £140-£242
(incl. bkfst)
Facilities: STV FTV Use of nearby health club Wi-fi
Parking: 26

This superbly restored Regency townhouse is in the city but feels just like an inviting country house. Open fires in the cooler months in the sumptuous Morning Room and elegant Library and Drawing Room create an ambience perfect for those who wish to relax and unwind. Attention to detail is top priority here including efficient room service in the luxurious bedrooms, which include three with four-posters. Six rooms are air conditioned and feature waterproof plasma TVs at the foot of the baths. The Ivy Brasserie, with two AA Rosettes, complements the hotel's stylish character, serving classic brasserie dishes that make good use of the highest quality, locally-sourced, seasonal produce whenever possible. The relaxed and informal New York Grill and Cafe Bar in the brick vaulted cellars provides an alternative dining venue that offers brunch, light bites, afternoon tea, lunch and dinner. Open all day and evening Monday to Friday, for lunch and dinner on Saturday and dinner on Sunday, it proves popular with both guests and locals alike. There are first class facilities for conferences, meetings and private dining with free Wi-fi provided throughout. The Grange is licensed for civil wedding ceremonies and there is free private parking, subject to availability, at the rear of the hotel.

Recommended in the area

York Minster; National Railway Museum; Castle Howard

South Yorkshire

Damflask Reservoir, near Sheffield

Best Western Premier Mount Pleasant

★★★★ 80% ⊛ HOTEL

Address: Great North Rd, ROSSINGTON, DN11 0HW
Tel: 01302 868696 & 868219 **Fax:** 01302 865130
E-mail: reception@mountpleasant.co.uk
Website: www.mountpleasant.co.uk
Map ref: 7, SK69
Directions: On A638 (Great North Road) between Bawtry & Doncaster
Rooms: 56 (18 fmly) (27 GF) **S** £79-£99; **D** £99-£119 (incl. bkfst) **Facilities:** Spa STV Beauty salon Wi-fi
Parking: 140 **Notes:** ⊛

This charming 18th-century hotel, once a farm, stands in 100 acres of wooded parkland on the old Great North Road, now the quiet A638, thanks to the creation decades ago of the distant A1(M) motorway. Bedrooms and suites are beautifully and individually designed and furnished; standard bedrooms all have a double bed, en suite bathroom, hot drinks tray, desk or dressing table, hairdryer, wardrobe, trouser press, iron and ironing board. Executive rooms are the next step up, being more spacious with a settee and, in some, a special feature bed. A third of the rooms are the more opulently furnished Junior Suites, with a lounge area. Proud of its AA Rosette, the Garden Restaurant's dinner menu tempts with fresh fish every day; braised shin of beef; herb-crusted rack of lamb; and sweet onion and ricotta cheesecake. Dishes like these are complemented by pastas, risottos and other light snacks and bar meals in the lounges, where you can also sup hot beverages and alcoholic drinks at any time of day. Carvery meals are served to parties of six and more, but must be pre-booked. For pure self-indulgence, the Therapie Health and Wellness Centre offers a variety of treatments to benefit the body, and possibly even the soul.

Recommended in the area

Darlington Railway Museum; Raby Castle; South Yorkshire Aircraft Museum

Whitley Hall

★★★★ 78% ◎◎ HOTEL

Address: Elliott Ln, Grenoside, SHEFFIELD, S35 8NR
Tel: 0114 245 4444 & 246 0456
Fax: 0114 245 5414
E-mail: reservations@whitleyhall.com
Website: www.whitleyhall.com
Map ref: 7, SK49
Directions: A61 past football ground, 2m, right just before Norfolk Arms, left at bottom of hill. Hotel on left
Rooms: 32 (3 annexe) (2 fmly) (8 GF) **S** fr £80.25; **D** fr £90.50 (incl. bkfst) **Facilities:** STV FTV Wi-fi
Parking: 100 **Notes:** ⊗

Peacocks strut across the lawns of this 16th-century, ivy-clad mansion, where you can walk in the footsteps of Mary Queen of Scots. Standing proudly in 20 acres of landscaped grounds and gardens in the rolling countryside of South Yorkshire, it would be easy to forget that the M1 motorway is less than two miles away. Of its many attractions, the very pretty grassed courtyard between the two wings takes some beating, while in the older part of the hotel, the public rooms are full of dark wood and interesting architectural features, and command some great views. The individually styled bedrooms, two with four-posters, are furnished in keeping with the country house setting. Some in the recently opened Parker Wing have a Juliet balcony, and regular guests apparently always book well in advance to secure their favourite room and its special view. The oak-panelled restaurant has two AA Rosettes for its frequently changing menus, on which might appear starters of shredded slow-cooked ham hock; and seared Scottish king scallops; followed by charred sirloin of Charolais beef; and fillet of line-caught sea bass; and dessert of peach carpaccio, accompanied by a wine from the internationally stocked cellar. Sunday lunch is popular and it is wise to book.

Recommended in the area

Botanical Gardens; Peveril Castle; Kelham Island Museum

Langsett, on the edge of the Peak District National Park

Isle of Man

Snaefell Mountain Railway, Laxey

Sefton

★★★★ 81% ◉◉ HOTEL

Address: Harris Promenade, DOUGLAS,
Isle of Man, IM1 2RW
Tel: 01624 645500
Fax: 01624 676004
E-mail: info@seftonhotel.co.im
Website: www.seftonhotel.co.im
Map ref: 5, SC37
Directions: 500yds from ferry dock on promenade
Rooms: 96 (3 fmly)
Facilities: ◉ Gym Cycle hire Steam room
Library ♫ Wi-fi
Parking: 36 **Notes:** ◈

This finely restored, grand Victorian hotel is right
on the prom overlooking the Irish Sea, close to
the island capital's main shopping and business
districts. A modern extension is centred round a
striking atrium and water garden. Standard rooms
offer plenty of space, and each is provided with
wireless internet, fridge, safe, ironing board and
the latest in TV entertainment options. Those that
overlook the atrium have their own balconies and
king-size bed, while each of the nine suites offers
up to 90 square metres of high-ceilinged, period-
detailed space overlooking Douglas Bay. The Gallery
Restaurant was recently awarded its second AA
Rosette for the quality of the locally sourced dishes,
such as pan-fried sea bream; fillet of Manx beef;

and roasted loin of Yorkshire red deer. Sir Norman's,
named after the late Norman Wisdom, who lived
much of his later life on the island, is open all
day for meals, snacks and drinks; on Fridays and
Saturdays a resident pianist ivory-tickles away.
Consider a three-course set dinner before a show
at the magnificent old Gaiety Theatre next door. The
ground floor library provides two internet access
PCs for use free of charge, daily newspapers and
reading material, and board games.

Recommended in the area

Coastal path walks; Peel Castle; Steam Railway trip
to Port Erin

Channel Islands

A golden-sand beach on the island of Alderney

Cobo Bay Hotel

★★★ 84% ◉◉ HOTEL

Address: Coast Rd, Cobo, CASTEL, GY5 7HB
Tel: 01481 257102
Fax: 01481 254542
E-mail: reservations@cobobayhotel.com
Website: www.cobobayhotel.com
Map ref: 15
Directions: From airport turn right, follow road to
W coast at L'Eree. Turn right onto coast road for 3m
to Cobo Bay. Hotel on right
Rooms: 34 (4 fmly) **S** £49-£89; **D** £79-£190 (incl.
bkfst) **Facilities:** STV FTV Gym 2 exercise bikes
Sauna Wi-fi **Parking:** 60 **Notes:** ⊗

A modern, family-run hotel on the seafront overlooking a beautiful sandy beach. The well-equipped en suite bedrooms are tastefully decorated, the most sought after, of course, being those with a sea-facing balcony. Amenities rank alongside those you'd expect in a higher rated hotel, including plasma screen satellite TV, free Wi-fi, personal safe, bathrobes and slippers. Some offer wet rooms with a shower only; rooms for families and the disabled are available too. The stylish restaurant, one of only four on Guernsey with two AA Rosettes, specialises in fresh local fish and shellfish. Their brand new menu features seared diver-caught scallops, a pan fried fillet of brill, chargrilled prime Irish beef and an aubergine and ratatouille stack with warm pesto dressing. The Beach Terrace is also open all day throughout the summer for al fresco dining and afternoon tea, whilst the elegant Chesterfield lounge creates a warm and friendly atmosphere for a relaxing drink in the evening. A complimentary health suite featuring a hot tub, sauna and steam room is available, as well as a private sun terrace and the use of the heated outdoor pool at Cobo Bay's sister hotel, The Farmhouse.

Recommended in the area

Saumarez Park and Guernsey Folk and Costume Museum; Fort Hommet

La Barbarie

★★★ 81% ◎ HOTEL

Address: Saints Rd, Saints Bay, ST MARTIN,
Guernsey, GY4 6ES
Tel: 01481 235217
Fax: 01481 235208
E-mail: reservations@labarbariehotel.com
Website: www.labarbariehotel.com
Map ref: 15
Rooms: 30 (8 GF) **S** £38.50-£75.50; **D** £77-£136
(incl. bkfst)
Facilities: ⚲ Wi-fi
Parking: 50
Notes: ⊗

This fine hotel is named after the Barbary Coast pirates who kidnapped and held to ransom the house's owner in the 17th century. A hotel since 1950, it lies in a peaceful green valley close to some of the lovely bays, coves and cliffs in the south of the island, and retains all of its historic charm, not least in the lovely residents' lounge, with its old beams and open fireplace. The en suite accommodation comes with every modern comfort, and includes some two-room suites with inter-connecting doors, ideal for families with children. Some self-catering apartments are also available. Dining here is serious but far from pretentious – there are excellent choices and fresh local ingredients form the basis of the interesting menus. The fixed-price four-course dinner menu is very good value, while for something lighter you can choose from the bar or poolside menu. For seafood lovers, La Barbarie Seafood Extravaganza is an absolute must and features the freshest of produce. The poolside patio is the perfect secluded spot for a lazy lunch or quiet aperitif before dinner. The hotel is ideally placed for walkers, cyclists, horse riders and joggers.

Recommended in the area

Saumarez Manor; Castle Cornet; South Coast
Cliff Path

Fermain Valley

★★★★ 79% ◎◎ HOTEL

Address: Fermain Ln, ST PETER PORT, Guernsey,
GY1 1ZZ
Tel: 01481 235666 & 0800 316 0314
Fax: 01481 235413
E-mail: info@fermainvalley.com
Website: www.fermainvalley.com
Map ref: 15 **Directions:** Turn left from airport, take
Forest Rd, turn right on Le Route de Sausmarez, then
right into Fermain Lane. Hotel 100mtrs on left
Rooms: 43 (11 annexe) (2 fmly) (6 GF) **S** £102-£184;
D £135-£245 (incl. bkfst) **Facilities:** STV FTV ⓧ
Cinema Sauna Wi-fi **Parking:** 40 **Notes:** ⊗

Peaceful and secluded yet conveniently situated
just five minutes from Guernsey's charming harbour
capital, St Peter Port, the four-star Fermain Valley
Hotel offers the perfect place for a relaxing break.
The hotel has 43 exquisitely decorated bedrooms,
all unique and designed with comfort in mind.
A long list of thoughtful in-room extras includes
bathrobes, fridge, flat-screen TV, Wi-fi, hairdryer,
sherry decanter and complimentary tea and
coffee. Some rooms even benefit from private
balconies. The award-winning Valley Restaurant
offers elegant surroundings and a sophisticated
menu complemented by fine wines. In summer, the
Terrace – a mulit-level outside decking area – offers
alfresco dining with the wow factor of stunning and

far-reaching views down the pretty valley and out to
sea. The chic Rock Garden bar and restaurant is a
stylish place for a drink with a snack or a meal. The
hotel also has an indoor heated pool and sauna, a
residents' private cinema showing the latest films,
complimentary Wi-fi throughout, and ample facilities
for meetings and functions. The friendly staff are
dedicated to providing the very highest standards
of personal service, whether your stay here is for
business or pleasure. Special offers and breaks are
also available.

Recommended in the area

Castle Cornet; tax-free shopping; cliff walks

Farmhouse Hotel

★★★★ 82% ◎ SMALL HOTEL

Address: Route Des Bas Courtils, ST SAVIOUR,
Guernsey, GY7 9YF
Tel: 01481 264181
Fax: 01481 266272
E-mail: enquiries@thefarmhouse.gg
Website: www.thefarmhouse.gg
Map ref: 15
Directions: From airport, left to 1st lights. Left then
left again around runway perimeter. After 1m left at
x-rds. Hotel 100mtrs on right
Rooms: 14 (7 fmly) **D** £69-£250 (incl. bkfst)
Facilities: STV ↺ ⅃ ♫ Wi-fi **Parking:** 80 **Notes:** ⊗

Originally a 15th century farmhouse, three
generations of the Nussbaumer family have
overseen its transition into the beautiful hotel it is
today, having created a mix of individually designed
boutique bedrooms and suites complete with
luxury bathrooms featuring large walk-in showers
and under-floor heating. Some offer balconies
overlooking the gardens, the heated outdoor pool
and the surrounding countryside, whilst beautiful
natural prints, oak beams, warm stone tiles and
Egyptian cotton sheets all come as standard. The
cuisine is worthy of an AA Rosette and can be
enjoyed in a variety of dining areas, inside or out.
The seasonal menu may feature a loin of hogget
with smoked shoulder, neck fillet and kidney
pudding with cassis vinegar jus to be enjoyed by
the fire, whilst during the summer months you
might enjoy a whole roasted Dover sole on the
poolside terrace or a delicious picnic on the lawn.
Surrounded by tranquil lanes,in the rural heart of
Guernsey, The Farmhouse is perfectly placed for the
many attractions this wonderful, friendly little island
has to offer – just minutes from beautiful sandy
beaches, spectacular cliff walks and the island's
busy capital, St Peter Port.

Recommended in the area

Bruce Russell & Son goldsmiths; The Little Chapel;
German Occupation Museum

St Brelade's Bay Hotel

★★★★ 80% HOTEL

Address: ST BRELADE, Jersey, JE3 8EF
Tel: 01534 746141
Fax: 01534 747278
Website: www.stbreladesbayhotel.com
Map ref: 15
Directions: The hotel is positioned on the southwest corner of the island
Rooms: 74 (8 fmly) **D** £140-£304 Suites from £246
Facilities: STV ⚲ Putt green 🛶 Games room Table tennis ♫ Wi-fi
Parking: 60
Notes: ⊗

Separated by no more than a lawn from one of the most stunning beaches in the Channel Islands, and set in five acres of beautiful gardens, this 19th-century hotel could hardly be better positioned. The entire building was lavishly refurbished in early 2011 and offers a good choice of accommodation: there are family rooms, which share a connecting bathroom, rooms with a view of the garden, and rooms with a balcony overlooking the sea. More exclusive are the five spacious suites, each of which is provided with a telescope for scanning the bay. Formal dining takes place in the Bay Restaurant, where the wide menu choice ranges from simple and light to modern 'Jersey-inspired' dishes using locally sourced produce, such as its take on 'surf 'n' turf', grilled tournedos with grilled lobster tails, tarragon jus and chilli hollandaise. Lunch in the Petit Port Café is a more casual affair where food is cooked on the outdoor grill, overlooking the sparkling heated swimming pool, and with the bay in the background, this offers open-air potential, whatever the weather. During the high season there is a disco, a magician, jazz, or entertainment of some sort most evenings.

Recommended in the area

Corbière Lighthouse; St Brelade's Bay Beach; Jersey Lavender Farm

The Club Hotel & Spa

★★★★ ◎◎◎◎ TOWN HOUSE HOTEL

Address: Green St, ST HELIER, Jersey, JE2 4UH
Tel: 01534 876500
Fax: 01534 720371
E-mail: reservations@theclubjersey.com
Website: www.theclubjersey.com
Map ref: 15
Directions: 5 mins walk from main shopping centre
Rooms: 46 (4 fmly) (4 GF) (5 smoking) **S** £99-£215;
D £99-£215 (incl. bkfst)
Facilities: Spa STV FTV ⊗ ↖ Sauna Steam room
Salt cabin Hydrothermal bench Rasul room Wi-fi
Parking: 32 **Notes:** ⊛

This swish, town house hotel in the centre of Jersey's capital features stylish, contemporary decor throughout. The fully air-conditioned bedrooms and suites have large, full-height windows opening on to a balustrade, while the beds are dressed with Frette Egyptian cotton sheets and duck-down duvets. All rooms are equipped with safes, flat-screen TVs, DVD/CD players, Bang & Olufsen portable phones and private bars. Granite bathrooms include power showers, robes, slippers and aromatherapy products. Free Wi-fi access is available throughout the hotel. The dining choice includes the award-winning Bohemia Bar and Restaurant, where a typical main course might be roast local turbot with braised frog's leg, minted peas, herb gnocchi and chicken emulsion. Overlooking the outdoor pool is The Club Café, a contemporary New York-style restaurant offering breakfast, light lunches and dinner. Several hours might easily be spent in The Spa, starting with a relaxing swim in the salt pool, followed by mud treatment in the rasul (a traditional Arabian ritual cleansing) room, and finally a spell on one of the luxurious loungers. Two luxury meeting rooms with oak tables and stylish leather chairs can accommodate 50 attendees theatre style or up to 32 as a boardroom.

Recommended in the area

German Underground Hospital; Jersey Zoo; Mount Orgeuil

Pomme d'Or Hotel

★★★★ 80% @@ HOTEL
Address: Liberation Square, ST HELIER, Jersey,
JE1 3UF
Tel: 01534 880110
Fax: 01534 737781
E-mail: enquiries@pommedorhotel.com
Website: www.pommedorhotel.com
Map ref: 15
Directions: Opposite harbour
Rooms: 143 (3 fmly) **D** £89-£200 (incl. bkfst)
Facilities: STV Use of Aquadome at Merton Hotel.
Wi-fi
Notes: ⊗

Splendidly located in the centre of the island capital, this landmark hotel has been looking after business and leisure travellers for more than 175 years. Impressively appointed, air-conditioned rooms include a writing desk, flat-screen TV with movies on demand, free broadband internet, quadruple-glazed windows and all-cotton linen. The twin beds in the Harbour View rooms can be zipped together to form a super-king, and in the larger Premier rooms, which look out over Liberation Square and the yacht marina, there's a raised lounge area with a sofa and writing desk. Such is the hotel's place in island life that most Jersey residents have probably dined in the two-AA Rosette restaurant at some stage, or eaten Sunday lunch in the Harbour Room, or even

indulged in a Friday seafood buffet of gravadlax, gambas, langoustines, mussels, crab claws, oysters, whole dressed salmon, and much more. In the evenings, with its fine wines, beers, spirits and cocktails, the Café Bar becomes a focal point for St. Helier's social scene. Hotel guests can enjoy the swimming pool with water slides, spa pools, sauna and steam room, and fitness centre at nearby sister hotel, the Merton, which has the Leisure Club and Aquadome, where guests can learn how to 'ride a wave'.

Recommended in the area

Elizabeth Castle; Corbière Lighthouse; St Brelade's Bay Beach

The Royal Yacht

★★★★ 83% ◉◉ HOTEL

Address: The Weighbridge, ST HELIER, Jersey,
JE2 3NF
Tel: 01534 720511
Fax: 01534 767729
E-mail: reception@theroyalyacht.com
Website: www.theroyalyacht.com
Map ref: 15
Directions: In town centre, opposite marina
and harbour
Rooms: 110 **S** £135; **D** £175-£750 (incl. bkfst)
Facilities: Spa STV ⑤ Gym 𝄞 Wi-fi
Notes: ⊗

What is thought to be St. Helier's oldest hotel, having been founded in the 1820s, reopened as this modern luxury hotel in 2007. Back in 1848, members of the French Royal Family, forced to flee trouble at home, took refuge here, and during World War II it was commandeered by the German Navy. Public areas are decorated and finished to a high standard in a warm, modern style. Bedrooms are air conditioned, with separate bath and, in most, a shower, satellite TV, DVD/CD player, free Wi-fi, hairdryer, hot drinks tray and use of the hotel's luxury Spa Sirène. Rooms with a balcony or terrace overlook the harbour, a tranquil park or the courtyard of Jersey Museum. There are several bars – The Drift, P.O.S.H and The Cabin, and three

places to eat. Chic and sophisticated Restaurant Sirocco looks out over the glittering waterfront and serves a six-course tasting menu with wines. Dishes from the Sirocco kitchen are classic Jersey style with a modern twist . The open-air Café Zephyr's brasserie menu is known for its breakfasts and all-day hot oriental salads, sushi and sashimi, Asian-spiced meats, and its signature dish of chilli squid. And finally, there's The Grill, which serves what you would expect and maintains the standard of cuisine served throughout the hotel.

Recommended in the area

St Brelade's Beach; Jersey War Tunnels;
The Maritime Museum

Longueville Manor

★★★★★ ◉◉◉ HOTEL

Address: ST SAVIOUR, JE2 7WF
Tel: 01534 725501
Fax: 01534 731613
E-mail: info@longuevillemanor.com
Website: www.longuevillemanor.com
Map ref: 15
Directions: A3 E from St Helier towards Gorey.
Hotel 1m on left
Rooms: 30 (1 annexe) (7 GF) (6 smoking)
S £195-£370; **D** £220-£630 (incl. bkfst)
Facilities: STV ↖ ♨ ☞ Wi-fi
Parking: 40

For more than 60 years this charming hotel has been run by the Lewis family, and is currently owned by Malcolm and Patricia Lewis. The refurbished 14th-century manor house is set in its own wooded valley, with 15 acres of grounds including vibrant flower gardens and a lake complete with black swans, yet is only five minutes from St Helier. The hotel is stylishly presented, with warm colour schemes, fine antique furnishings and lavish floral displays. The tranquil location, historic setting and excellent food invite complete relaxation, with a tennis court and a heated swimming pool to enjoy, plus a poolside bar and barbecue. The bedrooms are each named after a type of rose and come with a chaise longue, Egyptian cotton sheets, wide-screen TV and DVD/CD player and a cordless phone. Delicate touches include fruit, flowers and homemade biscuits. Additional in-room equipment includes a safe, hairdryer, iron and ironing board, and rooms on the ground floor have a private patio overlooking the garden. The hotel's restored Victorian kitchen garden provides abundantly for the dining room, including delicacies from the Victorian glass houses. The restaurant offers a fine dining experience with a Master Sommelier to advise on wines.

Recommended in the area

Royal Jersey Golf Club; Durrell Wildlife Conservation Trust; Mont Orgeuil Castle

SCOTLAND

Eilean Donan Castle, Loch Duich, on the west coast of Scotland

Raemoir House Hotel

★★★ 85% ◎◎ COUNTRY HOUSE HOTEL

Address: Raemoir, BANCHORY, AB31 4ED
Tel: 01330 824884
E-mail: hotel@raemoir.com
Website: www.raemoir.com
Map ref: 14, NO79
Directions: 2 miles north of Banchory at the junction of the A980 and B977
Rooms: 20 (6 annexe) (2 fmly) **S** fr £125; **D** fr £140 (incl. bkfst)
Facilities: FTV Putt green ⚓ Wi-fi
Parking: 20

The recently refurbished Raemoir, once known as the Claridges of the North, stands in eleven acres of secluded lawns and parkland, surrounded by 3,500 acres of hills and forest. Two distinct buildings house the bedrooms: the older is the Ha'Hoose (Hall House), built in 1715, and in front of it is the Georgian Mansion, a hotel since 1943. Elegantly traditional in style, most rooms have a bath and a shower, flat-screen digital TV and Wi-fi. Some have a four-poster, and others overlook the gardens and beyond. Meals are served in three areas: the Big Fish Bar, dominated by a 96lb monster that didn't manage to get away; the Drawing Room, historically the Oval Ballroom, and still used as such, with Victorian flocked walls and gilt-wood mirrors; and finally, the wood-panelled Dining Room, whose vast windows look out over the grounds. Holding two AA Rosettes for its food since 1996, it offers a short fixed-price dinner menu, typically featuring chump of lamb; fillet of veal; supreme of chicken; and truffle, green pea and tarragon risotto. Weather permitting, outdoor dining brings with it a chance of spotting the resident family of woodpeckers. Near Banchory is the hotel's sister restaurant, the award-winning Milton.

Recommended in the area

Drum Castle & Garden; Falls of Feugh; Banchory Museum

Meldrum House Country Hotel & Golf Course

★★★★ 79% ◎◎ COUNTRY HOUSE HOTEL

Address: OLDMELDRUM, AB51 0AE
Tel: 01651 872294
Fax: 01651 872464
E-mail: enquiries@meldrumhouse.co.uk
Website: www.meldrumhouse.com
Map ref: 14, NJ82 **Directions:** 11m from
Aberdeen on A947 (Aberdeen to Banff road)
Rooms: 24 (13 annexe) (1 fmly) (6 GF) **D** £120-£180
(incl. bkfst)
Facilities: FTV ↕ 18 Putt green ॐ Wi-fi **Parking:** 70

Standing in 240 acres of parkland and considerably remodelled since it was built in the 13th century, the L-shaped baronial mansion of today largely took shape in the 1830s. It opened as a hotel in the 1950s. Stay overnight in one of the individually designed, en suite bedrooms in the main building, some of which contain old Meldrum artefacts; or in one of the five en suite rooms in the spacious private Chain Lodge, with a fully fitted kitchen, large lounge and separate dining area. Alternatively, you might prefer a large, modern double room with a luxury bathroom in The Stables, adjacent to the conference centre. In the dining room, lofty ceilings and intricate cornicing illustrate the Scottish baronial look the Victorians loved so much. On

the lunch and dinner menu, expect dishes such as sirloin of Aberdeen Angus with mushrooms and hand-cut chips; a selection of market-fresh fish with saffron potatoes, fennel, samphire and avruga caviar; and goat's cheese Wellington. As the name of the hotel suggests, there is a golf course, a championship one, no less, with a world-class practice facility and teaching centre. Golfers can stroll straight from the breakfast table to the first tee.

Recommended in the area

Glen Garioch Distillery; Aberdeen; Banff

Falls of Lora

★★★ 77% HOTEL

Address: CONNEL, Connel Ferry, PA37 1PB
Tel: 01631 710483
Fax: 01631 710694
E-mail: enquiries@fallsoflora.com
Website: www.fallsoflora.com
Map ref: 9, NM93
Directions: From Glasgow take A82, A85.
Hotel 0.5m past Connel sign (5m before Oban)
Rooms: 30 (4 fmly) (4 GF) (30 smoking)
S £29.50-£69.50; **D** £59-£159 (incl. bkfst)
Facilities: FTV Wi-fi Child facilities
Parking: 40

Personally run, this long-established, thriving holiday hotel on Loch Etive was built in 1886 and extended in the 1970s. A short distance away are the Falls of Lora themselves, which can be seen when the tide level in the Firth of Lorn drops below the level of the water in the loch. On the ground floor is a comfortable, traditional lounge and a cocktail bar offering more than a hundred whiskies, and an open log fire. Across the road is a pleasant two-acre loch-side garden, with a slipway for launching small boats. Bedrooms come in a variety of styles, ranging from standard doubles to luxury suites. All have private bathrooms; those in the new wing have baths with shower attachments, those in the older part have baths only, while hairdryer, trouser press, hot drinks tray, TV, radio and direct-dial phone incorporating a baby-listening facility are standard. Adjoining the cocktail bar is the all-day Bistro, with an extensive à la carte and 'specials' menu featuring locally sourced meat and seafood. A seven-course Scottish Dinner, served in the formal Dining room, is available by prior arrangement for parties of 10 or more. Wines from a 'specials board' are excellent value at under £8 a bottle.

Recommended in the area

Oban Distillery; Iona Abbey; Ben Nevis, Inverary Castle

The Ardanaiseig

★★★ ◎◎◎ COUNTRY HOUSE HOTEL

Address: by Loch Awe, KILCHRENAN, by Taynuilt,
PA35 1HE
Tel: 01866 833333 **Fax:** 01866 833222
E-mail: ardanaiseig@clara.net
Website: www.ardanaiseig.com
Map ref: 9, NN02 **Directions:** A85 at Taynuilt onto
B845 to Kilchrenan. Left in front of pub (road very
narrow) signed 'Ardanaiseig Hotel' & 'No Through
Road'. Continue for 3m
Rooms: 18 (4 fmly) (5 GF) **S** £73-£113; **D** £146-£226
(incl. bkfst) **Facilities:** FTV Fishing 🚣 Boating Clay
pigeon shooting Bikes for hire Wi-fi **Parking:** 20

Ardanaiseig is a baronial-style, country house
hotel, nestled within densely wooded gardens
on the shores of Loch Awe. The hotel is adorned
with beautiful antiques and offers a choice of 16
individually designed bedrooms, each with views
to the loch or magical gardens. A contemporary
boat shed suite offers a private balcony over the
loch – and a self catering two-bedroom cottage
sits peacefully within the well-maintained grounds.
As well as being a delight to behold, Ardanaiseig
is firmly established as a food-lovers hotel. The
five-course gourmet meals never fail to delight,
thanks to the unique culinary flair of Gary Goldie,
and his use of the finest, fresh, local ingredients in
the three-AA Rosette restaurant. Whilst for some,

Ardanaiseig is the perfect romantic, relaxing or
culinary getaway, for others it is the perfect resting
place after a day of Highland adventure. A number
of activities can be arranged as part of a stay
here, from clay pigeon shooting, fishing and deer-
stalking, to horse-riding, hiking, mountain biking,
climbing and kayaking. Many guests also indulge in
chauffeured local tours and boat rides, or classes
on foraging, cookery and wildlife photography.
Ardanaiseig can be hired for exclusive use and is
particularly popular for weddings and celebrations.

Recommended in the area

Inveraray Castle; Cruachan Power Station; Kilchum
Castle

Taychreggan

★★★★ 76% ◉◉ COUNTRY HOUSE HOTEL
Address: KILCHRENAN, PA35 1HQ
Tel: 01866 833211 & 833366
Fax: 01866 833244
E-mail: info@taychregganhotel.co.uk
Website: www.taychregganhotel.co.uk
Map ref: 9, NN02
Directions: W from Crianlarich on A85 to Taynuilt,
S for 7m on B845 (single track) to Kilchrenan
Rooms: 18 (1 fmly) **S** £91-£176; **D** £122-£292 (incl.
bkfst) **Facilities:** FTV Fishing ⏳ Air rifle range
Archery Clay pigeon shooting Falconry Mock deer
stalk Wi-fi Child facilities **Parking:** 40

Taychreggan Hotel is a romantic 300-year-old
drover's inn situated on the shores of Loch Awe
and offers true Highland hospitality. The comfy
bedrooms have breathtaking views of Scotland's
longest inland loch from most windows. Rooms
in the original 17th-century part of the hotel have
made good use of space and some have four
poster beds, from which you can gaze across the
loch. The (much) newer part of the hotel has been
beautifully refurbished and offers some junior
suites. All bedrooms are en suite, and have tea and
coffee making facilities, flat-screen TV, hairdryer
and complimentary fluffy bathrobes as well as very
comfortable beds. Dining is a delightful experience
at the two-AA Rosette restaurant – head chef John

Sherry uses fresh, local produce in an imaginative
way. Guests can enjoy cuisine that will tempt the
robust appetite, fine wines and a dram or two from
Taychreggan's shamefully large selection of malt
whiskies. Snooker, sailing (boats are available on
site), fishing rights, clay pigeon shooting and hawk
handling are all available. Or you could just relax in
an overstuffed armchair looking out across the loch
and enjoy a spot of afternoon tea.

Recommended in the area
Inverary Castle; Cruachan Power Station;
Oban War Museum

Stonefield Castle

★★★★ 73% ⊛ HOTEL

Address: TARBERT LOCH FYNE, PA29 6YJ
Tel: 01880 820836
Fax: 01880 820929
E-mail: reservations.stonefieldcastle@ohiml.com
Website: www.oxfordhotelsandinns.com
Map ref: 9, NR86
Directions: From Glasgow take M8 towards Erskine
Bridge onto A82, follow Loch Lomond signs. From
Arrochar follow A83 signs through Inveraray &
Lochgilphead, hotel on left 2m before Tarbert
Rooms: 32 (2 fmly) (10 GF)
Facilities: Wi-fi **Parking:** 50

In 1837, the Campbell family built this outstanding example of Scottish baronial architecture on the Mull of Kintyre, overlooking Loch Fyne – and, although stunning views are around every corner in the west of Scotland, you know immediately why they chose this 60-acre spot. If you walk the short distance through the rhododendron-rich gardens – they're at their best in late spring – to an isthmus that connects with Barmore Island, you reach the beautiful loch itself, stretching far away to your right and left. The one-AA Rosette restaurant is all period grandeur and sweeping picture windows (so expect more inspirational views). The kitchen successfully juggles its cooking output between classical and modern British, while always ensuring a prominent role for Scottish ingredients, particularly locally sourced beef and game, and fish and seafood landed at the pretty village of Tarbert nearby. After dinner, relax in the traditional elegance of the wood-panelled bar, warmed externally by an open log fire, internally perhaps by a wee dram of locally distilled malt whisky. The tastefully decorated en suite bedrooms are split between the main house and a purpose-built wing, with, yes, even more expansive panoramas of the gardens and Loch Fyne.

Recommended in the area

Corryvreckan Whirlpool; Springbank Distillery; Islay

The Balmoral

★★★★★ ◎◎◎ HOTEL

Address: 1 Princes St, EDINBURGH, EH2 2EQ
Tel: 0131 556 2414
Fax: 0131 557 3747
E-mail: reservations.balmoral@roccofortehotels.com
Website: www.roccofortechotels.com
Map ref: 10, NT27
Directions: Follow city centre signs. Hotel at E end of Princes St, adjacent to Waverley Station
Rooms: 188 (22 fmly) **S** £395-£2100; **D** £395-£2100
Facilities: Spa STV ⊛ Gym ♬ Wi-fi
Parking: 100
Notes: ⊛

The Balmoral is a luxury hotel in the true sense of the word. With its majestic clock tower, the hotel is a contemporary, luxurious five-star property set in the very heart of Edinburgh which offers 188 opulent suites and rooms, many with views towards Edinburgh Castle and the Old Town. The stylish rooms feature fine Italian marble bathrooms and are designed to reflect the earthy colours of the moors, mists and heathers associated with Scotland. When it comes to fine-dining, The Balmoral's three-AA Rosette restaurant, number one, offers attentive but non-intrusive service and outstanding Scottish cuisine provided by Executive Chef Jeff Bland. For more informal dining, the elegant Hadrian's Brasserie serves delicious cuisine in a relaxed atmosphere. The Balmoral's Palm Court is home to Scotland's only Bollinger Bar, serving traditional Afternoon Tea, an extensive range of single malt whiskies and vintage champagne. The glamorous Balmoral Bar is perfect for a relaxing afternoon or evening with a wide range of premium spirits and innovative cocktails. For the ultimate in relaxation, spend time in the Balmoral Spa, where there are five treatment rooms, ESPA and SUNDARI treatments, a 15 metre swimming pool, sauna, steam room, gymnasium and exercise studio.

Recommended in the area

Holyroodhouse; St Giles Cathedral; Royal Mile

Prestonfield

★★★★★ ⑳⑳ TOWN HOUSE HOTEL

Address: Priestfield Rd, EDINBURGH, EH16 5UT
Tel: 0131 225 7800
Fax: 0131 220 4392
E-mail: reservations@prestonfield.com
Website: www.prestonfield.com
Map ref: 10, NT27
Directions: A7 towards Cameron Toll. 200mtrs
beyond Royal Commonwealth Pool, into Priestfield
Road
Rooms: 23 (6 GF) **D** £295-£365 (incl. bkfst)
Facilities: STV FTV ⌁ 18 Putt green ⚑ Free bike hire
Wi-fi **Parking:** 250

This centuries-old landmark has been lovingly
restored and enhanced to become a truly luxurious
five-star hotel. Built in 1687 as the grand baroque
home of Edinburgh's Lord Provost, its current
manifestation is the creation of owner, James
Thomson, who wanted to create a glamorous,
stylish and luxurious place to stay. In Prestonfield
he has achieved his objective with this extravagant
fusion of historic architecture, art and antiques,
and décor every bit as opulent and colourful as
the history of the house itself. It will not disappoint.
Bedrooms are furnished in trademark rich, warm
colours and fabrics; the modern technology is all
there, but it's hidden away behind coverings on
silk-covered walls. Moreover, the rooms all feature

antiques, a desk, beds dressed with fine linen and
piled high with cushions, and a mini-bar. Windows
look out over secluded gardens and parkland
to Edinburgh's iconic hill, Arthur's Seat, to Royal
Holyrood, or to the historic ruins of Craigmillar
Castle. In the highly memorable, award-winning
Rhubarb restaurant, where the walls are adorned
with pictures of former owners, dishes such as roast
red grouse with sauerkraut, prunes and Armagnac;
and roast rack of Dornoch lamb with dauphinoise
potatoes give an idea of the cuisine.

Recommended in the area
Edinburgh Castle; National Museum of Scotland;
Palace of Holyrood House

The Scotsman

★★★★★ 83% ◉ TOWN HOUSE HOTEL

Address: 20 North Bridge, EDINBURGH, EH1 1YT
Tel: 0131 556 5565
Fax: 0131 652 3652
E-mail: reservations@thescotsmanhotelgroup.co.uk
Website: www.thescotsmanhotel.co.uk
Map ref: 10, NT27
Directions: A8 to city centre, left onto Charlotte
St. Right into Queen St, right at rdbt onto Leith St.
Straight on, left onto North Bridge, hotel on right
Rooms: 69 (4 GF)
Facilities: Spa STV ⏺ supervised Gym Beauty
treatments Wi-fi **Notes:** ⊗

A boutique hotel in a majestic building in the heart of Edinburgh's Old Town. Grade II-listed, it was the offices of *The Scotsman* newspaper from 1905 until 2001, when it became the only hotel in Edinburgh that can boast views over Edinburgh Castle, Princes Street, Calton Hill, the Firth of Forth and Leith. To those who know the city, that's some view. During renovation, careful attention was paid towards preserving the magnificent Italian marble staircase, oak panelling, marble pillars and ornate ceilings. No two bedrooms or suites are alike, and each has its own quirky features, such as curved corner window bays, as well as marble bathrooms and free Wi-fi. Naturally, *The Scotsman* is delivered free every morning. The two-floor Penthouse suite, with

its own sauna, used to be the pigeon lofts, from where the birds flew the news far and wide across Scotland. The North Bridge Bar and Brasserie, once the newspaper's reception room, features original wood panelling, a hand-carved wooden balcony and lots more marble pillars. The seating area is split into two levels, with the quieter balcony offering a bird's-eye view of the buzzing main restaurant and cocktail bar below. The Health Club and Spa now occupies the old press room.

Recommended in the area

Edinburgh Castle; St Giles' Cathedral; Royal Botanic Gardens

Balcary Bay

★★★ 86% ◉◉ HOTEL

Address: AUCHENCAIRN, DG7 1QZ
Tel: 01556 640217 & 640311
Fax: 01556 640272
E-mail: reservations@balcary-bay-hotel.co.uk
Website: www.balcary-bay-hotel.co.uk
Map ref: 10, NX75
Directions: On A711 between Dalbeattie &
Kirkcudbright, hotel 2m from village
Rooms: 20 (1 fmly) (3 GF) **S** £78; **D** £140-£170
(incl. bkfst)
Facilities: FTV
Parking: 50

At the end of a narrow lane on a beautiful bay stands this secluded hideaway in over three acres of gardens. Dating from 1625, it faces the Solway Firth and the old smugglers' hideout of Heston Isle, beyond which rise the majestic peaks of the Lake District. The well-appointed twin and double-bedded rooms all have en suite bathrooms, TV and radio, hairdryer, telephone, complimentary toiletries and hot drinks tray. On the ground floor, three superior rooms, each with a patio, overlook the bay, while rooms without a sea view overlook the gardens instead. Dining in the restaurant gives guests the opportunity to dress smartly for Craig McWilliam's award-winning cuisine, based on fresh, locally sourced ingredients. His menus change daily to offer such starters as baked Dunsyre cheese custard and toasted walnut crust; and pan-fried king scallops, pea purée and black pudding. Typical mains include Stewartry lamb with turnip fondant, roast potatoes, Savoy cabbage and Madeira sauce; Galloway beef fillet with Pont Neuf potatoes, wild mushrooms and tarragon sauce; and grilled monkfish on herb risotto with saffron sauce. A hundred world bins appear on the wine list. Afterwards, relax in one of the comfortable lounges with a warming malt whisky selected from the many available.

Recommended in the area

Auchencairn Bay; Rockcliffe (NT); Dundrennan Abbey; the Artists' town of Kirkcudbright

Fairmont St Andrews, Scotland

★★★★★ 85% ◉◉ HOTEL

Address: ST ANDREWS, KY16 8PN
Tel: 01334 837000
Fax: 01334 471115
E-mail: standrews.scotland@fairmont.com
Website: www.fairmont.com/standrews
Map ref: 11, NO51
Directions: Approx 2m from St Andrews on A917 towards Crail
Rooms: 209 **S** Fr £159 **D** Fr £159
Facilities: Spa STV FTV ⓧ ♨ 36 Putt green Gym Wi-fi
Parking: 150

On a 520-acre estate overlooking the rugged Fife coastline and two world-class golf courses, this is very much a golfer's hotel. Spacious and elegantly decorated bedrooms have under-floor heating in the bathroom, walk-in shower (some also have a bathtub), and each offers the latest in-room amenities, including satellite TV, dual phone lines, work desk and speakerphone. For a special occasion, consider the Kingdom of Fife Suite, with a large bedroom, separate living room, dining room and individual changing rooms. There are also two four-bedroom Manor Homes, with a farmhouse-style kitchen, dining room and large open-plan living room. Guests can choose from several dining options, each individually styled, but having in common their use of the best local produce, expertly prepared and creatively served. Esperante, the jewel in the crown, holds two AA Rosettes and offers Mediterranean-influenced dishes and wines from the New and Old Worlds. The Squire, for brasserie-style food, is named after golfing legend Gene 'The Squire' Sarazen. Beers, 'wee nips' and snacks are available in Kittocks Den (in old Scottish a kittock was a flighty lady). Take afternoon tea and Dundee cake in the glass-topped Atrium, or play pool in The Rock & Spindle bar.

Recommended in the area

West Sands Beach; Blackfriars Chapel; St Andrews Castle

The Old Course Hotel, Golf Resort & Spa

★★★★★ ◉◉◉ HOTEL

Address: ST ANDREWS, KY16 9SP
Tel: 01334 474371
Fax: 01334 477668
E-mail: reservations@oldcoursehotel.co.uk
Website: www.oldcoursehotel.co.uk
Map ref: 11, NO51
Directions: M90 junct 8, A91 to St Andrews
Rooms: 144 (5 fmly) (3 GF) **S** £170-£1535;
D £200-£1535 (incl. bkfst)
Facilities: Spa STV FTV ⊛ ♨ 18 Putt green Gym
Thermal suite ♫ Wi-fi
Parking: 125 **Notes:** ⊗

A haven for golfers, this internationally famous hotel stands alongside the renowned 17th 'Road Hole' of the championship course. Also within view are West Sands Beach and miles and miles of the Fifeshire coast. Bedrooms vary in size and style, although they all, with their gold and antique-style lamps, provide near-decadent levels of luxury. Twenty-three of the suites were recently completely redesigned by Jacques Garcia (of Hôtel Metropole, Monte Carlo, fame) in rich, signature hotel-red and silk-lined walls. Many have a private balcony. Public rooms include intimate lounges, a bright conservatory, the luxury Kohler Waters Spa and a range of pro golf shops. Holder of three AA Rosettes, the fine-dining Road Hole Restaurant retains its original open kitchen,

and its floor-to-ceiling windows frame views of the Old Course, the *auld grey toon* of St Andrews and the sea. It offers three seasonal menus based on Scottish and, where possible, organic ingredients – a fixed-price, an eight-course tasting and a vegetarian. The informal Sands Grill specialises in seafood and steaks, the Jigger Inn is the popular in-house pub, and is effectively the 19th hole. Champagnes and wines are hand-picked by an expert sommelier, and the Road Hole Bar's malt whiskies come from over 200 Scottish distilleries.

Recommended in the area

St Andrews Cathedral; St Andrews Links; West Sands

Moorings

★★★ 82% ® HOTEL

Address: Banavie, FORT WILLIAM, PH33 7LY
Tel: 01397 772797
Fax: 01397 772441
E-mail: reservations@moorings-fortwilliam.co.uk
Website: www.moorings-fortwilliam.co.uk
Map ref: 13, NN17
Directions: Take A830 (N from Fort William), cross
Caledonian Canal, 1st right
Rooms: 27 (2 fmly) (1 GF) **S** £49-£138; **D** £70-£148
(incl. bkfst)
Facilities: STV Gym Wi-fi
Parking: 60

Just three miles from Fort William and alongside
the famous Neptune's Staircase on the Caledonian
Canal, this hotel offers high standards of
accommodation and panoramic views, which
take in not only the canal, but also Aonach Mor
and the UK's highest mountain, Ben Nevis. Each
bedroom is individually designed and has satellite
TV, a hospitality tray, direct-dial telephones, and
free Wi-fi. The executive rooms also have 32"
flat-screen LCD TVs, bathrobes, slippers and iron
facilities plus wonderful panoramic views of the
mountains and the canal. The dining options are
Neptune's Restaurant, awarded an AA Rosette,
that offers a fine dining experience with a menu
based on west coast seafood and salmon, and
locally sourced venison and game; alternatively the
informal split-level Upper Deck Lounge Bar serves
seasonally created bar menu choices. Wines from
around the world feature on the interesting wine list
and complement the food perfectly. In the summer
guests can relax in the secluded garden or enjoy a
delightful canalside stroll. The area is, of course, a
mecca for outdoor pursuits including climbing, hill
walking, fishing and mountain biking. Residents can
enjoy free golf at the Fort William Golf Course.

Recommended in the area

West Highland Museum; Ben Nevis Distillery;
Jacobite Steam Train; Nevis Range; Treasures of
the Earth

Inver Lodge Hotel

★★★★ ◉◎ HOTEL
Address: LOCHINVER, IV27 4LU
Tel: 01571 844496
Fax: 01571 844395
E-mail: stay@inverlodge.com
Website: www.inverlodge.com
Map ref: 13, NC02
Directions: A835 to Lochinver, through village,
left after village hall, follow private road for 0.5m
Rooms: 21 (11 GF) **S** £115-£150; **D** £215-£480
(incl. bkfst)
Facilities: FTV Sauna Wi-fi
Parking: 30

A delightful, purpose-built hotel on a hillside above the fishing village, with wonderful views across the clear waters of Loch Inver to the distant outline of the Western Isles. Rooms called Assynt, Canisp and Suilven, and indeed others, named after nearby mountains and lochs, enjoy similar views. Well-equipped and generously proportioned, they easily accommodate a six-foot double bed or an extra-wide twin, a writing desk, dressing and coffee tables, and comfortable chairs. Private bathrooms have superior fittings and toiletries. Downstairs, the bar provides opportunities to sample the region's distinctive malt whiskies, including the hotel's own special blend. Dinner in Chez Roux is prepared by legendary chef, Albert Roux. When his appointment was announced, he declared he would provide "Hearty country cooking using all the wonderful products from the sea, which is literally at the doorstep". In addition to a speciality fish dish of the day, he may suggest his classic soufflé Suissesse; slow-cooked local beef cheek with glazed carrots and lardons; or pan-fried potato gnocchi with sautéed wild mushroom fricassée. Guests may relax with a game of snooker on a full-size table, have a sauna or enjoy a holistic massage. A drying room is available for wet clothes.

Recommended in the area

Fishing from Lochinver Port; Assynt Visitor Centre; Loch Kirkaig, Inverkirkaig

Glenmorangie Highland Home at Cadboll

★★★ ◎◎ COUNTRY HOUSE HOTEL

Address: Cadboll, Fearn, TAIN, IV20 1XP
Tel: 01862 871671
Fax: 01862 871625
E-mail: relax@glenmorangie.co.uk
Website: www.theglenmorangiehouse.com
Map ref: 13, NH88 **Directions:** A9 onto B9175
towards Nigg. Follow tourist signs
Rooms: 9 (3 annexe) (4 fmly) (3 GF) **S** £225;
D £350-£400 (incl. bkfst & dinner)
Facilities: FTV ᗺ Archery Beauty treatments Clay
pigeon shooting Falconry Wi-fi
Parking: 60 **Notes:** ⊗ ◃ᵗ under 15yrs

From the moment one is greeted, it's clear that guests are not in for a run-of-the-mill hotel experience. Evenings are dominated by the 'house party', where everyone socialises over malt whiskies in the drawing room, then dines together around one long table. Afterwards comes the big test – is your bedroom in the main house (parts of which date back to the 17th century) or in one of the cosy cottages in the grounds? Each room has its own character and all the expected en suite comforts. There is also an extra touch – a complimentary dram of (yet more) Glenmorangie. The daily changing menu is created with enthusiasm and to discover why the food here is so celebrated, start by wandering down to the centuries-old walled garden and look at the quality of the vegetables, herbs and soft fruit. Then remember that fresh seafood comes from 200 yards away, world-renowned beef and lamb from the coastal grazing pastures, and ample supplies of game from neighbouring estates. Breakfast includes home-made porridge, fresh fruit, scrambled fresh farm eggs with smoked salmon, tea and home-made preserves. Hotel staff are happy to organise fishing and shooting parties for guests that want to experience these classic country pursuits.

Recommended in the area

Dunrobin Castle; Falls of Shin; Dornoch Cathedral

Craigellachie

★★★★ 72% ◎ HOTEL

Address: CRAIGELLACHIE, AB38 9SR
Tel: 01340 881204
Fax: 01340 881253
E-mail: reservations.craigellachie@ohiml.com
Website: www.oxfordhotelsandinns.com
Map ref: 14, NJ24
Directions: Hotel situated on A95 between
Aberdeen & Inverness
Rooms: 26 (1 fmly) (6 GF)
Facilities: Wi-fi
Parking: 30

How many malt whiskies are there? If somewhere near 700 is the answer, then they're all here at the Quaich Bar in this impressive and popular, 1893-built hotel in the heart of Speyside, home to more distilleries than anywhere else in Scotland. An in-house whisky specialist conducts nosing and tasting sessions for up to around 20 people, but be prepared to pay anything from £2 to £275 per nip. Near to the picturesque village of Elgin, the hotel has all the expected modern-day facilities while retaining a timeless elegance. Bedrooms come in various sizes but all are tastefully decorated and the en suite bathrooms are of a high specification; the master bedrooms have wonderful views of the River Spey and Thomas Telford's famous 1814 bridge.

The Ben Aigen restaurant, a long-term AA Rosette holder, does a mean line in traditional Scottish cooking, making full use of local meats, game and seafood. Start with Buckie potted crab, crisp croutons and pea shoots, followed by seared rump of Cabrach lamb with Arran mustard mash and red wine jus. The hotel's fishing beat on the Spey, right in front of the hotel, is predominantly time-share, but rods can usually be hired.

Recommended in the area

Strathspey Railway; Cairngorm ski area; RSPB Loch Garten

Alona Hotel

★★★★ 77% HOTEL

Address: Strathclyde Country Park, MOTHERWELL, ML1 3RT

Tel: 01698 333888

Fax: 01698 338720

E-mail: gm@alonahotel.co.uk

Website: www.alonahotel.co.uk

Map ref: 10, NS75

Directions: M74 junct 5, hotel approx 250yds on left

Rooms: 51 (24 fmly) (17 GF) **D** £75, Family room £85

Facilities: FTV ♫ Wi-fi

Parking: 100 **Notes:** ⊗

Strathclyde Country Park, where you'll find this modern hotel, was created in the early 1970s from the grounds of the now-demolished Hamilton Palace. Alona is a Gaelic word meaning 'exquisitely beautiful', a description that unquestionably applies to the hotel's views over the loch and surrounding forests. A circular glass atrium prepares guests for the contemporary interior, from the open-plan public areas to the spacious and well-appointed bedrooms. These all have flat-screen TV with Freeview, direct-dial phone, free Wi-fi, personal safe, hairdryer, iron and ironing board, and hot drinks tray. Parents with children under 12 will find the Lochside rooms ideal as they contain a sofa bed, and others have interconnecting doors. There are also three suites with access for the disabled. The Glasshouse Restaurant and Bar offers a main menu with a broad range of familiar, locally sourced dishes, including chicken Kiev; beef Stroganoff; steak and ale pie; grills and vegetarian options. There's also an express, two-course lunch menu. The huge Banqueting Suite can seat up to 300 guests for a meal, and 400 for a reception. Among local attractions are watersports on the loch and M&D's–Scotland's Family Theme Park, just next door.

Recommended in the area

New Lanark World Heritage Site; Glasgow; Edinburgh

The Gleneagles Hotel

★★★★★ ◎◎◎◎ HOTEL

Address: AUCHTERARDER, PH3 1NF
Tel: 01764 662231
Fax: 01764 662134
E-mail: resort.sales@gleneagles.com
Website: www.gleneagles.com
Map ref: 10, NN91 **Directions:** Off A9 at exit for A823 follow signs for Gleneagles Hotel
Rooms: 232 (115 fmly) (11 GF) **S** fr £315; **D** fr £315 (incl. bkfst) **Facilities:** Spa STV FTV ◎ supervised ⌁ ♨ 54 ⛳ Putt green Fishing ⛵ Gym Falconry Off-road driving Golf Archery Clay target shooting Gundog school Wi-fi Child facilities **Parking:** 277

When the former Caledonian Railway opened this grand hotel in 1924 it was described as 'the eighth wonder of the world'. In 850 acres of glorious countryside, it has a well-deserved international reputation, not least for its many sporting facilities, including the PGA Centenary golf course, where the 40th Ryder Cup will be played in 2014. Traditional or contemporary in style, the spacious bedrooms, with en suite bath and shower rooms, contain a king-size bed and extensive in-room accessories. Each of the restaurants presents different styles of cooking but the common hallmark is the use of the finest Scottish produce, particularly from Perthshire, as well as from specialist worldwide suppliers. The Strathearn, with fine views of the estate, has two AA Rosettes and offers classics such as Highland venison with Stornoway black pudding; fillet of Scotch beef; and langoustines flambéed in Pernod, as well as top wines and some of Scotland's rarest malt whiskies. Deseo 'Mediterranean Food Market' serves antipasti, tapas, fresh fish and meats, pizzas and homemade Italian desserts, and in Andrew Fairlie@Gleneagles – holder of four AA Rosettes – smoked lobster is his signature dish. There is also the Clubhouse and several bars. Espa Life offers naturopathy, acupuncture and other treatments.

Recommended in the area

Wallace Monument; Stirling Castle; Drummond Castle Gardens

Killiecrankie House Hotel

★★★ ◎◎ SMALL HOTEL

Address: KILLIECRANKIE, PH16 5LG
Tel: 01796 473220
Fax: 01796 472451
E-mail: enquiries@killiecrankiehotel.co.uk
Website: www.killiecrankiehotel.co.uk
Map ref: 13, NN96
Directions: Exit A9 at Killiecrankie onto B8079.
Hotel 3m on right
Rooms: 10 (2 GF) **S** £90-£100; **D** £180-£220
(incl. bkfst)
Facilities: FTV ➲ Wi-fi
Parking: 20

Small and friendly, this lovely hotel lies in four acres of grounds at the gateway to the Highlands. Opposite, beyond the Pass of Killiecrankie and the River Garry, is the wooded hillside of Fonvuik. Built in 1840 as a private residence for a church minister, the hotel is now owned by Henrietta Fergusson, who recently refurbished the all en suite bedrooms, decorating them in rich colours and fabrics. The beds are fitted with Egyptian cotton sheets, and there's a TV, radio, hairdryer, hospitality tray, shoe-cleaning materials and, as a nice touch, fresh flowers in every room. As a bonus, they all look out over the garden and surrounding countryside. Under head chef Mark Easton, the restaurant's reputation for excellent food is confirmed, among other awards, by its two AA Rosettes. Although based on local and traditional ingredients, his menus are likely to feature contemporary flavours too, so, to quote just one typical example, try pan-fried fillet of Highland venison and breast of wood pigeon with braised Savoy cabbage, carrot ribbons, chive mash and redcurrant and game jus, with a Côtes de Rhône Guigal 2003. The Conservatory Bar serves lunch and supper in more relaxed surroundings, and a snug sitting room with an open fire leads to a small patio.

Recommended in the area

Pass of Killiecrankie (NT); Blair Castle; Pitlochry Festival Theatre

Ballathie House Hotel

★★★★ 78% ◎◎ COUNTRY HOUSE HOTEL

Address: KINCLAVEN, Stanley, PH1 4QN
Tel: 01250 883268
Fax: 01250 883396
E-mail: email@ballathiehousehotel.com
Website: www.ballathiehousehotel.com
Map ref: 10, NO13 **Directions:** From A9, 2m N of
Perth, take B9099 through Stanley, follow signs. Or
from A93 at Beech Hedge follow signs for hotel, 2.5m
Rooms: 41 (16 annexe) (2 fmly) (10 GF) **S** £65-£130;
D £130-£290 (incl. bkfst)
Facilities: FTV Putt green Fishing ◡ Wi-fi
Parking: 50

Set in an extensive estate, this splendid turreted
mansion combines classical grandeur with modern
comforts. When the main railway line between
Glasgow and Aberdeen came through in the 19th
century, it even had its own train halt built. A luxury
hotel since 1972, the main house contains some of
the bedrooms, while others are in the purpose-built
Riverside development, with balconies and terraces
overlooking the River Tay. Further accommodation is
provided in the recently rebuilt Sportsman's Lodge.
Ranging from well-proportioned master rooms to
modern standards, many have antique furniture and
art deco bathrooms, while all provide bathrobes
and toiletries, trouser press, hairdryer, Freeview TV,
direct-dial phone and hot drinks tray. The kitchen
does full justice to Scotland's rich supply of fish,
game and meats with a fine-dining restaurant menu
that has helped it earn two AA Rosettes. Taken from
one example are seared calf's liver on truffle mash;
pan-seared salmon fillet with herb pappardelle; and
carved guinea fowl supreme with lemon and thyme
pomme mousseline. The wood-panelled, private
club-like Restaurant Bar stocks many malt whiskies,
including some from Perthshire. Sports lovers seek
Ballathie out as their base for golfing, fishing and
outdoor breaks. It's popular for weddings too.

Recommended in the area
Scone Palace; Huntingtower Castle; Glamis Castle

The Four Seasons Hotel

★★★ 83% ◉◉ HOTEL

Address: Loch Earn, ST FILLANS, PH6 2NF
Tel: 01764 685333
Fax: 01764 685444
E-mail: info@thefourseasonshotel.co.uk
Website: www.thefourseasonshotel.co.uk
Map ref: 10, NN62
Directions: The hotel is on the A85, towards the west of the village
Rooms: 18 (6 annexe) (7 fmly) **S** £54-£108; **D** £108-£166 (incl. bkfst)
Facilities: FTV Wi-fi
Parking: 40

Of countless highly desirable hotel settings in Scotland, this is unquestionably in the upper echelons. Looking southwest down beautiful Loch Earn, the views are almost too good to be true – they include spectacular sunsets, morning mists and snow-covered mountains. Built in the 1800s for the manager of the local lime kilns, the house has been extended over the years to become today's small but exceedingly comfortable hotel, with several individual sitting rooms, a choice of bedrooms and, out on the wooded hillside at the rear, six comfortable and well-equipped chalets. All bedrooms are spacious, most with bath and shower, and many have uninterrupted views down the loch. The chalets have a double or twin room and a bunk room, making them ideal for family use. When eating, choose between the more formal Meall Reamhar Room or the Tarken Room. Both offer the same high standard of contemporary Scottish cuisine, with much, as you might expect, coming from local sources. A large selection of malts is stocked in the bar. Dog owners will be gratified to know that resident canine Sham welcomes his cousins; he'll even tolerate cats, parrots and gerbils, depending on his current humour.

Recommended in the area

Loch Lomond & the Trossachs National Park; Stirling Castle; Famous Grouse Experience

Best Western Gleddoch House

★★★★ 73% HOTEL
Address: LANGBANK, PA14 6YE
Tel: 01475 540711
Fax: 01475 540201
E-mail: reservations.gleddochhouse@ohiml.com
Website: www.oxfordhotelsandinns.com
Map ref: 9, NS37
Directions: M8 to Greenock, onto A8, left at rdbt onto A789, follow for 0.5m, turn right, hotel 2nd on left
Rooms: 70 (22 fmly) (17 GF)
Facilities: Spa FTV ⊛ ♨ 18 Putt green Gym Steam room Sauna Wi-fi **Parking:** 150

Successful Clydeside shipbuilder Sir James Lithgow built this fine-looking house in the 1920s. A hotel since 1975, it stands in 360 acres of landscaped grounds and is high enough above Langbank and the Clyde estuary for clear views of Ben Lomond and the rolling Renfrewshire hills; the distant night-time glow of Glasgow also gets in on the act. Its en suite bedrooms are individually designed and elegantly furnished, and from most you can see across the hotel's 18-hole championship golf course, gardens and surrounding estate. The Crannog Brasserie offers menus that make good use of Scotland's natural produce to offer the highly tempting pork fillet wrapped in bacon with Stornoway black pudding, potato rösti and buttered greens; lamb rump with sweet potato dauphinoise, rosemary and red wine sauce; and pan-seared gnocchi with semi-dried tomatoes, rocket and Parmesan shavings. A perfect place to relax in, the Leisure Club has a 17-metre swimming pool, sauna and well-equipped gym, while golfers can take advantage of one-night golfing breaks, Sunday Drivers, residential courses and pro-lessons. Many arrive at Glasgow International Airport, which is about nine miles away.

Recommended in the area

Loch Lomond; Clydebuilt Maritime Heritage Centre; Kelvingrove Art Gallery & Museum

Uplawmoor Hotel

★★★ 81% ◉ HOTEL

Address: Neilston Rd, UPLAWMOOR, G78 4AF
Tel: 01505 850565
Fax: 01505 850689
E-mail: info@uplawmoor.co.uk
Website: www.uplawmoor.co.uk
Map ref: 9, NS45
Directions: M77 junct 2, A736 signed Barrhead &
Irvine. Hotel 4m beyond Barrhead
Rooms: 14 (1 fmly) (2 smoking) **S** £60-£70;
D £85-£95 (incl. bkfst)
Facilities: STV Wi-fi
Parking: 40 **Notes:** ⊗

Instantly recognisable by its whitewashed façade and prominent location in the village, this popular hotel dates back to the 1750s when it stood on the old road between Glasgow and Irvine. Over the years, from being a one-room coaching inn, it has been greatly expanded and upgraded, most extensively in 1958 when art nouveau touches, inspired by the designs of innovative Glasgow-born architect Charles Rennie Macintosh, were applied to the exterior. Once a barn, the comfortable restaurant is the holder of one AA Rosette, a delight to the owners, who set as their goal to run 'the best village eating place in Greater Glasgow'. Richly furnished, with a copper-canopied fireplace, it offers fillet steak with haggis among its traditionally Scottish cuisine, but there are contemporary dishes too, such as baked cod with tomato compote and saffron oil. The separate lounge is popular for freshly prepared bar meals. After a night in one of the comfortable modern bedrooms, the full Scottish breakfast may feature local black pudding or hot porridge oats, but there is also a cereal and buffet option. In the right sort of weather, visitors can also enjoy the beer garden, which leads to the village park.

Recommended in the area

Burrell Collection, Glasgow; People's Palace & Winter Gardens, Glasgow; Robert Burns' Cottage, Alloway

Glenapp Castle

★★★★★ ◎◎◎◎ HOTEL

Address: BALLANTRAE, KA26 0NZ
Tel: 01465 831212
Fax: 01465 831000
E-mail: enquiries@glenappcastle.com
Website: www.glenappcastle.com
Map ref: 9, NX08
Directions: S through Ballantrae, cross bridge over River Stinchar, 1st right, hotel in 1m
Rooms: 17 (2 fmly) (7 GF) **S** £265-£450; **D** £415-£620 (incl. bkfst & dinner)
Facilities: STV FTV ॐ ऄ Wi-fi
Parking: 20

Looking like something out of a fairytale, this Scottish baronial castle is hidden in 36 acres of glorious gardens and woodland on the ruggedly beautiful Ayrshire coast. The views across the Irish Sea to the island of Arran and the massive granite rock of Ailsa Craig are superb. Public areas are handsomely furnished with personally chosen antiques and fine oil paintings, while seemingly endless oak-panelled hallways and corridors lead to the impeccably furnished bedrooms and suites. Two of these, the Earl of Inchcape and the Earl of Orkney, are simply palatial. A ground-floor family suite has two connecting bedrooms, each with its own en suite bathroom. Rooms are bright and sunny thanks to the tall Victorian windows, and all include designer toiletries, direct-dial phone, wireless broadband internet access, TV, CD and DVD player. Accomplished cooking, using quality local ingredients characterises the dining experience; a well-crafted, six-course gourmet menu offers dinner possibilities of Ballantrae lobster with olive oil, lemon, spring roll and roasted lobster mayonnaise; and breast of grouse with beetroot, garden baby turnip, cobnuts and brambles. Guests should make a point of walking around the grounds to take a look at the gardens and restored Victorian greenhouses.

Recommended in the area

Walking and mountain biking in the Galloway Forest Park; Mull of Galloway; Culzean Country Park

WALES

Snowdonia National Park

Ivy Bush Royal

★★★ 77% HOTEL

Address: Spilman St, CARMARTHEN, SA31 1LG
Tel: 01267 235111
Fax: 01267 234914
E-mail: reception@ivybushroyal.co.uk
Website: www.ivybushroyal.co.uk
Map ref: 1, SN42
Directions: A48 to Carmarthen, over 1st rdbt, at 2nd rdbt right onto A4242. Straight over next 2 rdbts. Left at lights. Hotel on right at top of hill
Rooms: 70 (4 fmly) **S** £60-£115; **D** £80-£150 (incl. bkfst) **Facilities:** FTV Gym Wi-fi
Parking: 83 **Notes:** ⊗

Once a favoured retreat of Lord Nelson and Lady Hamilton, this friendly family-run hotel has been sympathetically modernised to blend its old-world charm with up-to-date facilities. The accommodation is spacious and well-equipped, and includes some family rooms, a four-poster suite, executive suites and the Merlin Suite with its own whirlpool bath. Dine in style in the restaurant, where the produce is locally sourced and the carte menu changes with the seasons. Welsh black beef is a particular speciality, and carvery lunches are extremely popular on Sundays. For guests looking for a more informal dining experience, the cosy bar and lounge area is open all day, every day, serving a full range of traditional meals. For those wanting to get active during their stay, the gym has all the latest cardiovascular equipment, and you can ease your tired muscles after a workout with a relaxing session in the sauna. The hotel is licensed for weddings and has an experienced team of staff to call on to help arrange your special day at the Ivy Bush Royal. There are also four meeting and conference rooms with facilities to accommodate up to 200 people.

Recommended in the area

National Botanic Garden of Wales; Aberglasney House & Gardens; Oakwood Theme Park

The Cliff

★★★ 75% HOTEL

Address: GWBERT-ON-SEA, SA43 1PP
Tel: 01239 613241
Fax: 01239 615391
E-mail: reservations@cliffhotel.com
Website: www.cliffhotel.com
Map ref: 1, SN14
Directions: A487, into Cardigan, take B4548 towards Gwbert, 2m to hotel
Rooms: 70 (6 fmly) (5 GF) **S** £59-£85; **D** £75-£135 (incl. bkfst)
Facilities: Spa FTV ⊗ ♪ 9 Putt green Fishing Gym
Parking: 100

Built in 1850 and originally known as the Gwbert Inn, this coastal retreat was renamed the Cliff Hotel in the early 1900s in a bid to become a seaside getaway to rival the holiday resorts of southern England. Whether the name change was enough to persuade holidaymakers away from the south coast and across into Wales, we don't know, but The Cliff Hotel is certainly in a prime sea-facing spot. The 70-bedroom hotel sits in 30 acres of land along south Ceredigion's beautiful coastline, with stunning views of Cardigan Island, Cardigan Bay and Poppit Sands. Most rooms benefit from those views and all are en suite and have tea- and coffee-making facilities. There is a state-of-the-art gym along with a hydro spa (built in the last few years),

sauna, Jacuzzi, steam room, heated loungers, and a beauty therapy suite offering a range of treatments. A day spent on the par 3, nine-hole golf course, which stretches along the cliff top, should give you a good appetite for a relaxing dinner in the restaurant or the Island Bar. The food is locally sourced and freshly prepared, and a meal here very often comes with the added bonus of watching the sun set over Cardigan Bay.

Recommended in the area

Clifftop walks; golf; dolphin, porpoise and seal watching

Royal Oak

★★★ 86% ⊛ HOTEL

Address: Holyhead Rd, BETWS-Y-COED, LL24 0AY
Tel: 01690 710219
Fax: 01690 710603
E-mail: royaloakmail@btopenworld.com
Website: www.royaloakhotel.net
Map ref: 5, SH75 **Directions:** On A5 in town
centre, adjacent to St Mary's church
Rooms: 27 (1 fmly) **S** £77.50-£80; **D** £95-£180
(incl. bkfst)
Facilities: STV ♫ Wi-fi
Parking: 90
Notes: ⊛

The wonders of Snowdonia National Park are right on the doorstep of this former Victorian coaching inn, which nestles at the foot of a wooded hillside in the heart of the picturesque village of Betws-y-Coed. Rooms have been designed with the heritage of the hotel in mind, with stylish fabrics and feature beds offering contemporary luxury in a period setting. For a special occasion book one of the four-poster rooms with Jacuzzi bathroom. Guests benefit from complimentary membership of the nearby Stations Leisure Complex, while free broadband is available in all rooms and Wi-fi in the lounge bar. The award-winning Llugwy Restaurant, which was beautifully refurbished in 2011, offers modern Welsh cooking via a set three-course menu.

Dishes might include locally smoked halibut or a trio of Welsh mountain lamb, and, if you're lucky, the bara brith-and-butter pudding with Welsh whisky ice cream. Alternative dining options are the relaxed and modern Grill Bar that prides itself on serving the best local Welsh produce, or the Stables Bistro, which has a rather special atmosphere with its regular music nights, plenty of cask ales and alfresco dining.

Recommended in the area

Snowdon Mountain Railway (or a walk to the summit); Conwy Castle; Llechwedd Slate Caverns

Castle Hotel Conwy

★★★★ 79% ◉◉ TOWN HOUSE HOTEL

Address: High St, CONWY, LL32 8DB
Tel: 01492 582800
Fax: 01492 582300
E-mail: mail@castlewales.co.uk
Website: www.castlewales.co.uk
Map ref: 5, SH77
Directions: A55 junct 18, follow town centre signs, cross estuary (castle on left). Right then left at mini-rdbts onto one-way system. Right at Town Wall Gate, right into Berry St then High St
Rooms: 28 (2 fmly) **S** £82-£92; **D** £130-£250 (incl. bkfst) **Facilities:** FTV Wi-fi **Parking:** 34

The distinctive building that houses the Castle Hotel hints at its long and fascinating history. Built on the site of a Cistercian abbey, it has welcomed many famous people through its doors, including Thomas Telford (who built the town's famous bridge), railway pioneer George Stephenson, William Wordsworth and the Queen of Romania. The current owners, the Lavin family and partner/head chef Graham Tinsley, have been very mindful of this important heritage while giving the place an attractive facelift. All of the bedrooms have en suite bathrooms and modern facilities. Deluxe rooms have spa baths, one has an ornately carved four-poster bed, and another enjoys a good view of the castle. Graham Tinsley MBE, and his award-winning kitchen team, have gained a reputation for serving excellent Welsh produce. Food is available in both Dawson's Restaurant and the bar, where the atmosphere is relaxed and the emphasis is on locally sourced ingredients. There's a real seasonal feel to the menu, with Conwy mussels featuring in the winter months, and Conwy Valley lamb in spring and early summer. There's also a good selection of vegetarian and organic food on the menu.

Recommended in the area

Conwy Castle; Caernarfon Castle; Snowdonia National Park; Bodnant Garden (NT); Anglesey

Dunoon

★★★ 82% HOTEL

Address: Gloddaeth St, LLANDUDNO, LL30 2DW
Tel: 01492 860787
Fax: 01492 860031
E-mail: reservations@dunoonhotel.co.uk
Website: www.dunoonhotel.co.uk
Map ref: 5, SH78
Directions: Exit Promenade at war memorial
by pier into Gladdaeth St. Hotel 200yds on right
Rooms: 49 (4 fmly) **S** £64-£98; **D** £108-£130
(incl. bkfst)
Facilities: FTV Pool table Wi-fi
Parking: 24

Close to the promenade in this well preserved Victorian seaside resort, the Dunoon has a certain old-world grace about it. Hushed and stuffy it isn't, though. In fact, the Williams family, who have been here a good while, make sure it offers a happy antidote to what they regard as anodyne modern living. For example, they treat returning guests like old friends, and first time customers as new ones. Their approach is evident too in the way they have styled the bedrooms, with no two alike, and in their attention to detail, with crisp Egyptian cotton bed linen, and Molton Brown toiletries in every bathroom. The same is true of the restaurant, where silver rings contain freshly pressed linen napkins, and white porcelain is used on the tables. Food and wine are the Williams' abiding passions. Cooking is unpretentious, using fresh ingredients sourced locally as far as the seasons allow, with specialities such as terrine of game, medley of local fish, ragout of Welsh lamb with mint dumplings and asparagus mousse. Their taste in wines is adventurous, with a list that, in their words, 'offers more than you would expect from a modest hotel in the sleepy outer reaches of Britain'.

Recommended in the area

Great Orme; Bodnant Gardens; Snowdonia National Park

Imperial Hotel

★★★★ 81% ◉ HOTEL

Address: The Promenade, LLANDUDNO, LL30 1AP
Tel: 01492 877466
Fax: 01492 878043
E-mail: reception@theimperial.co.uk
Website: www.theimperial.co.uk
Map ref: 5, SH75
Directions: A470 to Llandudno
Rooms: 98 (10 fmly)
Facilities: FTV ◉ Gym Beauty therapist
Hairdressing ♫ Wi-fi
Parking: 25
Notes: ⊗

An impressive hotel on the resort's famous promenade, with lovely views out to Llandudno Bay and its guardian headlands, the Great and Little Orme. It was built in the late 19th century, during the era when the Victorians helped make seaside holidaying fashionable. The guest rooms, including four suites with lounges, offer high levels of comfort; expect large flat-screen TV, bathrobes, slippers, hot drinks tray and mineral water as standard, and sea views in many. As dictated by its long-standing environmental policy, the hotel uses only ethically produced electricity, sets limits for water consumption and recycles zealously. Also, as a member of 'Wales the True Taste', the kitchen is committed to using local, seasonal and market-fresh Welsh produce, and thus food miles are kept to a minimum. The Chantrey Restaurant has an AA Rosette for dishes such as slow-braised shoulder of lamb; chargrilled prime steaks; and roast fillet of halibut with Conwy crab. As an alternative for a leisurely lunch, snack or afternoon tea, try The Terrace. Mint Condition, the Imperial's health and fitness centre, incorporates a 45ft ozone-treated swimming pool and two gyms. The Imperial was the AA Hotel of the Year for Wales 2010–2011.

Recommended in the area

Bodnant Gardens (NT); Conwy Castle; Snowdonia National Park

St Tudno Hotel and Restaurant

★★★ ⊛⊛ HOTEL

Address: The Promenade, LLANDUDNO, LL30 2LP
Tel: 01492 874411 **Fax:** 01492 860407
E-mail: sttudnohotel@btinternet.com
Website: www.st-tudno.co.uk
Map ref: 5, SH78
Directions: On Promenade towards pier, hotel opposite pier entrance
Rooms: 18 (4 fmly) **S** £67.50-£100; **D** £95-£215 (incl. bkfst)
Facilities: FTV ⊗ ♫ Wi-fi **Parking:** 12

Right on the Llandudno seafront, this outstanding hotel is personally run by the owner, Martin Bland, who has put together a loyal and caring team to look after guests. There is a delightful sitting room with sea views as well as a leafy coffee lounge and Victorian style bar lounge, the latter renowned for its afternoon teas. The restaurant transports you to northern Italy with its vast murals depicting Lake Como, but it is the food that has the greatest impact of all. With its two AA Rosettes it is clear that you are in for a treat, and this might include a warm salad of langoustines, duck ham and pea shoots with a nut-brown butter dressing, or a composition of game with a honey, blackberry and truffle dressing. The bedrooms are all en suite and half have spa baths. All are individually styled and have fine linen, bathrobes and Molton Brown toiletries, a Villeroy and Boch tea service and home-made biscuits, as well as facilities such as Wi-fi and flat-screen TV with a multitude of Freeview channels. Even more luxurious suites are also available. There is a heated indoor swimming pool in case the sea temperature is too bracing, and a delightful garden.

Recommended in the area

Great Orme Tramway; Conwy Castle; Snowdonia National Park

Tynedale Hotel

★★★ 80% HOTEL

Address: Central Promenade, LLANDUDNO, LL30 2XS
Tel: 01492 877426
Fax: 01492 871213
E-mail: enquiries@tynedalehotel.co.uk
Website: www.tynedalehotel.co.uk
Map ref: 5, SH78
Directions: On Promenade opposite bandstand
Rooms: 54 (1 fmly) **S** £40-£43; **D** £80-£122
(incl. bkfst) **Facilities:** FTV ♫ Wi-fi
Parking: 20
Notes: ⊛

On Llandudno's North Shore, this privately owned hotel enjoys a panoramic view from the Great Orme's Head in the west to the Little Orme in the east. Public areas are modern and bright, with bedrooms confirming its Victorian origins only in the sense that they come in all shapes and sizes. In every other respect they are bang up-to-date, with the first-floor Executive Bay rooms, for example, offering a twin or king-size bed, white bathroom with bath tub and over-bath thermostatic shower, large LCD TV, hair dryer, iron, hot drinks tray, and leather tub chairs for enjoying the views. The restaurant serves dinner from a daily changing menu that typically includes fillet of trout with leeks, bacon, and chervil and chive dressing; Welsh

lamb with a herb and mustard crust, scallion-crushed potatoes and red wine gravy; and zucchini herb pancakes with pan-fried broccoli, red onion, blistered red peppers, melting Brie and sour cream dressing. The ground floor Café Bar, leading out to a seafront patio garden with tables, chairs and parasols, provides all-day tea and coffee, a bistro-style lunch, and bar drinks until midnight. There's a cabaret every night of the year.

Recommended in the area

Rhuddlan Castle; St Asaph Cathedral; Plas Mawr

Bron Eifion Country House

★★★★ 77% ⊚ COUNTRY HOUSE HOTEL
Address: CRICCIETH, LL52 0SA
Tel: 01766 522385
Fax: 01766 523796
E-mail: enquiries@broneifion.co.uk
Website: www.broneifion.co.uk
Map ref: 5, SH43
Directions: A497 between Porthmadog & Pwllheli,
0.5m from Criccieth, on right towards Pwhelli
Rooms: 18 (1 fmly) (1 GF) **S** £95-£135; **D** £135-£185
(incl. bkfst)
Facilities: FTV Wi-fi
Parking: 50 **Notes:** ⊛

Bron Eifion, a delightful Grade II-listed country house hotel set in extensive grounds to the west of Criccieth, enjoys breathtaking views of the sea. Golfers are particularly well catered for here, with five of the best courses in North Wales in close proximity to the hotel; special golf packages can be arranged. Inside, guests will find a tranquil and relaxing atmosphere, with attentive and friendly service, and the interior style highlights the many retained period features. There is a choice of restful lounges, warmed by log fires, and the very impressive central hall features a minstrels' gallery. The attractive en suite bedrooms have been individually decorated to combine luxury and elegance, and tea- and coffee-making facilities as well as flat-screen TV, Wi-fi and hairdryers all come as standard. The Garden Restaurant, overlooking the spectacular grounds, is fresh and bright by day, candlelit and relaxed in the evening. The emphasis is on fresh Welsh produce, with dishes such as Llyn Peninsula Seabass, Tyddyn Mawr Welsh Beef and roast rack of Welsh lamb, followed by seasonal desserts, home-made ice creams and pastries. Afternoon tea includes a delicious selection of sandwiches and home-made sweet treats.

Recommended in the area

Portmeirion; Snowdonia National Park; Blaenau Ffestiniog Railway

Royal Sportsman

★★★ 80% ◉◉ HOTEL

Address: 131 High St, PORTHMADOG,
LL49 9HB
Tel: 01766 512015
Fax: 01766 512490
E-mail: enquiries@royalsportsman.co.uk
Website: www.royalsportsman.co.uk
Map ref: 5, SH53
Directions: At rdbt junct of A497 & A487
Rooms: 28 (9 GF) (7 fmly) (9 GF) **S** £62-£86;
D £88-£102 (incl. bkfst)
Facilities: STV FTV Wi-fi
Parking: 17

With Snowdonia as a backdrop, this former coaching inn, built from local Blaenau Ffestiniog slate in 1862, still retains the stone and slate fireplaces in Gelert's Bar and Lorenzo's Lounge. It is Porthmadog's premier hotel with two AA Rosettes, only one of five in Gwynedd to have achieved such status. Family owned and managed, the close-knit team of staff work with great attention to detail and maintain an extended family atmosphere for which the Royal Sportsman is renowned. Peppino's, the beautifully restored, 60-seat restaurant, serves highly regarded food to suit all tastes. All bedrooms are well-equipped and refurbishment was completed in early 2012. There is free Wi-fi, on-site covered parking and, as a family hotel, babies

and children are particularly welcome, as are pets in designated rooms. Drying and storage facilities are provided for golfers, cyclists and walkers and the hotel is an activity organiser, with considerable experience in looking after private groups. The Royal Sportsman is not a pretentious boutique nor fashionable hotel. It is simply a very good, honest and traditional hotel, well-managed and staffed by a team that cares about its customers.

Recommended in the area

Criccieth Castle; Rheiffordd Ffestiniog Railway; Moel Hebog

Castell Deudraeth

★★★★ 77% ◎ HOTEL

Address: PORTMEIRION, LL48 6EN
Tel: 01766 770000
Fax: 01766 771771
E-mail: castell@portmeirion-village.com
Website: www.portmeirion-village.com
Map ref: 5, SH53
Directions: A4212 for Trawsfynydd/Porthmadog. 1.5m beyond Penrhyndeudraeth, hotel on right
Rooms: 11 (5 fmly)**S** £119-£219; **D** £159-£259 (incl. bkfst)
Facilities: Spa STV ⤢ ⅃ Wi-fi
Parking: 30 **Notes:** ⊗

A castellated Victorian mansion built by David Williams, the first Liberal MP for Merionethshire, which architect Clough Williams-Ellis bought in 1931 in order to expand his Italianate village of Portmeirion. Briefly a hotel before the Second World War, it became a hotel again in 2001, when it was officially opened by Welsh opera singer, Bryn Terfel. The interior fuses traditional Welsh materials with cutting-edge technology and design, for example, the Welsh oak and original slate floors have modern under-floor heating. Stone fire surrounds, oak panelling, plasterwork cornices and ornate ceilings have been painstakingly restored. Bedrooms have real-flame gas fires, wide-screen TV with DVD and cinema surround-sound, and whirlpool baths have been installed in all the marble-tiled bathrooms. The brasserie menu is based on the best produce from the locality, especially the fish and shellfish. Guests have free access to all the village facilities, including the Mermaid Spa, outdoor swimming pool, gardens and beaches. The Williams-Ellis family connection remains strong with work on show by his elder daughter, Susan, and her husband Euan Cooper-Willis, founders of Portmeirion Potteries. All the buildings are listed and the whole estate is a designated Conservation Area.

Recommended in the area

Portmeirion Village; Ffestiniog Railway; Snowdonia National Park

The Hotel Portmeirion

★★★★ 79% ◎ HOTEL
Address: PORTMEIRION, LL48 6ET
Tel: 01766 770000
Fax: 01766 770300
E-mail: hotel@portmeirion-village.com
Website: www.portmeirion-village.com
Map ref: 5, SH53
Directions: 2m W, Portmeirion village is south
off A487
Rooms: 42 (28 annexe) (4 fmly)
Facilities: Spa STV ৲ ৪ Wi-fi
Parking: 40

There are two things people tend to know about the Italianate village of Portmeirion: one, that it was the creation, between 1925 and 1976, of architect Clough Williams-Ellis, and two, that it was where Patrick McGoohan's classic Sixties TV series 'The Prisoner', was filmed. The elegant hotel itself, which Williams-Ellis saved from dereliction, lies below wooded slopes and overlooks the sandy estuary and the mountains of Snowdonia. Many bedrooms have private sitting rooms and balconies with spectacular views, while all the cottages in the village either have individual guest rooms or are let complete as suites. The brasserie in neighbouring Castell Deudraeth sources its produce locally, including lobster, crab and scallops from the Lleyn Peninsula, oysters brought in daily from the Menai Straits, and lamb from Portmeirion's own pastures. Typically, the menu, which is printed in both Welsh and English, offers Thai-style salmon fishcakes; smoked duck breast with black pudding; and roasted squash risotto. Some dishes are available both as starters and main courses. The village has its own cafés, shops and the Mermaid Spa, which specialises in high quality bespoke treatments. The staff, most of whom are Welsh-speaking, provide a good mix of warm hospitality and efficient service.

Recommended in the area

Ffestiniog Railway; Llechwedd Slate Caverns; Llandudno Pier

Glen-yr-Afon House Hotel

★★★ 80% HOTEL

Address: Pontypool Rd, USK, NP15 1SY
Tel: 01291 672302 & 673202
Fax: 01291 672597
E-mail: enquiries@glen-yr-afon.co.uk
Website: www.glen-yr-afon.co.uk
Map ref: 2, SO03
Directions: A472 through High St, over river bridge, follow to right. Hotel 200yds on left
Rooms: 28 (1 annexe) (2 fmly) **S** £99-£123; **D** £136-£159 (incl. bkfst)
Facilities: STV FTV ◔ Complimentary access to Usk Tennis Club Wi-fi **Parking:** 100

Beautifully situated in rural Monmouthshire, overlooking the banks of the River Usk, this award-winning hotel offers relaxation and a high level of personal service and attention. The business opened its doors in 1974 and has welcomed thousands through them ever since for conferences, parties, weddings, dinner parties and accommodation. Surrounded by well-maintained grounds, the architecture of this stunning, privately owned Victorian villa means that no two rooms are the same, the angles creating rooms of individual character, style and space. A number of rooms have two floors, which can be ideal for families. The small picturesque town of Usk is just a five-minute stroll from the hotel. There's a choice of comfortable lounge areas, a stylish and spacious banqueting suite, and award-winning Clarkes restaurant. Typical dishes here include Brecon rib-eye steak with crispy bacon; Bwlch venison Wellington with port jus; cider-cured sea trout with crab sauce; and, for vegetarians, Glamorgan sausages with cheddar mash and onion gravy. Among the lighter options are chicken curry with rice, and smoked haddock with poached duck egg and crispy Parma ham. The library is a popular room for private dining, while the ballroom is the perfect location for parties.

Recommended in the area

Usk Rural Life Museum; Usk Castle; walks in the Vale of Usk

The Celtic Manor Resort

★★★★★ 85% ◉◉◉ HOTEL

Address: Coldra Woods, NEWPORT, NP18 1HQ
Tel: 01633 413000
Fax: 01633 412910
E-mail: bookings@celtic-manor.com
Website: www.celtic-manor.com
Map ref: 2, ST38 **Directions:** M4 junct 24, take
B4237 towards Newport. Hotel 1st on right
Rooms: 400 (34 fmly) from £110 (incl. bkfst)
Facilities: Spa STV FTV ◉ ⌀ 54 ◎ Adventure golf
Gym Golf Academy Mountain bike trails Forest
Jump treetop adventure ♫ Wi-fi Child facilities
Parking: 1300 **Notes:** ⊗

This hotel and leisure resort consists of two adjoining hotels, a country inn, two golf and country clubs, and a multi-purpose conference centre. It stands high above the M4 on the south-facing side of Christchurch Hill, and each of its distinctively furnished and decorated bedrooms is generously provided with facilities from an alarm clock to underfloor heating. Superior rooms offer a queen-size bed and a spacious marble en suite bathroom with separate shower; from those rooms with a balcony there are views over the golf courses or the Severn Estuary. The luxury suites have picture windows and terraces, while even more sumptuous are the two Presidential Suites, one with a baby grand piano. All guests enjoy complimentary phone calls to national landlines, high-speed internet access and use of The Forum Health Club and Spa. Extensive public areas are set around a spectacular atrium lobby that includes several eating options: The Crown fine dining restaurant, holder of three AA Rosettes; the Olive Tree & Garden Room; the Forum Café overlooking the swimming pool; and Merlin's Bar, with conservatory and sun terrace. There is also a choice of shops and boutiques. Three challenging golf courses include the Twenty Ten Course, designed for the 2010 Ryder Cup.

Recommended in the area

Caerphilly Castle; Millennium Centre, Cardiff; Tradegar House

St Brides Spa Hotel

★★★★ 82% HOTEL

Address: St Brides Hill, SAUNDERSFOOT, SA69 9NH
Tel: 01834 812304
Fax: 01834 811766
E-mail: reservations@stbridesspahotel.com
Website: www.stbridesspahotel.com
Map ref: 1, SN10
Directions: A478 onto B4310 to Saundersfoot. Hotel above harbour
Rooms: 46 (12 annexe) (6 fmly) (9 GF) **S** £125-£190; **D** £150-£280 (incl. bkfst)
Facilities: Spa FTV Gym Thermal suite Wi-fi
Parking: 65 **Notes:** ⊗

In a prime position overlooking Saundersfoot harbour and Carmarthen Bay, this luxury, destination spa hotel is its owners' dream come true. When they bought it in 2000 it was a traditional seaside hotel; today it has modern en suite bedrooms, the majority enjoying sea views from their balconies, and luxury apartments (where pets are welcome) in the grounds. Contemporary Welsh art hangs on the walls. The rooms are known simply as Good, Better and Best, depending on size and facilities, which are generous, with bath and shower, iron and ironing board, robes and slippers, hot drinks tray, TV and DVD player, hairdryer and fan. There are three places to eat: in the hotel itself is the Cliff Restaurant and Gallery Bar; down in the village is Mermaid on the Strand, specialising in locally landed sea food and traditional home cooking; and on the harbour is Marina, a modern take on the time-honoured British fish and chip shop. From over 400 Old and New World wines, choose a bottle of fizz for your room, perhaps, or something chilled for drinking on one of the outdoor terraces. Views from the treatment room and spa pool are among the hotel's best. St Brides is the AA Hotel of Year for Wales 2011–2012.

Recommended in the area

Barafundle Bay; Pembroke Castle; Tenby

Atlantic Hotel

★★★ 80% HOTEL

Address: The Esplanade, TENBY, SA70 7DU
Tel: 01834 842881
Fax: 01834 840911
E-mail: enquiries@atlantic-hotel.uk.com
Website: www.atlantic-hotel.uk.com
Map ref: 1, SN10
Directions: A478 into Tenby, follow town centre
signs (keep town walls on left) right at Esplanade,
hotel on right
Rooms: 42 (11 fmly) (4 GF) **S** £82-£93; **D** £114-£195
(incl. bkfst) **Facilities:** FTV ⊛ Steam room Spa bath
Wi-fi **Parking:** 25

Many hoteliers would probably give their eye-teeth for the cliff-top position of this privately owned, personally run hotel. Look one way and there's Castle Hill and the island fort of St. Catherine; look the other, and two kilometre-long South Beach stretches towards Caldey Island and its Cistercian monastery, which you can visit by boat from Tenby harbour. Bedrooms vary in size and style, although all are en suite with bath and shower, and are equipped with TV, radio, direct-dial phone, free Wi-fi access and hot drinks tray. A lift serves all but two rooms, many of which have sea views. In addition to the residents' bar, open for morning coffee and afternoon tea, there's Carrington's restaurant, where typical starters are Carmarthen dry-cured ham with red onion relish and side salad; and Pant Mawr goat's cheese: main dishes include Welsh lamb cutlets and potato cake with rosemary, redcurrant and port sauce; and breast of chicken stuffed with leeks and Caws Preseli cheese, wrapped in smoked bacon. Breakfast is served in Trayles restaurant. Make use of the in-house leisure facilities, including an indoor pool, spa bath, steam room and heated loungers. There is a 28-space car park, which is covered by CCTV.

Recommended in the area

South and North beach; coastal path walks; Caldey Island trip

County Map

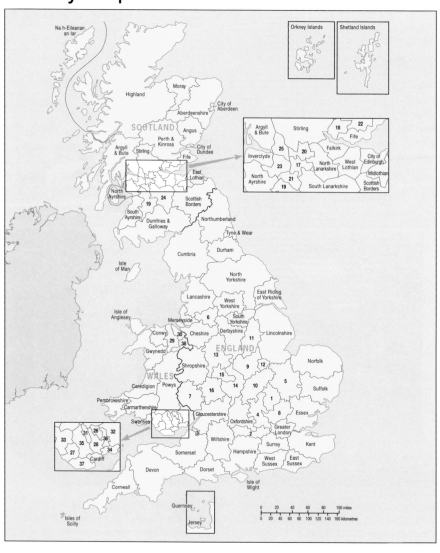

England
1 Bedfordshire
2 Berkshire
3 Bristol
4 Buckinghamshire
5 Cambridgeshire
6 Greater Manchester
7 Herefordshire
8 Hertfordshire
9 Leicestershire
10 Northamptonshire
11 Nottinghamshire
12 Rutland
13 Staffordshire

14 Warwickshire
15 West Midlands
16 Worcestershire

Scotland
17 City of Glasgow
18 Clackmannanshire
19 East Ayrshire
20 East Dunbartonshire
21 East Renfrewshire
22 Perth & Kinross
23 Renfrewshire
24 South Lanarkshire
25 West Dunbartonshire

Wales
26 Blaenau Gwent
27 Bridgend
28 Caerphilly
29 Denbighshire
30 Flintshire
31 Merthyr Tydfil
32 Monmouthshire
33 Neath Port Talbot
34 Newport
35 Rhondda Cynon Taff
36 Torfaen
37 Vale of Glamorgan
38 Wrexham

Maps

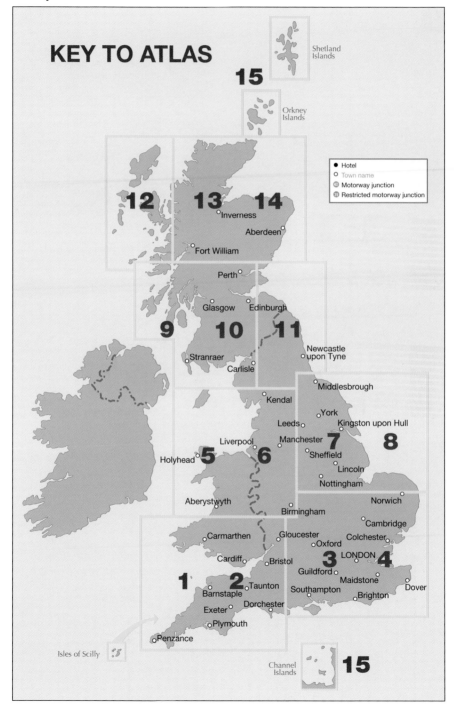

KEY TO ATLAS

Shetland Islands

15

Orkney Islands

- ● Hotel
- ○ Town name
- ⓜ Motorway junction
- ⓡ Restricted motorway junction

12 13 14
Inverness

Aberdeen

Fort William

Perth

Glasgow Edinburgh

9 10 11
Newcastle upon Tyne

Stranraer

Carlisle

Middlesbrough

Kendal

York

Leeds Kingston upon Hull

Liverpool Manchester 7 8

Holyhead 5 6 Sheffield

Lincoln

Nottingham

Aberystwyth Norwich

Birmingham

Cambridge

Carmarthen Gloucester Colchester

Oxford

Cardiff Bristol 3 LONDON 4

Guildford

1 2 Maidstone

Taunton Southampton Dover

Barnstaple Brighton

Exeter Dorchester

Plymouth

Penzance

Isles of Scilly

Channel Islands 15

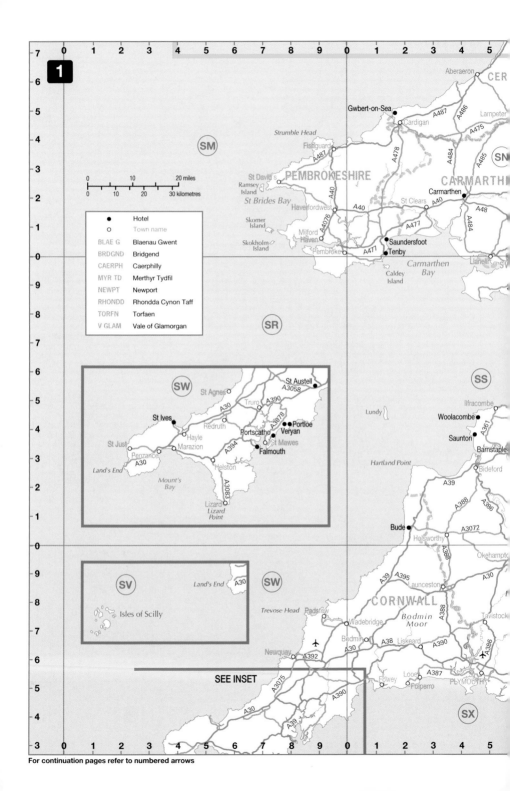

1

Aberaeron
CER

Gwbert-on-Sea
Cardigan
A487
A486
Lampeter
A475

Strumble Head

SM

Fishguard
A487
A478
A484
A485
SN

St David's
Ramsey
Island
PEMBROKESHIRE
St Brides Bay
A40
Haverfordwest
A40
St Clears
A40
Carmarthen
CARMARTH

A4076
A477
A48
A484

Skomer
Island
Milford
Haven
Saundersfoot
A477

Skokholm
Island
Pembroke
A477
Tenby
Carmarthen
Bay
Llanelli
SV

Caldey
Island

SR

	Hotel
○	Town name
BLAE G	Blaenau Gwent
BRDGND	Bridgend
CAERPH	Caerphilly
MYR TD	Merthyr Tydfil
NEWPT	Newport
RHONDD	Rhondda Cynon Taff
TORFN	Torfaen
V GLAM	Vale of Glamorgan

0   10   20 miles
0   10   20   30 kilometres

SW
St Agnes
St Austell
A3058
SS

St Ives
Truro
A390
Ilfracombe
Woolacombe
A361

Redruth
A30
A3078
Portloe
Portscatho
Veryan
Lundy
Saunton

St Just
Hayle
Marazion
A394
St Mawes
Falmouth
Barnstaple

Penzance
A30
Helston
Hartland Point
Bideford

Land's End
Mount's
Bay
A3083
A39

Lizard
Lizard
Point
Bude
A3072

Holsworthy
Okehampton

SV
Land's End
A30
SW
A39
A395
Launceston
A30

Isles of Scilly
Trevose Head
Padstow
CORNWALL
Bodmin
Moor
A388
Tavistock

Wadebridge
A388

Bodmin
A38
Liskeard
A390
A386

Newquay
A392

SEE INSET
A3075
Fowey
Looe
A387
PLYMOUTH
Polperro

A30
A390

A39

SX

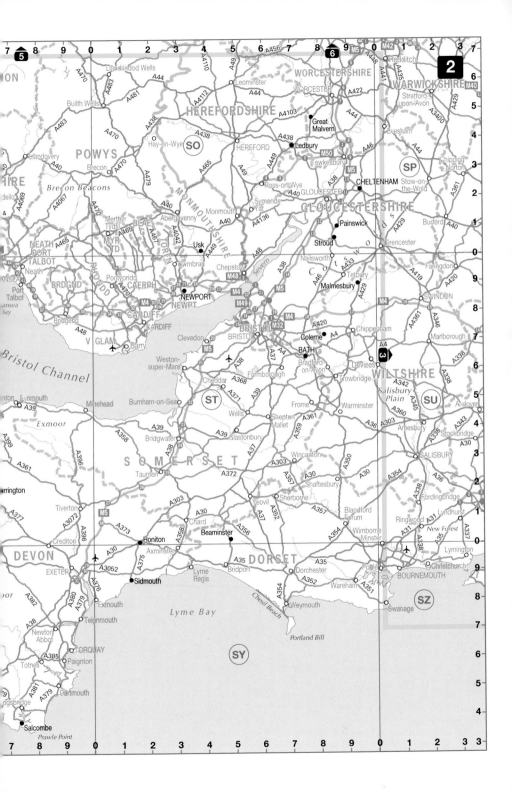

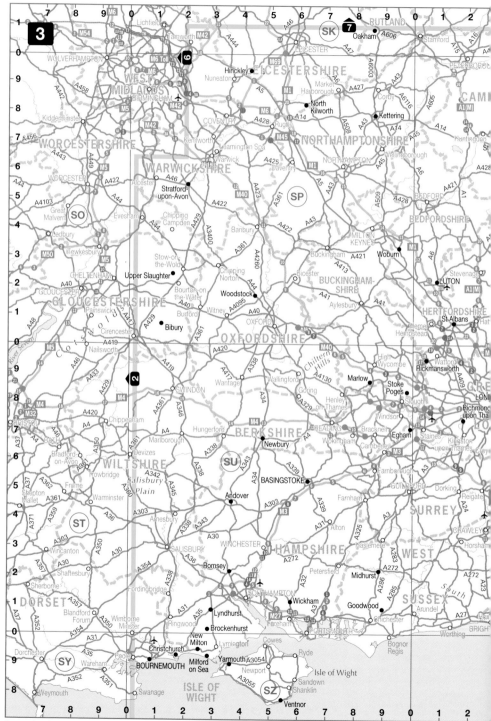

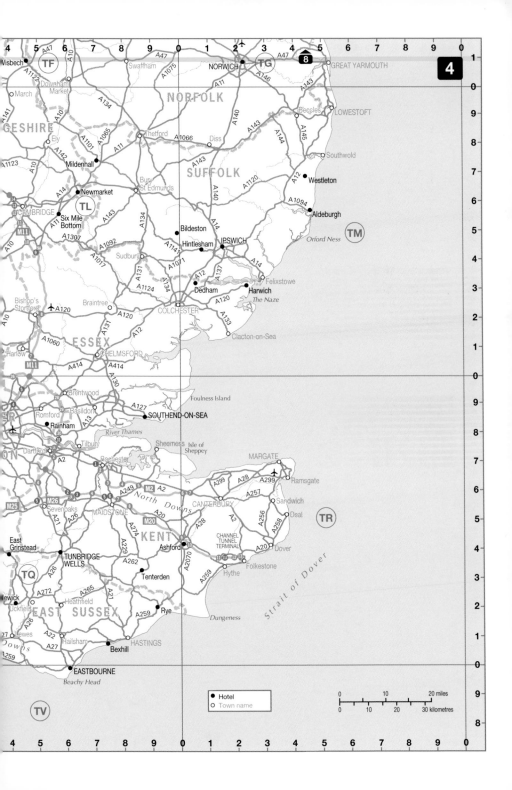

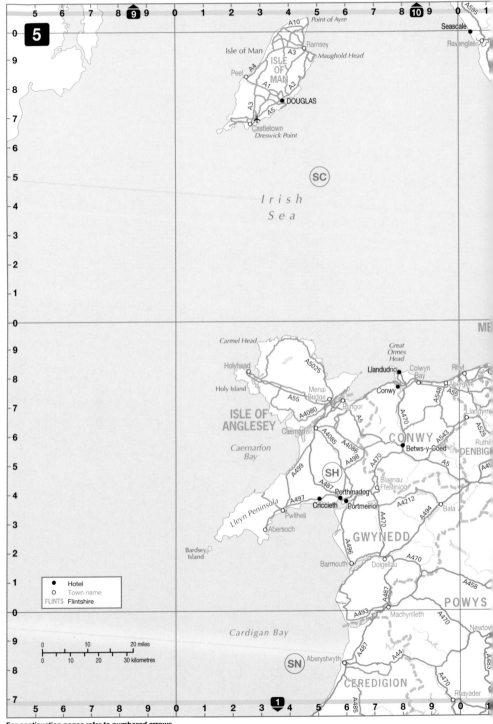

5

5 6 7 8 ⬆9 9 0 1 2 3 4 5 6 7 8 ⬆10 9 0 1

A10   Point of Ayre

Seascale

Isle of Man   Ramsey

Ravenglass

A3

ISLE   Maughold Head

Peel   A4

OF

MAN

A1   A2

A5

A3   A5   ● DOUGLAS

Castletown

Dreswick Point

(SC)

I r i s h

S e a

Carmel Head

Great Ormes Head

Holyhead

A5025   Llandudno●   Colwyn Bay   Rhyl

Holy Island   Conwy●

A55   Menai Bridge   A548   A55   Abergele

A55

ISLE OF   A4080   Bangor   Llandyrn

ANGLESEY   A5   A525

Caernarfon   A4085   A470   Ruthi

Caernarfon Bay   A4086   **CONWY**   A543   **DENBIG**

Betws-y-Coed

A499   A498   A470   A5   A49

(SH)

A487   Blaenau Ffestiniog

Porthmadog

A497   Criccieth   Portmeirion   A4212   A494   Bala

Lleyn Peninsula   Pwllheli

Abersoch   A496   **GWYNEDD**   A470

Bardsey Island

Barmouth   Dolgellau   A470

A458

	Hotel
○	Town name
FLINTS	Flintshire

A487   **POWYS**

A493   Machynlleth   A470   Newtow

Cardigan Bay

0   10   20 miles

0   10   20   30 kilometres

(SN)   Aberystwyth   A487   A44   A483

A470

CEREDIGION   Rhayader

5 6 7 8 9 0 1 2 3 ⬇1 4 5 6 7 8 9 0 1

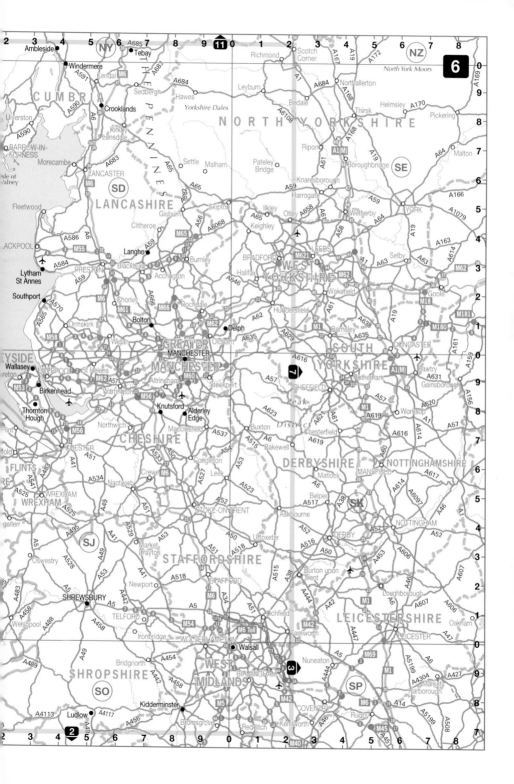

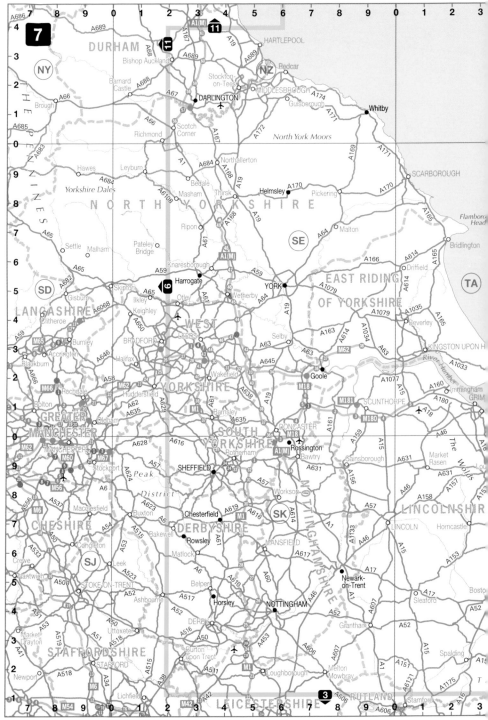

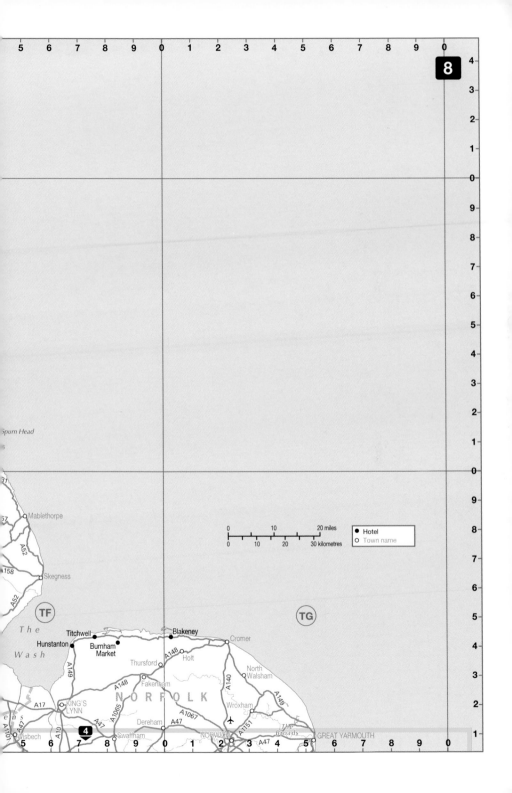

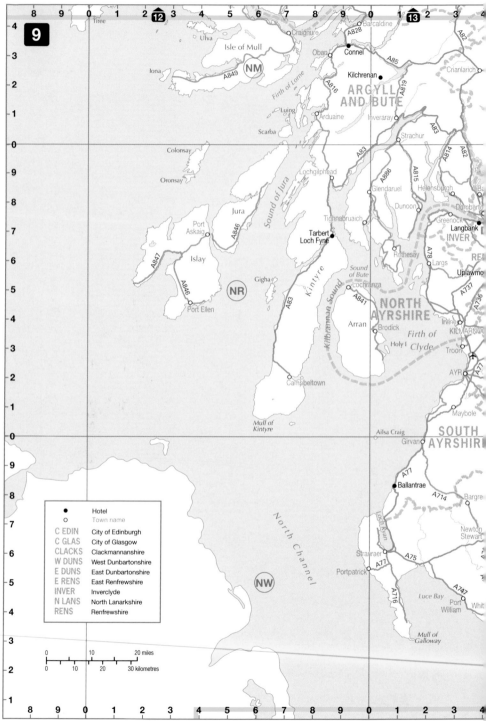

9

	Hotel
●	Hotel
○	Town name
C EDIN	City of Edinburgh
C GLAS	City of Glasgow
CLACKS	Clackmannanshire
W DUNS	West Dunbartonshire
E DUNS	East Dunbartonshire
E RENS	East Renfrewshire
INVER	Inverclyde
N LANS	North Lanarkshire
RENS	Renfrewshire

0   10   20 miles
0 10 20 30 kilometres

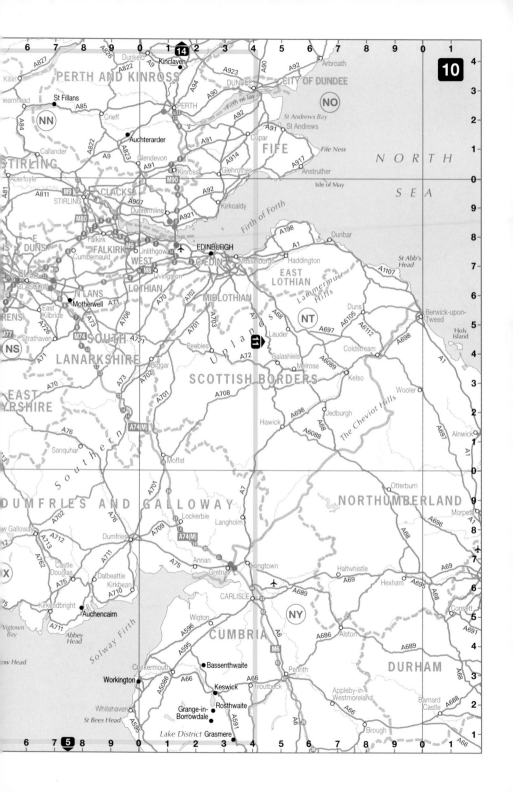

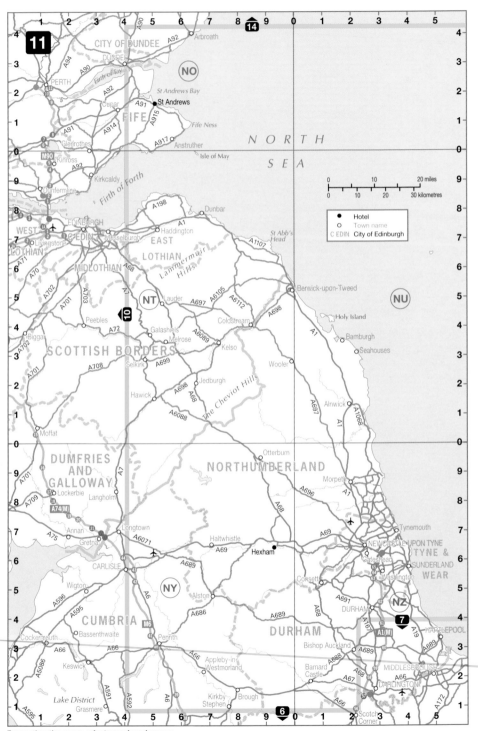

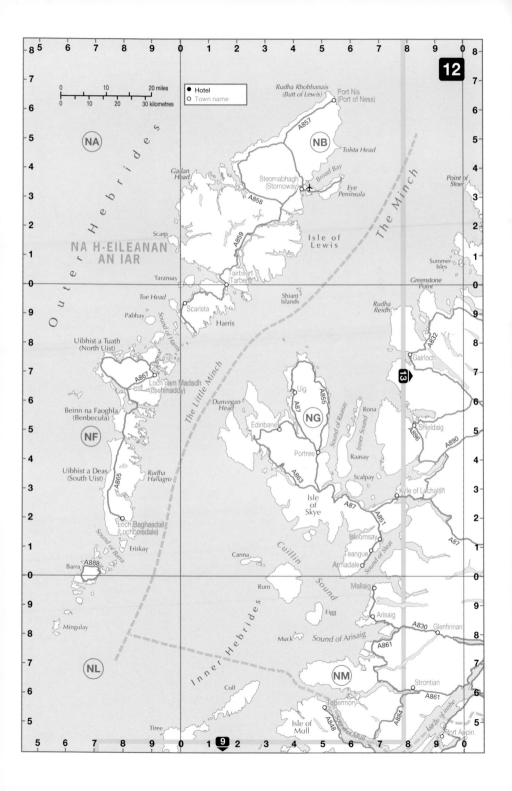

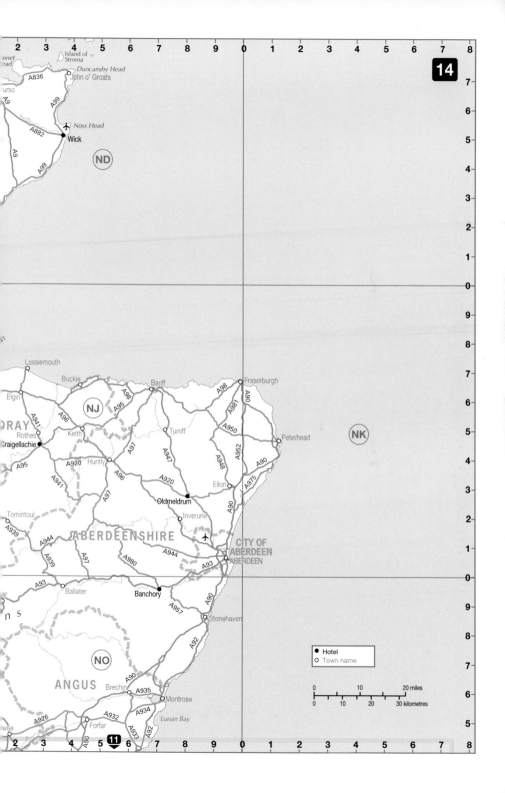

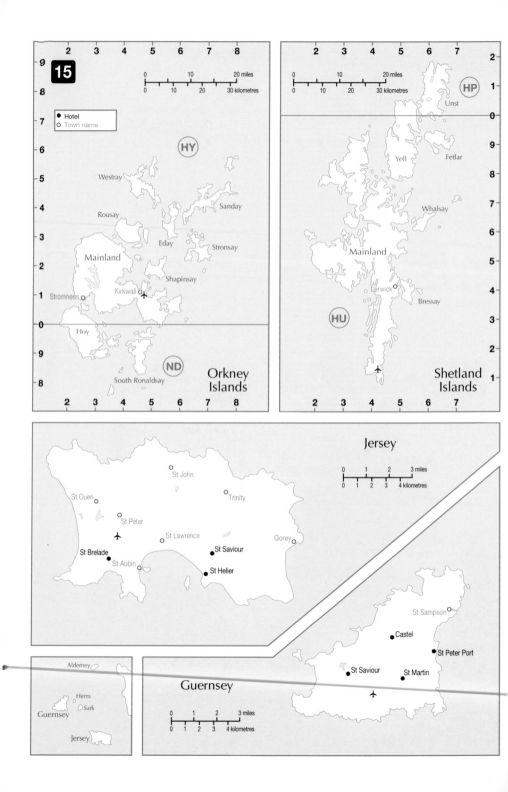

15

Hotel
Town name

Orkney Islands

HY

ND

Westray
Rousay
Sanday
Eday
Stronsay
Mainland
Shapinsay
Stromness
Kirkwall
Hoy
South Ronaldsay

Shetland Islands

HP

HU

Unst
Yell
Fetlar
Whalsay
Mainland
Lerwick
Bressay

Jersey

St John
St Ouen
Trinity
St Peter
St Lawrence
Gorey
St Brelade
St Aubin
St Saviour
St Helier

Guernsey

Alderney
Herm
Sark
Guernsey
Jersey

St Sampson
Castel
St Peter Port
St Saviour
St Martin

Establishment Index

Location Index

Acknowledgements

The Automobile Association would like to thank the following photographers, companies and picture libraries for their assistance in the preparation of this book.

Abbreviations for the picture credits are as follows – (t) top; (b) bottom; (c) centre; (l) left; (r) right; (AA) AA World Travel Library.

4/5 Courtesy Stoke Park Country Club & Resort; 9 Courtesy Danesfield House Hotel; 14 AA/James Tims; 16/17 AA/Mike Kipling; 18 AA/Derek Forss; 21 AA/James Tims; 24 AA/James Tims; 27 AA/Laurie Noble; 31 AA/Caroline Jones; 34 AA/Adam Burton; 43 AA/Anna Mockford & Nick Bonetti; 58 AA/Tom Mackie; 62 AA/Adam Burton; 72 AA/Max Jourdan; 78 AA/Roger Coulam; 81 AA/Neil Setchfield; 86 AA/David Hall; 92 AA/John Mottershaw; 96 AA/Adam Burton; 106 AA/Caroline Jones; 108 AA/James Tims; 111 AA/Laurie Noble; 115 AA/David Clapp; 118 AA/Peter Baker; 121 AA/Sarah Montgomery; 141 AA/Neil Setchfield; 142 AA/Neil Setchfield; 145 AA/David Clapp; 150 AA/Tom Mackie; 156 AA/M Birkitt; 158 AA/Roger Coulam; 160 AA/James Tims; 163 AA/James Tims; 164 AA/James Tims; 166 AA/M Birkitt; 168 AA/AA; 171 AA/Rebecca Duke; 175 AA/Tom Mackie; 183 AA/Tom Mackie; 184 AA/James Tims; 186 AA/John Miller; 191 AA/John Miller; 195 AA/John Miller; 196 AA/Caroline Jones; 198 AA/Caroline Jones; 200 AA/Andrew Newey; 203 AA/Michael Moody; 206 AA/Caroline Jones; 210 AA/David Clapp; 212 AA/Mike Kipling; 217 AA/John Morrison; 221 AA/AJ Hopkins; 222 AA/AA; 224 AA/Wyn Voysey; 234/234 AA/Stephen Whitehorne; 260/261 AA/Stephen Lewis